W9-BNY-922

DISCOVERING CAUSAL STRUCTURE

Artificial Intelligence, Philosophy of Science, and Statistical Modeling

DISCOVERING CAUSAL STRUCTURE

Artificial Intelligence, Philosophy of Science, and Statistical Modeling

**Clark Glymour, Richard Scheines,
Peter Spirtes, and Kevin Kelly**

Department of Philosophy
Carnegie Mellon University
Pittsburgh, Pennsylvania

With a Foreword by Herbert A. Simon

1987

ACADEMIC PRESS, INC.
Harcourt Brace Jovanovich, Publishers
Orlando   San Diego   New York
Austin   Boston   London   Sydney
Tokyo   Toronto

ACADEMIC PRESS, INC.
Orlando, Florida 32887

United Kingdom Edition published by
ACADEMIC PRESS INC. (LONDON) LTD.
24–28 Oval Road, London NW1 7DX

Library of Congress Cataloging in Publication Data

Discovering causal structure:

　　Artificial intelligence, philosophy of science,
　　and statistical modeling
　　Includes index.
　　1. Social sciences—Statistical methods.　2. Social
sciences—Data processing.　3. Social sciences—
Mathematical models.　4. Artificial intelligence.
I. Glymour, Clark N.　II. Title: Causal structure.
HA29.D495　1987　　300'.1'51　　87-1860
ISBN 0—12—286961—3 (alk. paper)

PRINTED IN THE UNITED STATES OF AMERICA

87 88 89 90　　9 8 7 6 5 4 3 2 1

For Alison, Patricia, Mort, Jessica, Thomas, and Kelly

Contents

Part III : Using TETRAD, EQS, and LISREL

About This Book

This book is about a computer program, TETRAD. The program is designed to assist in the search for causal explanations of statistical data. There are often many millions of possible alternative causal explanations for nonexperimental data; human researchers can only consider and evaluate a handful of these alternatives and hope that the best explanation they find is the best explanation there is. That hope is often in vain. The TETRAD program uses artificial intelligence techniques to help the investigator to perform a systematic search for alternative causal models using whatever relevant knowledge may be available.

A version of the TETRAD program, together with several data sets discussed in the book, are included on the floppy disk accompanying this volume. The version of the TETRAD program on the floppy will run on IBM personal computers and on IBM-compatible machines. We recommend 512K of RAM , but simple models can be run on machines with less memory. The TETRAD program is intended to be used in conjunction with programs for statistical estimation and testing, such as the LISREL [3] and EQS [1] programs.

The program on the floppy is limited to models with no more than nine variables. A version of the IBM program suitable for larger models (up to 23 variables) is available from Academic Press. Still larger models can be treated using a version of the TETRAD program for the DEC Microvax II Workstation, which will shortly be available.

Directions for running the program can be found in Chapter 12. Effective use of the program requires study of Chapter 5 and of some of the examples in Chapter 8.

Because the book was written as the program developed, output described in the book's examples may differ in minor ways from output obtained with the version of the program on the floppy disk.

Foreword

After a long period of neglect, the logic of scientific discovery -- the description and prescription of reasonable procedures for bringing new theories into being -- is now attracting increasing attention and effort in philosophy of science, in artificial intelligence and cognitive science, and in statistics. We are less and less satisfied to attribute discovery to an unanalyzed and unanalyzable miracle of "creativity" or "genius." We wish to know what constitutes sensible and effective ways of proceeding with scientific work, and why some scientists seem to succeed more often than others in making significant discoveries. We even aspire to bring our new intellectual workhorse, the computer, to our aid in inducing generalizations from our data and in formulating theories of possible value. This book represents an important contribution to this effort to understand the scientific venture and to provide it with new tools.

I need not repeat at length the authors' own description of their work and the way in which they report it in this book. At its center is a computer program, TETRAD, that can be viewed as a normative theory of how to induce causal models from empirical, nonexperimental data, and also as an engine for doing just that. But because of the skepticism that has prevailed in the past about the logic of discovery, the authors surround their description of TETRAD with a careful discussion of the discovery process and detailed answers to the objections that have been raised against aspiring to have a normative theory of discovery as well as those that have been raised against causal modeling. I find my own views in such close accord with this philosophical defense of their undertaking that my comments on this part of the book can be summed up in the one word: Amen! Or perhaps it should be: Right on!

My remarks here will be directed to another side of the matter that can hardly be emphasized too much because it has been so much misunderstood in the past. The goal of TETRAD is to discover one or more (usually more) models -- that is, systems of linear equations -- that are consistent with a body of correlational data. This is also the goal of the factor-rotation techniques employed in factor analysis, the techniques for adding variables successively in regression analysis, and others. The key question is this: On what basis should we prefer one of the models produced by these techniques over another?

In the data themselves there is a fundamental ambiguity. Given any set of linear equations, we can, by taking linear combinations of them, produce an infinity of alternative sets that have exactly the same solutions as the original set and, hence, fit exactly the same data. Why do we prefer one of these sets to another? What does it matter? And if we have some criteria of preference, how do we identify the preferred one?

The answer to the first question is embedded in the econometricians' idea of structural equations and the contrast between structural equations and reduced-form equations. In our interpretation of the equations that describe some empirical data, we like to imagine that each equation represents a specific one of several mechanisms that govern the behavior of the system from which the data derive. If the equations describe a bridge truss, we would like each equation to correspond to the stresses at some node in the bridge or the stresses on one particular member. If the equations describe the relation between weather and the price of wheat, we would like one equation to describe the relation between weather and the size of the wheat crop, another to describe the relation between the price of wheat and the amount of land that farmers will sow, and another to describe the relation between the price of wheat and the amount of wheat that consumers will buy. In the case of either of these models, we wish our individual equations to describe the specific direct causal mechanisms that are at work, interacting in the entire system of simultaneous relations.

The advantage of representing the system by structural equations that describe the direct causal mechanisms is that if we obtain some knowledge that one or more of these mechanisms has been altered, we can use the remaining equations to predict the consequences -- the new equilibrium. (A second advantage is that a description of a system in causal terms provides an explanation of the behavior of that system, while a description in terms of reduced-form equations does not.)

Now, since all of the equations we can obtain by linear combinations of the original set are equally consistent with the data, the data themselves cannot help us (directly) to choose the correct structural equations. We must add to the data additional information ("impose additional constraints," we usually say) in order to make a choice. But these additional data or constraints are not matters of form or syntax. They amount to empirical assumptions about the semantics of the situation, about the nature of the mechanisms that were actually at work in producing the data. There is no simple procedure for crank turning that will permit us to do automatic science here.

We see this problem clearly in the classical methods of factor rotation in factor analysis. For example, the criterion of "simple structure" amounts to an assumption of simplicity in the real world, the assumption that few things in the real world are directly connected with each other by mechanisms and, hence, that the model assuming the fewest connections (has the largest number of zero-factor loadings) is the correct structural model. Perhaps the criterion of simple structure is defensible as a criterion of desperation -- the rule we should apply if we know nothing about the phenomena beyond the statistical data that have been presented to us. But in most cases, we do indeed have knowledge beyond the data.

No experiment (as no man) is an island unto itself. We should hold in great suspicion statistical or other methods that treat experimental data as though we know nothing at all but what is contained in those data. Perhaps the strongest argument that can be made for the Bayesian position in statistics is that it provides us with a formal route for introducing prior information -- information about the world that we already possessed before we ran this particular experiment -- into our treatment of the experimental data. But there are many routes besides the Bayesian one for introducing such prior information. One way is to assume that certain variables are not directly connected, or that others are. We may make such assumptions, for example, because information from previous experiments or from other sources of knowledge about the world make us confident that such direct structural links do or do not hold.

A system like TETRAD enables us to introduce such additional information, in the form of constraints, into our system. When sufficient additional information has been added, the interpretation of the equation system is no longer ambiguous; the equations can no longer be combined and recombined without violating the constraints. If enough additional information is added, then the equations are overconstrained (or "overidentified," in the language of the econometricians), and we can test whether the equations are consistent with the totality of our assumptions -- whether, for example, certain partial correlations or tetrad functions are zero or nearly zero, as our constraints imply.

All of these matters, and the methods for introducing constraints and testing them against the correlational data, are treated at length in this book. The point I would hope to imprint in the reader, before he becomes fascinated with the powerful techniques that are provided for him, is that constraint specification is not a formal process. It cannot be guided by syntactical tests. It is fundamentally and intrinsically semantic. Constraints are assumptions about the phenomena that are under study, and the only legitimate sources for such assumptions are the data themselves and prior knowledge about the nature of the phenomena. But the techniques provide us with a powerful means of bootstrapping. If our prior knowledge is highly conjectural and uncertain, but there is enough of it -- however shaky -- to overidentify the equations, then our techniques allow us to test these assumptions not individually, but in their joint compatibility with the data.

We can classify the TETRAD system, then, as a member of the family of bootstrap methods of induction, and its justification is to be found in the general justification of bootstrap methodology. The bootstrapping procedures that TETRAD supports are described in Chapter 5 of this book, and a more general discussion of bootstrapping can be found in Clark Glymour's *Theory and Evidence* [2].

Under the guise of writing a foreword to this book, I have been seduced into emphasizing one particular component in its argument. If limits of length did not bar me, I could easily be seduced into discussing other components. The authors have not only provided us with TETRAD, a valuable new tool for statistical analysis, but they have also embedded TETRAD in a rich and thoughtful discussion of the philosophical and technical issues that it raises. Rather than comment on any more of these issues, I will now turn the book over to the reader, with the hope that it will provide him with as much stimulation and as many new ideas as it has given me.

Herbert A. Simon

Acknowledgments

The development of the TETRAD program has taken the better part of four years. We have been aided during that period both by people and by institutions. The National Science Foundation Program in History and Philosophy of Science provided support which led to the initial formulation of the TETRAD project. The NSF economics program in Measurement Methods helped to fund the development of the computer program. The University of Pittsburgh and Carnegie Mellon University provided computational resources. A second grant from the History and Philosophy of Science Program at NSF helped to support the writing of this book.

Jill Larken made equipment available for us, Preston Covey generously allowed us to use the printing facilities at the Center for Design of Educational Computing, Carol Scheftic and Chris Thyburg patiently helped us get over obstacles in Scribe, and Robert Daley kindly helped us with some computational needs. Rick Statman and Richmond Thomason gave us some valuable mathematical help. Alison Kost, Don Stoops, and Medellena Glymour assisted us with the many figures the book contains. Susan Trainer assisted us with preparing the tables. Many others have helped us through criticism, encouragement, data, or references. We thank William Bielby, Donald Campbell, Thomas Cook, Herbert Costner, Patrick Doreian, Thomas Ferarro, Steven Fienberg, Daniel Hausman, Max Henrion, Paul Humphreys, Jay Kadane, Melvin Kohn, Patrick Larkey, Peter Machamer, Paul Meehl, Jay Magidson, Merrilee Salmon, Wesley Salmon, Alan Sampson, Kenneth Schaffner, Ronald Schoenberg, William Shadish, Herbert Simon, and Jan Zytkow. Teddy Seidenfeld read through much of the manuscript and gave us valuable suggestions. Alison Kost, Martha Harty Scheines, and Jessica Feldman have patiently endured our obsession for several years.

This program and book could not have been developed in most places; only the special environment of Carnegie Mellon University has made it possible, and John Modell and Michael Salomone, respectively Acting Dean and Associate Dean at Carnegie Mellon University, deserve our special thanks, as do the editors of Academic Press, whose support and counsel were invaluable.

PART I

Artificial Intelligence
and
Nonexperimental Science

1. THE PROBLEMS OF SCIENCE WITHOUT EXPERIMENTS

1.1. The Limits of Experimentation

Modern science and experimental methods grew up together, and we cannot very well imagine empirical science without experimentation. Even so, much of what we want to know about our world cannot be answered by experiments, and much of what we know (or think we know) is not directly based on experimental studies. The limitations of experimentation are both practical and ethical. For practical reasons we cannot do real experiments with the economies of nations or with the arrangements of galaxies. For ethical reasons we cannot do all sorts of experiments on the causes of disease (on smoking and cancer, for example) or on causes of social conditions; neither the world nor conscience will let experimenters randomly assign infants to experimental and control groups for the purpose of studying the effects of poverty on delinquency.

Faced both with urgent needs for all sorts of knowledge and with stringent limitations on the scope of experimentation, we resort to statistics. In the nineteenth century there was a rapid development in the study of statistical data to answer causal questions. Statistical comparisons were made in epidemiology, to determine the effects of blood letting or of new surgical procedures, for example, and to attempt to estimate the effects of occupation on mortality. Later, nonexperimental statistical data were used to study heredity, the causes of differences in individual human abilities, and causes of economic change. By the early years of the twentieth century, nonexperimental statistics had made inroads into medicine, biology, psychology, and economics.

Today, statistical methods are applied to every public issue of any factual kind. The meetings of the American Statistical Association address almost every conceivable matter of public policy, from the safety of nuclear reactors to the reliability of the census. The attempt to extract causal information from statistical data with only indirect help from experimentation goes on in nearly every academic subject and in many nonacademic endeavors as well. Sociologists, political scientists, economists, demographers, educators, psychologists, biologists, market researchers, policy makers, and occasionally even chemists and physicists use such methods.

Nonexperimental statistical studies are only one way to get information that helps to decide questions of health or public policy. We could instead resort to fundamentalist revelation, or Marxist theory, or look entirely to political expediency. If we try to make science reach a little beyond our power to experiment, it is because we think such methods extend the scope of rationality, and because we wish to make social and individual decisions as rationally as we can. Even so, their reasonableness is not beyond dispute.

3

Controversy about the use of statistical methods to extract causal information from nonexperimental data is as old as the methods themselves. The controversy continues today, and it has many sources. Part of it may be no more than the continued resistance to quantitative methods by many of the practitioners of the "softer" sciences. Part of it is baldly political. The same methods that are used to study the spread of disease or the causes of economic change have also been used to argue for some very unpopular conclusions. Part of the opposition to causal inference in nonexperimental research is based on misconceptions about science. Critics unfamiliar with the history of science, or with practice in the natural sciences, sometimes make naive demands on applied statistics that are not met by even the most advanced of our sciences. But the most interesting and most important opposition derives from a justifiable sense that a good deal of applied statistics looks more like pseudo-science than like science. In many statistical studies in the social sciences, equations may be written down and references cited, but little or no justification is given for the assumptions that are made, the hypotheses put forward are not tested, and no predictions of any consequence are derived. The important question is not whether much of this work is poorly done, but why it is and whether it need be.

1.2. The Limits of Human Judgment

It is important to recognize the difference between practice and principle. If much of the quantitative work that aims to extract causal conclusions from nonexperimental data is not very convincing, then that might be either because of reasons of principle that cannot be overcome or because of individual lapses that can be overcome. The news is not very encouraging; some of the obstacles to good statistical modeling may be very difficult to overcome, no matter how fine our intentions may be. There are two distinct sources of discouragement, one from psychology, the other from elementary considerations of combinatorial mathematics.

The Psychological Problem

About thirty years ago, Paul Meehl [77] compared predictions obtained, on the one hand, by psychologists using clinical interviews and, on the other hand, by simple linear regression of the predicted attribute on any statistically relevant features of the population. He found that on the average the predictions obtained by linear regression were never worse, and were usually better, than those made by clinicians. Meehl's conclusion is one of the best replicated results in psychology. If the issue is selecting police officers who will perform their tasks satisfactorily, or graduate students who will do well in their studies, or felons who will not commit new crimes when paroled, a simple statistical algorithm will generally do better than a panel of Ph.Ds. Results of this sort are not confined to clinical psychologists. A growing literature on "behavioral decision theory" has found that people, even those trained in probability and statistics, perform well below the ideal in a variety of circumstances in which judgments of probability are called for [56]. One of the most resilient errors is the tendency to ignore base rates, or prior probabilities for various alternatives, and judge the probability of an alternative entirely by how likely that alternative renders the evidence.

The intellectual skills that are required to find, recognize, and establish a good scientific theory have many of the features of problems for which it has been shown that human decision making is less than optimal. There are a few studies which bear a little more directly on the capacity of humans to interpret scientific data. Studies of physicians' diagnostic behavior, for example, have shown that few alternative diagnoses are entertained and that evidence that is irrelevant to a preferred diagnosis is often erroneously taken to confirm it. Historical studies suggest much the same thing. Thus, in recent years philosophers of science have been stung by the historical criticisms of writers, such as Thomas Kuhn, who argue that the history of science does not fit very well with philosophical theories of scientific reasoning. The conflict is perfectly understandable if one realizes that philosophical methodologists have been concerned to characterize ideal, normative modes of reasoning, and if one supposes that the scientific community in any time and subject area typically falls well short of such ideals.

One major use of applied statistics is in economic forecasting. Forecasts are made in many ways: by the judgment of a human expert, by a variety of statistical time-series methods, some of which require a good deal of judgment on the part of the user and some of which do not, and by econometric methods that attempt to consider not only time-series but also causal factors affecting the variable to be predicted. The literature on the comparison of methods is large, complex, and especially controversial since forecasting procedures may involve large financial stakes. It seems fair to say, however, that there is considerable evidence that simpler procedures do as well or better than more complex procedures, and that statistical procedures requiring considerable judgment on the part of the user do little, if any, better than more fully automated procedures. There is little evidence that explicit consideration of causal variables significantly improves forecasting (see Makridakis, et al. [73] and Kmenta and Ramsey [59] for some recent comparisons and for references to the literature). What this suggests is that the causal theories produced for economic forecasting are not as good as we might wish.

Considerations such as these have led David Faust [25], a psychologist, to the conclusion that science itself is by and large too difficult for human cognitive capacities, and even Meehl takes this thought seriously. But there is a much more powerful combinatorial argument that leads to similar misgivings.

The Combinatorial Problem

The aim of science, whether physics or sociology, is to increase our understanding by providing *explanations* of the phenomena that concern us. The most common form of explanation in the sciences is to account for why things happen as they do by appealing to the causal relations among events, and by articulating generalizations about causal relationships. Causal claims alone are often insufficiently precise to give us the power to test them or to make important predictions from them. To gain that power, we usually embed causal claims, when we can, in a system of quantitative relationships. In considering nonexperimental data, the quantitative relationships are often in the form of a *statistical model* of some kind.

When we consider statistical models[1] in the social and behavioral sciences, we find everything from very small models in educational research with as few as six or seven measured variables, to econometric models containing several hundred vaiables. We can think of the causal part of any such theory as given by a **directed graph**, with the vertices of the graph representing the variables, and each directed edge in the graph representing a causal influence of one variable upon another. Such graphs look like arrow diagrams (Fig. 1-1).

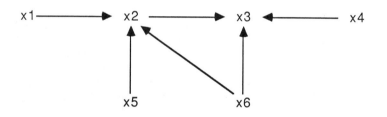

Figure 1-1: A directed graph.

Each distinct way of arranging a set of variables into a directed graph represents a

---

[1]The practice throughout statistics and much of the sciences is to term any specific theory a "model" and reserve the term "theory" for only the most general and sweeping of hypotheses. We will use "theory" and "model" interchangeably.

distinct model of the causal relationships among the variables, and thus an alternative causal theory of the data. The point is that even with a small collection of variables, the number of distinct possible causal arrangements, and thus the number of distinct, alternative causal models of the data, is astronomical. If we consider all of the *a priori* possibilities, then for each pair of variables A and B, there are four possible kinds of connection: A can have an effect on B but not B on A, or B can have an effect on A but not A on B, or A and B can each have an effect on the other, or, finally, A and B can each have no direct effect upon the other. The number of distinct possible causal arrangements of n variables is therefore 4 raised to the power of the number of pairs of variables. Thus with only 6 variables, there are 4^{15} different possible directed graphs or causal models. When we have it in our power to experiment, we are able to arrange circumstances so that we know most of these possibilities are excluded, and we can focus on whether a particular causal dependency does or does not occur. But without experimental control, the problem of determining the correct causal structure is far more difficult.

A social scientist or psychologist or epidemiologist or biologist attempting to develop a good statistical theory has many difficult tasks. He or she must choose what to measure and how to measure it, and worry about sampling technique and sample size. The researcher must consider whether the variables are multinormally distributed or have some other distribution. He or she must worry about whether measures of a variable in one individual or place or time are correlated with measures of that same variable in another individual or place or time. The researcher must consider whether the relations among the variables are linear, nonlinear, or even discontinuous. These are demanding tasks, but there are a variety of data analytic techniques to help one along and to test hypotheses concerning these questions. Suppose the investigator has passed these hurdles and has arrived, however tentatively, at some common statistical modeling assumptions: the relationships are linear (or close enough to linear) the distribution is multinormal (or nearly so) there is no autocorrelation (or at least not much). Assume that the investigator has covariance data for 6 variables. The troubles that now must be faced make the data analysis problems seem pale in comparison. There are 4^{15} alternative possible theories of the causal dependencies among the 6 variables, and only one of those theories can be true. How is the researcher to find the one needle in the enormous haystack of possibilities? Perhaps the goal need not be to find the one unique correct theory but only to reduce the possibilites to a handful, or to find a close approximation to the correct model. How is even that to be done? The usual thing to say is that the investigator must apply his or her "substantive knowledge" of the domain, but this is mostly whistling in the dark. To get the number of possiblities down to manageable size will take a lot more substantive knowledge than we usually have about social or behavioral phenomena. Suppose, for example, that one is quite certain that the causal relations do not form cycles. That is, there is no sequence of directed edges in the true graph of the causal relations that leads from one variable back to that same variable. Then the number of alternative causal models consistent with that restriction is still more than three million. Suppose, what is in fact rather unusual in many social science studies, that the variables are ordered by time of occurrence, and the researcher therefore knows that variables occuring later cannot be causes of variables occurring earlier. There are still 2^{15} alternative models.

Now repeat the same sequence of calculations when there are twelve variables in the data set. With no restrictions imposed, there are 4^{66} alternative causal models, only one of which can be true. If the researcher knows that there are no cyclic paths in the true model, the number of alternatives is still astronomical: 521,939,651,343,829,405,020,504,063.[2] If the researcher is lucky enough to be able to totally order the variables and knows that later variables cannot cause earlier variables, the number of alternatives is reduced to 2^{66}.

These counts are conservative. They do not not include the possibility, which every researcher considers, that some part of the correlations is due to unmeasured variables that have effects on two or more measured variables. Including such possibilities enormously increases the numbers. What can the investigator possibly do in the face of such an enormous number of possible causal models, no more than one of which can be correct? In practice, even the best researchers usually take a wild guess or indulge their prejudices rather than their knowledge. One causal model or at most two or three is suggested, appropriate equations are written down, parameters are estimated, and the model is subjected to some statistical test. If the test is passed, the researcher is happy and journal editors are happy and the thing is published. No one likes to mention the millions, billions, or zillions of alternatives that have not been considered, or the dark and troubling fact that among those alternatives there may be many which would pass the same statistical test quite as well, or even better, and which would also square with well-established substantive knowledge about the domain.

The practice of model building in the social and behavioral sciences looks very much like irrational judgment under uncertainty. The very phenomena that Kahneman and Tversky and many others describe in experimental subjects seem to be exemplified in the practice of social science. According to Bayes' theorem, the posterior probability of any particular model should take into account both the likelihood of the evidence on the model and the prior probability of the model. Much of current practice is to hit upon a model, somehow, and to advocate the model if it passes statistical tests, even when the tests are not powerful against all alternatives. In effect, those who follow this practice are ignoring the prior probabilities and judging a model to be good enough to accept if it yields a sufficiently high likelihood. Other workers may do much better than this and attempt to carry out a serious search for alternative explanations of the data. But in view of the vast numbers of possible models, we should wonder how anyone *could* carry out an adequate search.

---

[2]See Harary [42]

Some Examples

These arguments are not just idle combinatorics. The issue affects almost every piece of applied statistics addressing nonexperimental data. Consider just a few recent examples:

1. *The Census*

The national census is certainly not free of error. Some people are sure to be missed, and those most likely to be missed are often the least advantaged in our society: those without fixed abodes, those who live in isolated areas, those who live where census workers would as soon not go. Since census statistics are used to apportion all sorts of things, from votes to benefits, who is missed where is of considerable practical and political importance. The statistical task is to estimate the actual undercount in various places given both the actual count and estimates of undercounts based on matching studies.

For the 1980 census, the Census Bureau produced 29 matching studies (Post-Enumeration Program, or PEP studies), based on a variety of alternative assumptions. Using one of these PEP studies, Ericksen and Kadane [24] investigated a number of alternative linear models in which the actual undercount depends on geographic, social, procedural, or demographic variables, and the PEP estimates are a function of the true undercount. The distributions are assumed to be normal. They estimate the undercount by regression and argue that the undercount is robust over the alternative models they consider.

Ericksen and Kadane's work was criticized by Freedman and Navidi [28] on several grounds. One criticisms is that Ericksen and Kadane do not justify their assumptions. The point of the criticism is that allegedly, for all anyone knows, alternative PEP series have the correct assumptions, and alternative models are correct and would lead either to different estimates of the undercount or to no estimates at all (if the undercount is represented by an unidentifiable parameter). Kadane [55] replies that (among other things) there is a justification for the PEP series selected, that the conclusions he and Ericksen obtain are reasonably robust, and that the undercount estimate on any reasonable set of assumptions would be better than the Census Bureau's *de facto* estimate, which is that the undercount is zero. It is clear that the major issues in this dispute concern whether an adequate search can be made for plausible alternative linear models, and whether estimates of the undercount are reasonably robust over that collection of alternatives.

2. *Criminology*

McManus [76] (reported in Leamer, [61]) investigated the deterrent effect of capital punishment by regression on several subsets of variables. He obtained importantly different results according to the independent variables selected. It is, however, unclear why the sensible thing to do is not obvious: include all of the variables. Even so, many of the independent variables considered are undoubtedly correlated, and alternative assumptions about their dependencies can be expected to again give different estimates of the deterrent effect.

In one of the largest social experiments ever carried out (described by Rossi *et al.* [86]) newly released felons in Georgia and Texas received unemployment payments for a period of six months after their release. Legal requirements prevented those receiving payments from working. The rearrest rate was the same for the Texas group and for controls who received no payments, and nearly the same for the Georgia group and controls. The experimenters concluded that payments did decrease recidivism substantially, but that unemployment increased recidivism, and the two effects exactly, or almost exactly, canceled one another. They elaborated their conclusions in a path model. In effect, the experimental design failed to control for a relevant variable, unemployment, and thus left open many alternative explanations of the results. Zeisel [113], who served on an advisory committee for the experiment, vehemently objected to the conclusions drawn by Rossi *et al.* In his opinion the experiment established the obvious: payments have no significant effect on recidivism. Zeisel proposed a simple alternative path model to account for the data.

3. *Head Start*

Data on socioeconomic status variables and achievement and ability scores for Head Start participants and comparable nonparticipants have been much studied and discussed, and have had an effect on government policy. A principal difficulty with many analyses in the literature, beginning with the Westinghouse evaluation of the summer Head Start program, is that researchers have failed to carry out any systematic search for alternative models. Jay Magidson [71], in a study of the summer Head Start data, put the issue this way:

> The problem we face is that there is an infinite number of ways to formulate a causal model, and it is not a straightforward matter to determine how to go about doing it, particularly when the causes are unknown and/or unobserved. It is important for researchers to formulate not one but many models so that they can determine whether their conclusions may differ if they accept a different set of assumptions. It is also important to follow some general guidelines in building (formulating) models when the researcher has limited information about the causal process....

1.3. The Artificial Intelligence Solution

The problem we have described seems to us both urgent and difficult. In its way, the problem is far more difficult than that of getting people to do proper data analysis, to perform tests for linearity, for example, or for autocorrelation, or to select the most powerful test statistic. There are procedures for diagnosing erroneous statistical assumptions, and work has been done toward automating such procedures, especially in the context of regression analysis. Even so, the chief difficulty will usually remain: the number of alternative theories is astronomical, and it is beyond anyone's capacity to analyze and test any more than an insignificant fraction of the possibilities.

An ideal Bayesian solution would be to impose a prior probability distribution on all of the alternative statistical models that are consistent with prior knowledge (or with prior knowledge and some simplifying assumptions), compute the likelihood of values of an appropriate statistic as functions of the model parameters, obtain the evidence, and with the likelihood and the prior probability distribution, compute the posterior distribution.[3] One trouble with this solution is that the type of evidence we have may be insufficient to bring about reconciliation of agents with different priors. For example, Leamer [61] finds that representing the views of Keynesians and monetarists by different prior probability distributions and conditioning on time series evidence doesn't do much to change initial prejudices. Another trouble is computational. We don't possess a general procedure for quickly computing posterior probability distributions from arbitrary prior distributions and arbitrary evidence.[4]

Two procedures are in common use to help with this problem, and while they have their virtues, neither is adequate. One procedure is exploratory factor analysis, which is sometimes very useful in suggesting that groups of measured variables cluster together and may, therefore, have a common cause. But exploratory factor analysis does not consider the variety of possible causal relationships. As Blalock [8] points out, factor analytic procedures do not consider the possibility that measured variables may have direct causal effects on one another, nor do they allow that measured variables may have direct effects on unmeasured variables, nor do they consider the different possible causal relationships among the unmeasured variables. Factor analysis procedures rule out a variety of realistic possibilities *a priori*.

Another procedure commonly used to help search for alternative models is the formation of *nested sequences* of models. The idea is really quite old and goes back at least to Harold Jeffreys' *Scientific Inference* [51]. There are many different

---

[3]This strategy was suggested to us by our colleague, Jay Kadane.

[4]And, given results in computation theory, we never will.

technical forms of the idea, but the basic notion is that one starts with a simple theory having only a few free parameters or, equivalently, with a theory that postulates only a few causal relationships among the variables it considers. One then introduces a new free parameter into the model (a new causal connection among the variables). Sometimes the parameter freed is chosen by a formal procedure. Some statistical test is used to compare the new model with the model that precedes it, and the process is continued until eventually the statistical test is failed. A procedure like this is carried out automatically by the LISREL program, which is widely used for certain kinds of statistical modeling. While the general strategy is admirable, and the TETRAD program described in this book has an analogous architecture, in practice there are severe difficulties. The trouble with the procedure is that there are generally far too many possible nested sequences to be explored in this way. The results obtained depend on the order in which the parameters are freed, and the formal procedures for choosing which parameters to free are too fragile, and tend to overlook the best options. Some of these difficulties were noted by those who introduced the technical procedures (see Sorbom [100] and Byron [13]).

This book proposes a new solution, or, more accurately, a partial solution to the problem of searching for alternative models. That solution has two parts. The first is to consider formal aspects of *scientific explanation* in comparing alternative models. The idea is simply that we should prefer those models that offer the best explanation of our data, and that important aspects of explanation can be represented by formal, mathematical relationships between a model and the data it is to account for. "Explanation" is not a methodological notion that plays a major role in statistics, and the theory of scientific explanation upon which we rely is not contained within any of the familiar schools of statistics. By broadening the methodological viewpoint we do not intend to neglect statistical inference where it is applicable and useful, but we do intend to make use of an understanding of scientific explanation that is familiar to philosophers and historians of science and that is common in the natural sciences.

The second theme is to use artificial intelligence techniques to help search for models that will provide the best explanation of our data. The very idea owes a great deal to Herbert Simon [95], who also contributed to the understanding of connections between causal relationships and multivariate analysis. Simon takes one of the hallmarks of artificial intelligence to be *heuristic search*. A heuristic search is a computer procedure that applies plausible steps to hunt through an enormous space of alternatives in order to locate the best (or a collection of the best) alternatives for some purpose. What makes the search *heuristic* is that the procedure does not *guarantee* that the outcome will be the best alternative or will be a collection that includes the best alternative, but the procedure will typically produce the best alternative, or come rather close. The search procedures may, in various respects be less than rigorous and may not always deliver the optimal solution, but they will typically yield outcomes that are both good enough and better than can be obtained without heuristic search. Simon calls the strategy "satisficing." It amounts to settling for what is feasible and good enough rather than insisting on what is optimal but infeasible. A philosopher, Wilfrid Sellars, puts the same point in a simple imperative, upon which we will have several occasions to rely: do not let the best be the enemy of the good.

Simon's idea is that scientific discovery is a kind of heuristic search through alternative hypotheses or theories. If that is so, then there is a formal structure to scientific discovery, and if we can get a grip on that computational structure, then computer programs can make scientific discoveries. And indeed they already have. In chemistry, logic, and geometry, artificial intelligence programs have made discoveries of various kinds, and Simon [96] and his associates have written a series of programs that simulate many of the discoveries in the history of science.

The aim of artificial intelligence programs need not be to do things in quite the way that humans do them, especially if humans do the thing rather poorly and the computer can be made to do it better. Humans cannot do large sums very accurately; we do not want our pocket calculators to simulate our own inadequacies. Humans also seem not to be able to search through the space of alternative statistical models very adequately. Our claim is that a computer program, using heuristic search techniques, can help do it better. This book is a defense of that claim. Our argument is based on an actual program, TETRAD, a copy of which is included with this book. The program is intended to assist in the search for adequate statistical models of a very general kind, including factor analytic models, path analytic models, structural equation models, and many other varieties of linear statistical theory. They do not include statistical theories that cannot be put in additive form. A TETRAD user can learn more in an afternoon about the existence and properties of alternative linear models for covariance data than could an unaided researcher in months or even years of reflection and calculation. The TETRAD program is offered as a useful working tool, but it is also offered as an example. We think the same very general ideas about heuristic search can be, and ought to be, applied to develop artificial intelligence aids for other kinds of statistical models.

The notion of applying artificial intelligence techniques to problems of statistical model specification is not really novel. Several programs have been developed or proposed that apply artificial intelligence techniques to statistical modeling. Systems have been developed to test automatically the adequacy of common modeling assumptions, such as linearity and normality, and to suggest transformations of variables or other changes where these assumptions fail (see Gale and Pregibon [31] for a review). A great deal is known about statistical diagnostics, and the aim of these programs is to make that information, or appropriate conclusions, automatically available to the inexpert. One example is the REX program developed at Bell Labs by Gale and Pregibon. The program is designed to assist in regression modeling and will actively transform variables (to their logarithms, for example) to satisfy regression assumptions.

In principle, computer-aided search for causal relations has important applications beyond aiding researchers in finding better explanations. Fully automatic programs of this kind can function as inference modules in robotic systems. More immediately, fully automatic search for causal relations holds the promise of unlocking large data bases. In medicine, social science, astrophysics, in fact almost every domain, we have managed to collect more data than we have time and power to analyze. Potentially valuable causal knowledge is effectively locked up by the sizes of the data bases. Computer discovery procedures that are fully automated and reasonably reliable seem the only hope for making real use of the information we continue to acquire and store.

The problem of automatic computer search for causal relations has barely been scratched. Perhaps the best known piece of work in this line is Blum's [11] RX program. The RX program uses prior knowledge about a particular domain, rheumatoid diseases, together with a statistical package and a large data base. The variables in the data base are indexed by time, so that a variable with a later index cannot be a cause of a correlated variable with an earlier time index. The program looks for correlations that may be due to causal relations. When a correlation is found, the relationship is tested and compared with the program's current knowledge to determine whether the correlation may be due to common causes acting on the variables. If not, a causal conclusion is added to the knowledge base and the program continues. The statistical analyses are restricted to multiple regression models, and therefore a great many alternative causal explanations of correlation are never considered.

The program we describe in this book, TETRAD, is a continuation of the tradition of work on automated discovery carried out by Simon, Buchanan [68] , Blum, and others. TETRAD is not fully automatic and does not proceed without the active engagement of the user's judgment. But neither is the TETRAD program confined to searching for multiple regression models. Instead, the program is intended to help the user search through the vast space of alternative linear causal models that might explain a body of covariance data.

2. THE CASE AGAINST CAUSAL MODELING

2.1. The Critical Reaction

Causal modeling of nonexperimental data has been controversial since its beginning, and it is no less controversial today. The controversies are very philosophical, and they involve fundamental differences about what makes for science. The social and behavioral sciences are inevitably compared with the natural sciences, and disputes about methodology in social and behavioral science are often essentially disputes about what it is that has made the natural sciences so successful in understanding, predicting, and controlling the physical world. Paul Meehl [78] is fond of pointing out the discrepancies between the methodological procedures of chemists and physicists and biologists, on the one hand, and the methodological practices of the "soft sciences" on the other hand. Many natural scientists would be altogether puzzled by what goes on in quantitative sociology or social psychology or econometrics, and they would be unlikely to recognize some of it as science.

The essential question we shall pursue is whether, in the many criticisms of causal modeling *practices*, there are good reasons to think that the entire endeavor is suspect, or whether the valid criticisms are only evidence that social and behavioral scientists sometimes labor with misconceptions as to what science requires. That an enterprise is sometimes badly conducted is no sufficient argument that it is inherently unscientific or that it could not, in principle, be done well. Our view is that there are many well-founded criticisms of particular studies, and of various common practices in causal modeling, but none of the criticisms gives reason to think that the very idea is mistaken. We will also argue that the critics are often nearly as confused as those they criticize, and that many of the principled criticisms of causal modeling derive from mythology about the natural sciences. Our opinion is that there is nothing philosophically or methodologically wrong with applying statistical models to nonexperimental data or with the attempt to uncover causal structure. But doing it well, so that the result contributes to the progress of knowledge, is very hard, and there are many ways to go astray.

We will consider in turn the following criticisms of causal modeling:

1. Causal modeling involves a mistaken, or incoherent, conception of causal relations.

2. Theories with latent variables should be rejected on methodological or semantic grounds.

3. Only experimental data can contribute to our knowledge of causal relationships.

15

4. Those who advocate causal models do not, and presumably cannot, make a case for the assumptions of their models.

5. Linear causal models should be rejected because they are always literally false.

2.2. Making Sense of Causality

Some social scientists prefer to avoid causal language. They assume it is enough to give a set of structural equations, estimate the coefficients of the model, and perhaps subject the system of equations to a statistical test or tests. Some statisticians regard causal inferences drawn from nonexperimental data with the assistance of statistical models as an abuse of their subject.[5] These harsh judgments seem to spring from a vague sense that causal talk is unscientific or "metaphysical," or at best a gratuitous and unclear addition to the much clearer system of equations of a structural model.

In fact, the very logical structure of most social science models requires mathematical structure beyond that of a system of equations. Econometricians distinguish exogenous from endogenous variables, others distinguish independent from dependent variables. These distinctions are not given by the equations themselves. It makes no difference to the algebra which variables are written on the left hand side and which on the right hand side of the equality sign. When social scientists introduce such distinctions they are providing, in addition to the equations, a partial ordering of the variables. That partial ordering has a natural causal interpretation.

The application of most social science models depends on drawing causal conclusions from them. That is because we are usually interested in applying such models in situations where we have the possibility of changing some features of the social or economic system, and our concern is to know what other changes will result if we do so. This sort of application is routine with econometric models of national economies. Parameters representing policy variables are run with hypothetical rather than actual values in an attempt to predict the effects of changes in policy. Again, with models of the Head Start data, we are concerned with whether or not Head Start participation *causes* improvement in school and test performance. In studies of the American occupational structure, we may be interested in whether the educational system *causes* social mobility. In criminological studies, we are often concerned with whether specific penalties

---

[5]For some more optimistic recent discussions of statistics and causal inference, see Holland [47] and Glymour [37].

(e.g., the death penalty) *deter* certain crimes. To deter is to cause not to happen. Correlations and regression coefficients don't give us that information. Only causal conclusions will do so.

There are some contexts in which social science models are of practical importance even without causal conclusions. In estimating the undercount in the census, for example, we are not principally interested in drawing a causal conclusion. But more often, we want causal knowledge, however much our language may disguise that fact. Causal relations are either asserted or presupposed in almost every circumstance in which the application of social theory leads to a *counterfactual* assertion, that is, to an assertion roughly of the form "If A had happened, B would have happened." Causal conclusions are usually implicit when *future conditionals* are asserted, for example, in sentences such as "If the death penalty is enforced for murder, fewer homicides will occur." If social science could never lead to these sorts of conclusions (or their denials), we would not have much practical use or hope for it.[6]

The idea that causal discourse is somehow unscientific is rather wild. The determination of causal relations and causal structure remains a principal part of the enterprises of physics, chemistry, biology, engineering, and medicine. Causal talk is used without a qualm in many scientific papers on these subjects as well as in every laboratory. Why is it improper, then, in social science? It is sometimes claimed that causal talk is "meaningless," but that is itself a sloppy expression that cannot be taken seriously. We use causal talk all the time in everyday life, with pretty fair mutual understanding. We have good formal semantical theories of causal discourse (see Lewis [64] and Cross [21]). In innumerable cases we know how to determine causal relationships. What more could be required for intelligibility?

Interpreting Causal Claims

Many philosophers have attempted to explicate the notion of causality in terms of the notion of probability (see Suppes, Skyrms and Good, [106, 99, 38]). A probabilistic characterization of causality has been introduced into econometrics by Clive Granger [40] and developed by others (see Sims [97]). We do not assume that causal relations can be reduced to probabilistic relations of any kind, but neither do we contradict such assumptions. Instead, we assume that the theorist imposes certain connections between causality and probability. The most important of these connections is that, *ceteris paribus*, correlations are to be explained by causal relationships of one or another kind.

---

[6]For a careful discussion of the confusions about causality in the recent methodological literature in economics, see Hausman [44].

We assume that a causal claim implies a functional dependence, although not every functional dependence is a causal dependence. If A causes B then some changes in A must be accompanied by changes in B, if other variables are held constant; if A is a cause of B, then B is a function of A and (quite possibly) other variables. If B changes, then A must have changed if the other variables of which B is a function did not change. So we say that if A is a cause of B, then, *ceteris paribus*, a change in B must be accompanied by a change in A. Or, put another way, if A causes B, then, *ceteris paribus*, if a change in A had not occurred, a change in B would not have occurred.[7]

Mathematically, the representation of causal relationships in combination with linear structural equation systems is very simple. The causal relations are represented by a labeled directed graph, and the directed graph uniquely determines the structural equations of the statistical model. But mathematical representation is the easiest part; the hard part concerns what inferences are to be drawn from causal claims. One of the inferences to be drawn from the claim that A causes B is that, *ceteris paribus*, if B has changed then A must have changed. In the context of causal modeling the claim is ambiguous. There is a strong version:

> For any member of the population, *ceteris paribus*, if the value of B for *that* individual has changed, then the value of A for that same individual has changed.

There is also a weaker interpretation of the claim that variable A has an effect on variable B:

> For any two members of the population, *ceteris paribus*, if they differ in their values of B, then they differ in their values of A.

The two versions are not the same, and one can be true when the other is false. The first sense presupposes that if feature A is a cause, then it makes sense to talk of changing A for particular individuals. Sometimes that doesn't make sense: for example, it doesn't seem to make sense to talk of substantially changing the

---

[7]It might be claimed that we have it backwards and that A causes B means that, other things being equal, a change in A is accompanied by a change in B. But if A causes B does imply that B is a function of A and other variables, then (unless the function is one to one) a change in the value of A can occur without any change in the value of B, as in $B = A^2$. If the relations are linear then the relation is of course symetrical, and if A causes B then, ceteris paribus, if A changes B will change. And, of course, if, *ceteris paribus*, A causes B then some changes in A must be accompanied by changes in B.

genetic structure of one and the same individual. Some writers, such as Holland [47], contend that only when one is prepared to assert the strong claim is one really talking of causality. Terminology aside, it is important to recognize that the weaker claim might be correct even though the stronger one fails.

A related consideration is that causal claims may be true only historically. Lieberson [66] points out, correctly, that many causal processes are not reversible. So if values of B came to obtain historically because of what appears to be a linear dependence of B on A and changes in the value of A, a reversal in the value of A might not bring about a concomitant reversal in the values of B. When that occurs the dependence of A on B is not, in fact, linear.

These points are really cautions rather than objections to the notion of causality or to the search for causal explanations of nonexperimental data. They remind us that in understanding causal claims we must pay attention to what is being talked about. Lieberson enters another caution of a similar kind: If one knows that A causes B, one cannot conclude that a change in a third variable, C, that has not hitherto varied in the population or sample, will not cause a change in A or in B or in both.

All of these cautions are valuable, but there is no reason to suppose that they must necessarily bring trouble for causal modeling. Anyone considering genetic causes of phenotypic traits, for example, will be unlikely to confuse the weak and strong *ceteris paribus* conditionals. We can consider what differences in genotype between individuals may produce differences in phenotypic traits, but we are not likely to confuse ourselves into thinking we can change the genotype of a particular individual. No one is likely to think that the claim that Head Start participation improves school performance implies that a sixteen-year-old who did not participate in Head Start will have his school performance improved by reversing that condition and entering Head Start at age sixteen. Few of us are likely to think that, because nutritional levels did not vary in a sample of students obtained in a study of school performance, major changes in nutrition would have no effect on school performance. The cautions are sound, and important, but there is nothing in them to make us abandon the enterprise of causal modeling.

Baumrind and the Concept of Causality

In the course of a criticism of a paper by O'Donnell and Clayton [82] arguing that marijuana use is a stepping stone to heroin use, Diana Baumrind mounts a vigorous attack on causal modeling. She has interesting substantive objections to their argument, and she proposes an alternative causal model of the data, which we will not consider here. The chief burden of her essay, however, is that causal modeling of nonexperimental data can never justify drawing causal conclusions.

In particular, Baumrind criticizes the idea that causal relations consist in certain sorts of probabilistic relations, an idea which she (mistakenly) thinks is essential to causal modeling. The proposal, to which she objects, is that A's cause B's, where A and B are kinds of events, if the occurrence of an A event increases the probability of a subsequent B event and there are no events $C_1,...,C_n$, such that, conditional on prior events of kinds $C_1,...,C_n$, events of kinds A and B are statistically independent. Her criticisms of probabilistic accounts of causal relations are as follows:

1. It is a "parochial model of causality shared by neither laypersons nor philosophers of science." (p. 1289)

2. Shultz [91] has performed experiments that appear to show that people of all ages prefer a "generative" model of causal relations over covariation.

3. The correct account of causation is generative: "The generative approach to causation refers to the notion that the cause *produces* the effect.... Within the generative model the event called the *cause* acts to change or to produce the event called the *effect*" (p. 1291).

4. A parable. "The number of never-married persons in certain British villages is highly inversely correlated with the number of field mice in the surrounding meadows. Marital status of humans was considered an established cause of field mice by the village elders until the mechanisms of transmission were finally surmised: Never-married persons bring with them a disproportionate number of cats relative to the rest of the village populace *and* cats consume field mice. With the generative mechanisms understood, village elders could concentrate their attention on increasing the population of cats rather than the proportion of never-married persons. Note that although the correlation between marital status and incidence of field mice is *not* a joint effect caused by incidence of cats and is therefore a true association...the explanation that marital status is a cause of incidence of field mice is at best trivial, whereas the generative explanation that cats consume mice is valuable." (p.1297)

We cannot speak for laypersons, but we can speak for philosophers of science. Baumrind's claim is false. Several (rather more precise) versions of the probabilistic account of causality sketched above are advocated by some of the most prominent contemporary philosophers of science (for example, Suppes [106], Salmon [87], and Skyrms [99]). We can speak *about* lay-persons. What Schultz's experiments show is hard to say. No one should be surprised if in some circumstances laypeople systematically violate probabilistic criteria for causal attributions. There is considerable evidence that lay, and even expert, judgments about probability and causality violate almost every normative standard (see Kahneman, [56], and Faust, [25]).

Baumrind's characterization of the "generative" model of causality is not very helpful because it is not very clear. There are a few contemporary philosophers who analyze causal relations in terms of an unanalyzed oomph [43], but the closest thing to a clear and influential philosophical account that bears any connection to Baumrind's is the counterfactual analysis of causation developed by Lewis [65]. On these accounts, A causes B if and only if A occurs and B occurs, and if A had not occurred then B would not have occurred. (In Lewis' theory a model-theoretic semantics is developed for the counterfactuals that arise in this analysis of causation.) But this account allows increases in never-married persons to cause declines in the population of field mice.

What Baumrind really seems to mean by "generative" causation is that causal attributions should come with a specified *mechanism* by which the causal relation occurs. The intervening steps should all be spelled out and verified if possible. That is a perfectly sensible request, but it is part of *methodology*, not part of the meaning of "cause." It is a request that can only be satisfied, in any subject, by the examination of correlations, experimental or otherwise, and the application of prior knowledge. Baumrind's parable is bootless. In the story, variations in never-married persons *do* cause variations in field mice, even if the causation is indirect, and nothing in the story prevents the use of covariance analysis on uncontrolled samples to discover that the intervening variable is the density of cats.

Lots of models derived from nonexperimental data come with plausible speculations about the process by which the causal relation comes about. Thus, the apparently astonishing conclusion (see Crain [20]) that annual automobile safety inspections actually tend slightly to increase highway accidents rather than to decrease them is elaborated with possible mechanisms. For example, inspections may tend to give automobile drivers an erroneous view of the safety and reliability of their machines. There are obvious psychological mechanisms for the apparent effects of responses to some questionaire items on responses to other items. Blau and Duncan occasionally suggest mechanisms for the causal relations they argue for in *The American Occupational Structure*.

The importance of establishing the details of a causal process depends on the context. In many cases we are perfectly happy to know that plausible mechanisms can be conceived, and don't much care what the actual mechanism may be. In other cases, we may doubt a causal claim exactly because no plausible mechanism can be thought of. In still other cases, we may not have much doubt about the genuineness of the causal connection but may be especially concerned to discover its mechanism of action. In these respects, sociological and psychological and epidemiological mechanisms are no different from chemical mechanisms.

2.3. Causes, Indicators, and the Interpretation of Latent Variables

General Objections

Many linear models, including those for which TETRAD analyses are most useful, contain variables that have not been measured. Mathematically, models with such latent variables often specify that some of the measured variables are linear functions of one or more of the latent variables. Further, the latent variables are often given a causal interpretation--their variation causes variation in the measured variables--and this causal interpretation is represented in the directed graph of the model. Finally, latent variables are routinely given a title that carries some meaning with it: "socioeconomic status," "industrial development," "Authoritarian-Conservative personality trait."

A long tradition in philosophy of science holds that what cannot be measured or seen directly is not worthy of *belief*. Philosophers (and they have included many distinguished scientists, such as Pierre Duhem) of this persuasion usually hold that theories postulating unobserved objects and properties and relationships are useful and valuable *instruments* for prediction and control, for generating new experiments, and for guiding the development of still further theories, but they deny that these virtues give grounds for belief. They distinguish belief from *acceptance*. We may have good practical reasons for accepting theories as good empirical predictors and as useful tools, they hold, but no reason to go further and actually believe our theories. The best contemporary defense of this antirealist conception is in Bas Van Fraassen's *The Scientific Image* [109].

Realist philosophers of science think otherwise. They think we can have as much, perhaps more, reason to believe in our theories as we do to believe in everyday claims made outside of science. They distinguish *credence* from *certainty*. Belief has to do with credence, and we can allot more or less of it to a proposition without taking that proposition to be *certain*.

Realists and antirealists in philosophy of science agree that theories going beyond observation are useful and inevitable, and they largely agree as well on what virtues make one theory preferable to another. What they disagree about, for the most part, is whether those virtues give us reason to believe our best theories.

In the social and behavioral sciences, and in applied statistics generally, there is a much more radical train of thought which holds that, in constructing theories, *we should not postulate unmeasured features or properties or entities*. This view is very different from the philosophical antirealism we have just discussed, for it amounts to claiming that not introducing unobserved features is an overriding virtue of any theory: any theory that introduces unobserved features is inferior to any theory that does not. These critics think that it is somehow unscientific to introduce theoretical causes that are not directly measured. For example, Holland [47] rejects the introduction of any causal factors that cannot be manipulated and many econometricians and statisticians object to latent variables on the grounds that they do not give any novel predictions. The most famous modern rejection of latent variables came from B.F. Skinner [98] on the grounds that anything that can be predicted with latent variables can be predicted without them.

For two reasons, the critics of latent variables have things backwards. One is that latent variables often do not represent variables that are unobservable, whatever that may mean. They represent variables that are, in a particular study, not observed. In many empirical studies the variables measured form a rather small subset of those that *could* have been measured, and that might be relevant to the data obtained. It would be silly to omit, *a priori*, such unmeasured variables from all explanations of the data.

The second reason is as follows. *The natural sciences are successful exactly because of their search for latent factors affecting the phenomena to be explained or predicted.* Newtonian dynamics and celestial mechanics, the theory of electricity and magnetism, optics, chemistry, genetics, and the whole of modern physics would not have come to pass if natural scientists behaved as the critics of latent variables prefer. Gravitational force, electrical fluids and particles, electromagnetic fields, atoms and molecules, genes and gravitational fields, none of them could be directly measured or manipulated when they initially became part of modern science. Few of these notions were introduced initially because they predicted anything; they were introduced because they *explained things*. Newtonian theory explained Kepler's laws, and did so beautifully; Daltonian atomism explained (then controversial) regularities of chemical substances, such as the law of definite proportions; general relativity explained the anomalous advance of the perihelion of Mercury; Bohr's quantum theory explained spectral series of hydrogen. Of course these theories did eventually lead to important predictions, but they did so exactly because people who investigated the latent factors postulated by the theories sought laws about them and their properties, and sought to test those generalizations.

Critics may grant that the introduction of latent variables has been essential in the natural sciences, but maintain that they are inappropriate in the social and behavioral sciences. It is hard to think of any convincing reason for this view, however, and we should demand *very* convincing reasons for any methodological strictures that contradict the methodology of our most succesful sciences. Critics may doubt that statistical theories of nonexperimental data can *explain* in the same way that theories in the natural sciences do, or that the explanations can lead to novel predictions. In Part II of this book we will show that linear causal models can explain in the same fashion that, say, Daltonian atomism explained the law of definite proportions, that Maxwell explained electromagnetic phenomena, or that Copernican theory explained regularities of planetary motion. We will also show that theories with latent variables can lead to novel predictions that would be unlikely to be found without them.

Interpreting Latent Variables

In the social sciences, latent variables are routinely given some gloss. They are labeled "socioeconomic status," or "cognitive ability." In describing the TETRAD program, and in applying it to actual cases, we will follow the common practice, but with serious qualms. It is important to understand some difficulties with the practice, and to beware of certain confusions that may result from it.

Consider socioeconomic status. It is routinely used in sociological studies as a latent variable that affects education, income, occupation, and other variables. The implicit or explicit causal assumptions are:

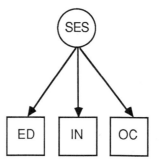

Figure 2-1: Standard causal interpretation of socioeconomic status.

Our understanding of the latent variable in fact often conflicts with this causal representation. If we think of socioeconomic status as a conglomeration of socioeconomic indices, and thus a function of education, income, and occupation, the causal dependencies are the reverse of those above.

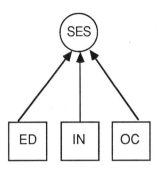

Figure 2-2: Alternative causal interpretation of socioeconomic status.

The same is true if we think of socioeconomic status as other's perceptions of a subject's status, perceptions influenced by education, income and occupation.[8] Of course models should be considered in which measured variables such as income and occupation are affected by a latent variable, but that variable cannot be interpreted as socioeconomic status in either of the above senses.

There is nothing amiss, logically or scientifically, in having latent variables that one is not quite sure how to interpret. Surely that is better than having latent variables with an interpretation that cannot be sustained. There is nothing wrong with supposing that something, for which we have no convenient name but which is *not* socioeconomic status, acts as a common cause of parental education, occupation, and income.

The most important error that inappropriate interpretations of latent variables may occasion is the failure to consider alternative models. Often variables are clustered together and specified to be the effects of a common latent variable because there is some common content to their description. In a study of school children, for example, Maruyama and McGarvey [74] group together a number of variables because they have to do with popularity, group other variables because they have to do with achievement, and group still others because they have to do with socioeconomic status. Within the causal model, these groupings carry a causal significance. They say that these features have a common cause. That may be correct, but it is not necessarily correct. That schoolwork popularity and playground popularity are both forms of popularity does not imply that they have a common cause, "popularity," or that they have any common cause at all. There is

---

[8]See Blalock [9].

no *a priori* warrant, therefore, for failing to search for other groupings of variables.

2.4. The Importance of Experiment

Diana Baumrind [3] said, "The objective of the traditional social psychology experiment is to enable the experimenter to infer unambiguously the existence and direction of causal relations by ruling out alternative causal explanations" ([3], p.1290). The objective may not often be literally achieved, but she is surely right that one of the advantages, perhaps the principal advantage, of experimental procedures is that they help to reduce the number of alternative causal models that might account for a body of phenomena. From a Bayesian perspective, experimental data may give narrower posterior distributions than nonexperimental data (compare Leamer [61]).

The advantages of experimental control can be seen from simple combinatoric considerations, provided we suppose that the outcome of each experiment is unambiguous. If we have four variables of concern to us, then there are $4^6 = 4096$ distinct possible causal graphs. If, however, we can control each variable experimentally, then we can consider them two at a time, making sure that other variables do not change, and test whether wiggling variable X makes variable Y wiggle, and whether wiggling Y makes X wiggle. Twelve experiments, two for each pair of variables, will therefore determine the pairwise causal dependencies. Of course it will take many more experiments than that to determine the form of the dependency of X and Y over a range of values, and far more measurements still to determine all possible nonadditive relations among variables. But experiments aren't always unambiguous, which is the point to which we next turn.

Zeisel on Experimentation and the TARP Experiment

In criticisms of causal modeling, judgments about issues of *principle* are often entangled with criticisms of particularly bad practices. One particular example has played a role in controversies over the advantages of experimental methods in social science. The Transitional Aid Research Project (TARP) was one of the largest social experiments ever conducted. The experiment, and the treatment of the data, are described in Rossi *et al., Money, Work and Crime* [86]. The experiment was intended to test the effects of financial support for newly released felons on recidivism rates. Payments to newly released felons in Texas and Georgia were made through the state unemployment commissions for a period of six months. Control groups in both states received no such payments. The outcome was nil: payments made no difference to recidivism. Rossi *et al.* concluded that unemployment, which was a condition of receiving the payments in the experiment, increased recidivism, while the payments themselves decreased recidivism, and the two effects simply happened to cancel one another out. Hans

Zeisel was originally on the advisory panel for the experiment, but resigned in protest over the treatment of the data. He objected, because, among other things, there was a better account of the outcome, namely the obvious one that payments have no effect on recidivism.

Rossi *et al.* responded by citing a previous, smaller scale experiment which they claimed supported their interpretation. (That effort, the LIFE experiment conducted in Maryland, is also discussed in their book). They further argue that their model is to be preferred to Zeisel's hypothesis because:

> ...the counterbalancing model and related specification were postulated before the structural equations were estimated and were constructed both on the basis of the result of the prior LIFE experiment in which a payment plan did have a recidivism reducing effect and by drawing on social science theory concerning the possible competition between legitimate and illegitimate income producing activities. There is a vast difference between posing a theory before examining the data and posing one after examining them. On that basis alone, Zeisel's post hoc models cannot stand on equal footing with our a priori model. Furthermore, our modeling was tested through replication, being first constructed on the data derived from the Texas experiment and then tested on the data from the Georgia experiment.

On the substantive argument, Zeisel wins hands down. The LIFE experiment, performed under conditions that permitted those receiving payments also to seek legal employment, showed an 8% differential recidivism rate for crimes of theft and no difference for other categories of crime. The difference was statistically significant, but only barely ([86], p. 37-43). The TARP experiment showed no significant difference. The only evidence the two experiments together provide for the effect of payments on recidivism is the weak evidence of the LIFE experiment, and that evidence is weakened further, not strengthened, by the TARP outcome. The temporal argument just cited is fallacious. It certainly makes an important difference if one theory uses the data to adjust a lot of parameters and another theory accounts for the data without such fiddling, but in fact it is the hypothesis of Rossi *et al.* that seems to require the most fiddling. But in this case, even the premises of the argument given by Rossi *et al.*, are false. The counterbalancing model was not obtained before examining the data. It seems clear that the model was developed after the null effect of the payments was known, and was developed in order to save the experimenters' hypothesis in the face of apparently refuting evidence. The puzzling claim that the model was postulated before the structural equations were estimated (how *could* one estimate equations before obtaining them?) indicates a confusion of estimation with testing.

The claim that the counterbalancing model was tested in any way is charitably described as Pickwickian. Rossi *et al.* begin their section on "Testing the TARP Counterbalancing Model" ([86] pp.108-112) as follows:

> So far the counterbalancing model... is a reasonable but not yet demonstrated hypothesis that can seemingly account for both the TARP and LIFE results. However, the model need not remain on the level of an unproven hypothesis since it is possible to use the TARP data to estimate coefficients for each of the links....

The authors then proceed to "test," "demonstrate," and "prove" their model *simply by estimating its coefficients!* No statistical test of the model is reported, save for t tests of the coefficients. Any mathematically consistent, identifiable model whatsoever can pass the "test" of parameter identification, and the t tests of coefficients are only tests of the significance of the parameters *given* the assumptions of the whole "counterbalancing model."

The claim that the model is tested because the same model was used on both the Texas and the Georgia data is smoke in logical eyes. Any identifiable model can be estimated on two different samples. We are not told whether the small differences in coefficient estimates are significant, but sameness of the coefficient estimates in the two populations would show little more than that the measured correlations are the same. That might indicate that the data are reproducible and give some confirmation of the appropriateness of linear modeling assumptions, but it has no other bearing whatsoever on the truth of the counterbalancing model.

Zeisel's methodological conclusion is more sweeping and less tenable than is his criticism of the arguments given by Rossi *et al.* He claims that there is a difference in kind between correlational and experimental data, and that experiments are always unequivocal.

> To interpret correlational data a theory is needed, and unless the theory is correct the interpretation will not be correct. It is the beauty of the controlled experiment that all the theorizing goes into its design. The result of the experiment, though more limited in its scope than correlational speculation, speaks for itself and needs no further theoretical support.

Would that it were true. It is not even close to the truth. Take any experimental subject you please, and its history and contemporary practice will show the reverse.

Chemistry. Robert Boyle's "pigeon" experiment, in which water boiled in a closed flask left a solid residue, was taken by Boyle to show that water could be turned into earth. Others disagreed. Dumas' measurements of the vapor density of phosphorus and sulfur in the 1830s were taken by Dumas, and others, to refute the atomic theory. The experiment was interpreted consistently with atomism by

Gaudin shortly after, but the interpretation remained controversial for thirty years. More recently, the interpretation of experiments that were purported to demonstrate the existence of a new physical state of water ("polywater") was controversial.

Physics. In the late nineteenth century, the foundations of electrodynamics turned on the interpretation to be given to a large number of optical and electrical effects, effects that could be produced at any time in almost any laboratory or observatory. Not least among them was the outcome of the Michelson-Morley experiment, whose interpretation was doubly controversial: many physicists disputed what the experiment demonstrated, and some (e.g., Miller) disputed that the experiment had revealed any real (null) effect at all. The significance of experimental comparisons of the solar spectrum with terrestrial spectra was disputed from 1914 into the 1920s, at least. Recently the interpretation of experiments that purported to detect gravitational waves has been disputed, and so has the interpretation of measurements of the shape of the sun. These are not isolated cases. They are typical cases.

Should one think that subjects, such as biology and psychology and sometimes even sociology, in which experimental and control groups are formed and given different treatments, somehow provide more certainty about the interpretation of their experimental outcomes? It seems unlikely that biologists, psychologists and experimental social scientists somehow provide a certainty that physicists and chemists cannot.

Control group experiments cannot be isolated from controversy for several reasons. Two prominent considerations are sample dissimilarity and unintended treatment effects. That samples are drawn from a population at random does not guarantee that they are representative. That subjects are assigned to various treatment classes at random does not guarantee that the class memberships are matched on all relevant nontreatment variables. Controversies can arise not simply because of statistical considerations about sample size, but also because of sampling methods, properties of the actual samples selected, etc. When a "treatment" is given to an experimental group, whatever is done is a complex event, with many facets. Separating out which facets are responsible for any differences found between experimental and control groups on outcome variables is not always trivial or obvious. The behavior of the experimenter's themselves may be the most important facet, as Rosenthal's [85] experiments suggest. The knowledge of the subjects themselves about their role in the experiment may be significant. It is exactly these concerns that are responsible for the double-blind design often used in medical research, in which neither experimenter nor subject is supposed to know which subjects are receiving the experimental treatment and which are controls. Even so, many medical experiments are anything but decisive.

The TARP study itself conflicts with Zeisel's opinion of the value of experiments. The explanation proposed by Rossi and his associates is *ad hoc*, and their arguments for it are egregious, but that does not show that their explanation is false. An *ad hoc* hypothesis can nonetheless be true, and bad arguments can be given for true hypotheses as easily as for false ones. Rossi *et al.* in effect suppose that a lot of leisure and absence of work discipline increases the propensity of felons to commit new crimes, that some cash in the pocket decreases that propensity, and the contrary effects are about equal. These are not absurd hypotheses, and they cannot be dismissed out of hand.

Zeisel and Baumrind seem to share the view that without experimental controls there is no science, and causal conclusions are never warranted. Their opinion is shared by others who do not bother to argue for it (e.g., Ehrenberg [23]). This is not a sustainable position. Most of astronomy developed without experimental evidence: Copernican theory was established without experimental evidence, as were Kepler's laws. Newtonian celestial mechanics had for *experimental* support only the law of the pendulum. The principal early argument for general relativity was its explanation of the anomalous advance of Mercury's perihelion, a phenomenon established by statistical analysis of nonexperimental data using a lot of assumptions. The first clearly *experimental* evidence for the theory, Pound and Rebka's, was not obtained until 1960. Darwin had the experience of animal breeders and his own uncontrolled experiments with pigeons, but his major evidence was the observation of variation and speciation in nature. Contemporary cosmologists observe; they cannot wiggle the entire universe, or build another cosmos for a control group. Good experiments are to be treasured, but science does not cease without them.

2.5. Justifying Assumptions

Ling on Causal Modeling

Robert Ling's [69] review of David Kenny's [58] *Correlation and Causation* is less a review than a call to arms against statistical and causal modeling. Despite its brevity, Ling's review seems to have caught the sentiments of the critics, and it is cited with approval both by Baumrind and by Freedman. The real substance of Ling's criticism turns on the existence of alternative models of data and on the failure to search for such alternatives, a failure sometimes justified simply by appeal to "assumptions."

> The logical fallacy underlying path analysis and other forms of inference from correlation can be illustrated by the following.... A researcher believes that malaria may be caused directly by exposure to swampy air.... Having specified the causal assumption by a path diagram, he finds a significant correlation between the incidence of malaria (Y) and the swampiness index of numerous locations sampled in the study. Ergo, the researcher concludes that "mal air" is the direct cause of malaria.
>
> The foregoing example is not atypical of the manner in which theories are

established by those employing the techniques described in this book. Not infrequently, the causal assumption (theory) is suggested by correlational data, which are then used (tautaulogically) as if the data were sufficient evidence to confirm the causal theory. In the path analysis methodology, the researcher can never disconfirm a false causal assumption, regardless of the sample size or evidence, so long as the variables alleged to be causally related are correlated.

There is a great deal of hyperbole in these paragraphs. Of course the assumptions of path models and other linear causal models can be, and often are, tested. But testing is not nearly enough. Often the tests applied to causal models are of low power given the sample size, meaning that for all anyone knows there may exist many, many alternative models that would also pass whatever test has been applied. A set of assumptions in a causal model cannot be justified merely by statistical testing without a search for alternative explanations of the data or without direct arguments from other sources. It remains true, however, that some of the most objectionable procedures in the social science literature are exactly as Ling describes them. The TARP experiment is a vivid example.

The examples could easily be multiplied. They can be found in economics quite as well as in political science and criminology. Ling's accusations are a fair complaint in many cases. That doesn't make them good logical objections to the technique of causal modeling, or establish that path analysis is "at best a form of statistical fantasy." Failures of practice do not establish a failure of principle. Contrary to Ling, nothing in statistical causal modeling prevents researchers from disconfirming, or even rejecting, direct causal relations between correlated variables. From early days (see Simon [94]) theorists knew that the hypothesis of direct causal relations could be disconfirmed by discovering other appropriate variables showing the association to be "spurious," i.e., the result of a common cause rather than a direct connection. Hypotheses about causal relations, direct or not, can be disconfirmed by the discovery of alternative models that give better accounts of the data and do better by statistical tests. They can be disconfirmed either by examining new samples from the population, or special subpopulations in which some variables do not vary, or by deriving from them predictions (or retrodictions) which prove to be false. Ling should have blamed some of the singers, not the song.

2.6. Linear Theories Are Literally False

Anyone who thinks there is any point or justification for statistical modeling and causal inference from nonexperimental data should be prepared to give an example of good modeling and good inference. There are many dimensions of goodness, and a good study is not necessarily, or even usually, one that is uncontroversial or unobjectionable. It is one that enhances our predictive ability, makes a persuasive case, or undermines our previous assumptions, and does so by reasonable scientific standards. By those criteria, it is easy to find good examples of causal inference from nonexperimental data. In return, serious criticism of causal modeling methodology (rather than practice) should turn on the best cases, not the worst.

Blau and Duncan's [10] study of the American occupational structure was recently cited by the National Academy of Sciences [75] as an exemplary piece of social science. Since it makes heavy use of causal modeling techniques, it is the sort of example that critics should consider. David Freedman [29] has done just that. Freedman levels a great many criticisms, which we will consider one by one. His principal objections, however, are that Blau and Duncan do not justify the assumptions used in their model and that the model is literally false. So let us first consider the value of literal truth.

The Aims of Linear Models

Nothing is more important in considering the value and limitation of a form of theorizing than keeping its *aims* clearly in mind. A procedure should not be dismissed for failing to do what it does not aim to do, or for not aiming and succeeding at what is impossible to do. In the case of linear causal modeling, the most important point is that little theories of this kind are *approximations*. They do not contain the exact truth or the whole truth.

Linear models are used throughout the sciences because they are conceptually simple, computationally tractable, and often empirically sufficiently adequate. They are almost never true in every detail. Of course a model that is not true in every detail can still be approximately true and close enough to the truth to be relied upon in reasoning about action and policy. What we want from social science is not truth in every detail, but theories that are close enough to the truth to be reliable guides in understanding and decision making. There need not be a unique theory that answers our need in any case. If two theories are both literally true, then they must be consistent with one another, but if two theories are each only approximately true, and thus literally false, they need not be consistent with one another. Any of several alternative theories may therefore sometimes meet our need for an approximately true theory on which to base action and policy. As long as each of them would lead to the same practical decision, it makes little difference which one we choose. But when the alternatives give different results relevant to decision making and action, it makes every difference which we choose.

This is not any kind of special pleading for weaker standards in the social sciences than in the natural sciences. In the natural sciences, nearly every exact, quantitative law ever proposed is known to be literally false. Kepler's laws are false, Ohm's law is false, Boyle's law is false, Maxwell's equations are false, nearly every physicist believes that general relativity is false (because it is not a quantum theory), and on and on (see Cartwright [15]). These theories are still used in physics and in chemistry and in engineering, even though they are known to be false. They are used because, although false, they are approximately correct. Approximation is the soul of science.

Blau and Duncan's Model

Blau and Duncan's conclusions are often summarized with a simplified path model relating father's education, father's occupational status, son's education, status of son's first job, and son's occupational status in 1962 (Fig. 2-3). The model is elaborated in several ways in the course of Blau and Duncan's book.

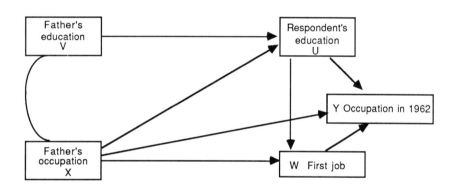

Figure 2-3: Blau and Duncan's model.

Freedman observes, correctly, that Blau and Duncan do not explicitly give a system of structural equations and distribution assumptions. He charitably, and so far as we can see correctly, ascribes to them the set of structural equations obtained from the directed graph above by applying the rules we describe in Chapter 4. Freedman supposes the equations are meant to apply to individuals in the population, the error terms for different individuals are uncorrelated and normally distributed, and the error terms for distinct variables are also uncorrelated. Save possibly for the normality assumption, this seems a fair account of what Blau and Duncan intended. We will consider in sequence Freedman's objections, and some pertinent responses.

Objection 1

There is no justification for the equations.

> ...the modelers have to make some showing that the structure of the equations reflects the structure of the phenomena.... The only relevant considerations are presented on pp. 166-168. In effect, Blau and Duncan argue that V_i and X_i are determined prior in time to U_i; likewise, except "for an appreciable minority," U_i is determined prior to W_i; and W_i is determined prior to Y_i. This is the whole of the argument....

Freedman suggests that the argument is supposed to lead to the structural equations by a recursive calculation of values of later variables from earlier variables, and he concludes:

> Of course, this parallelism does not establish [the equations] as the right model, since many other systems of equations have the same recursive structure. For example, the effects could be quadratic rather than linear, or multiplicative rather than additive. To sum up, the equations proposed by Blau and Duncan do not have any adequate theoretical foundation.

Response to 1

Blau and Duncan have a pretty clear idea as to how both the structural equations and the stochastic assumptions are to be justified, and how justifiable they are:

> As in the case with the assumption of linearity, we may for most assumptions adopt the pragmatic attitude that some departure from their literal truth may be tolerated if the assumptions facilitate an analytical objective. Yet it is often difficult to know if one has exceeded a legitimate level of tolerance and, especially, to comprehend what the consequences of sizeable violations of assumptions may be.
>
> We have sought a way out of this dilemma that will put some burden upon the reader. Instead of using only one or two techniques, with attendant greater or lesser severity of assumptions, we have varied the techniques and consequently the assumptions. With some techniques we clearly go well beyond the point where the requisite assumptions can be at all rigorously justified. This venture, however, will--to the extent possible--be counterpoised by alternative treatments of the same data, avoiding at least some of the questionable assumptions. (pp. 116-117)

The response is, first, that the model is offered as an approximation. Indeed, the model Freedman focuses on is offered as a very first approximation, which is elaborated in the course of the book. Blau and Duncan never suggest that it is literally true. Second, they test their assumptions, linearity for example, against other, weaker assumptions that lead to nearly the same results. They explicitly address both the suggestion that the effects could be in some power of the variables and the suggestion that they could be multiplicative. The power function hypothesis is checked by performing a multiple classification analysis which assumes that the effects are additive but not necessarily linear (pp.132-139; for a detailed treatment of these and related techniques see [92]). It is further checked by supposing that the effects are only piecewise linear in categories of independent variables and showing that the slopes in the several pieces are very nearly the same, save for thinly populated extreme values of the variables. We find these arguments convincing. A weaker argument is given regarding multiplicative effects. Blau and Duncan argue that a logarithmic transformation of variables from similar data gave correlations very close to those they obtain without such a transformation (pp. 139-140).

The strategy of using one set of assumptions, preferably weaker assumptions, to test other assumptions in a theory is ubiquitous in the sciences, and there is nothing wrong with it in principle, although like any strategy it can be practiced well or badly. It is the strategy Cannizaro used to argue for his system of atomic weights, and the strategy Jean Perrin used to determine Avogadro's number. Without it, much of the history of science would perish. The strategy, and some of its historical and contemporary applications, has been described in detail by Glymour [35, 36].

Linearity is well short of entailing the particular theory Blau and Duncan propose with this model. They have a further argument, of which they perhaps do not make enough. No one, apparently not even Freedman, disputes that the variables they choose as exogenous and intervening have a direct or indirect effect on occupational status. The issue is what the causal relations are. The principal justification for the model is that it explains the correlation data for these variables very well, and *no alternative linear model seems available which gives a comparably good explanation of the correlations.* Even before the parameters are estimated, and independently of any normality assumptions, the model implies constraints on the covariance matrix that are very closely approximated in the data. After estimation, the model accounts for almost--but not quite--all of the empirical correlations.

Any alternative linear model must do as well. It must also satisfy the temporal constraints on the variables which Freedman alludes to. The real point of time order is not that it establishes Blau and Duncan's model but that it constitutes a powerful constraint on any alternative. Freedman admits in a footnote that he could not find an alternative eight parameter model that fits the data as well as Blau and Duncan's initial model. Neither could we. Nor could we find a model with fewer parameters--such models tend to imply additional correlation constraints that are not very closely approximated by the data. A model with additional parameters can be made to fit the data, but such models either sacrifice simplicity while gaining nothing in their capacity to reproduce the correlations or they sacrifice simplicity while losing the nice explanation of the constraints satisfied approximately by the sample correlations. Blau and Duncan's model is certainly not true, but it bears the marks of an elegant linear approximation to the truth, and that is even more than they claim for it.

Objection 2

The assumption that there is no autocorrelation in V or in X is violated by the sampling technique, since the data were collected from households and the different respondents (all male) from the same household will surely have correlated values for these variables.

Response to 2

We cannot find any data in Blau and Duncan's book on what proportion of respondents were members of the same household or how they were distributed. The objection is sound, but its importance depends on that information.

Objection 3

There is no justification for assuming that the disturbance terms associated with the dependent variables are uncorrelated. There are, for example, famous dynasties in banking, politics, and film, and the corresponding error terms for education, first job, and occupational status in 1962 will surely be correlated for members of such dynasties.

Objection 4

Part of the error terms represent omitted variables, and these variables may act on several of the variables included in the model:

> Still more generally, the model omits families, neighborhoods, geographical regions. It does not consider the quality of education, or when education was obtained, or when respondents entered the labor force.... There is nothing of history in the model, and nothing of the economy.

Response to 3 and 4

Of course one can find cases in which there is good reason to think there are common sources of variance for the dependent variables. Once again, the model is not assumed to apply universally and literally. Blau and Duncan explicitly consider in later models the effects of age, race, ethnic group, geographic region, farm versus nonfarm background, marital status, father-in-law's occupational status, parental family size, birth order, family climate, family type (divorced, not divorced, etc.), and more. Historical factors are discussed throughout the book, and historical considerations enter explicitly in the justification of the scales. It is true that these factors do not enter explicitly in the model Freedman attends to, but why then complain of it when it is offered as a very first approximation and the factors of concern are investigated as modifications and qualifications of the simple model?

Objection 5

Significantly correlated errors will result in major changes in the estimated values of the parameters of the model.

Response to 5

Absolutely. Changes in specification will affect parameter estimates. There seems to be no evidence, however, that any of the variables Blau and Duncan consider produce a substantial correlation of the disturbance terms.

Objection 6

Blau and Duncan make no predictions from their model.

Response to 6

No predictions are made. Perhaps some could be. Principally, that improvements in the educational level of a subpopulation in one generation will have little effect on the occupational status of their descendents if structural social factors prevent the members of the first generation from using their education to improve their occupational status and if the educational improvements are not sustained in the second generation. It is, we suppose, one consideration pertinent to affirmative action and quota programs, although we have no idea what role, if any, Blau and Duncan's work has had on such practices.

Objection 7

Their model ignores their own data analysis.

> A fair summary is that the data clearly but narrowly violate the assumptions of the model: the regression curves are nonlinear (pp. 137, 144); the residuals are heteroscedastic (pp. 139, 144); the slopes vary across subgroups (p. 148). The path coefficients...therefore have no real existence. What are Blau and Duncan talking about?

Response to 7

Freedman's point is that Blau and Duncan's data analysis shows that their assumptions, in particular their assumption of linearity, is literally false. It also shows that it is a *very good approximation* to the truth, and that is all Blau and

Duncan claim for it. We should add that it appears to be at least as good an approximation to the data as are most of the simple classical chemical and physical laws. Physical chemistry would not be better off without the ideal gas law, or without the law of Dulong and Petit, but we very much doubt that the data available in the nineteenth century gave a substantially better fit for these laws than Blau and Duncan's data do for the linearity assumption.

Objection 8

The model fails a bootstrap statistical experiment [22] of a correlation constraint it implies.

Response to 8

Of course the model fails a significance test. Any false model that is very close to the truth and implies overidentifying constraints will fail a significance test if the test is powerful enough and the sample size is large enough. In this case the sample size, 20,700 is very large indeed. The important thing is that any alternative explanatory linear model would almost certainly fare worse.

Objection 9

Blau and Duncan claim that "the entire influence of father's education on son's occupational status is mediated by father's occupation and son's education," i.e., V has no direct effect on W or on Y. But the regression coefficient of V in a regression of Y on V, X, U and W is -.014 and the regression coefficient of V in a regression of W on V, X and U is .026, and both are statistically significant.

> The conclusion drawn by Blau and Duncan is unwarranted... But a fair statement of their results is only as follows: Roughly, the data conform to the equations ... as depicted in the path diagram, although the differences are highly significant...Blau and Duncan seem to have been misled by their methodology into confusing assumptions with conclusions.

Response to 9

The objection that Blau and Duncan draw an unwarranted conclusion is pedantic. The regression coefficients are indeed *statistically* significant. They are also dinky, and in any ordinary sense they are not significant at all. Blau and Duncan's statement is a fair summary of the facts they find.

Objection 10

The causal interpretation of path coefficients is nonsensical.

Suppose U, V and X are all functions of a more primitive variable τ, which is uniformly distributed over [0,1]. More specifically, let V be τ, let X be τ^2, and U be τ^3, but standardized to have mean 0 and variance 1....

Do we really want to say that the direct effect of τ on τ^3 is -.611, while the direct effect of τ^2 on τ^3 is 1.578? How can we vary τ while keeping τ^2 fixed?

The idea must be that structural equations are different from this artificial example. We need to have the difference spelled out.

Response to 10

It is essential to the usual representation of linear causal models that every variable have a unique exogenous source of variance. Freedman's "artificial example" violates this condition, and it is essential to his argument that it do so. That aside, suppose his conditions did actually obtain for some set of variables and some system. Then the causal claims would simply be false. That doesn't make the causal claims associated with real path models either false or nonsensical.

Real science has always proceeded by approximation and idealization. Many of Freedman's objections fail to appreciate that Blau and Duncan were doing, in a different setting, exactly what Newton, Dalton, Gay-Lussac, Hertz, and Eddington did in theirs: approximating and idealizing, looking for simple, elegant, plausible, and probably not literally correct theories that explain the phenomena. By the standards the natural sciences impose on themselves, the *American Occupational Structure* is not bad work at all, not even statistically. As one example, the Lick expedition of 1922 produced the best data on the gravitational deflection of light that were available until recent times. We guess that the gravitational effect accounted for less than 40% of the measured displacements of star images. The residuals of the least squares fit to the data were essentially unaltered if the relativistic deflection, which varies inversely with the square of the distance from the limb of the sun, was replaced by a simple inverse distance decay. Statistics does science many services, but it does no service at all if it keeps social science in thrall to a false and fantastic image of how science works.

2.7. Conclusion

The critical attack on the very idea of drawing causal conclusions from nonexperimental data is miles short of convincing. Criticisms of actual practice are something else. The principal faults that beset linear modeling in practice and are seized on by critics appear to be these:

1. Insufficient data analysis is done to justify the linear approximation

and the stochastic assumptions.

2. Alternative models are not considered, and structural equations are not justified.

3. Inadequate consideration is given to variables that are not included in the model but may be sources of covariance among variables included in the model.

4. No testable predictions are made.

TETRAD cannot help those who have not helped themselves about linearity and about stochastic matters. It can help substantially on the other counts. Later chapters demonstrate that the program can help to find good alternative models where they exist, and can help detect the existence of important neglected variables, although TETRAD will not tell the user what those variables are. We will show at least one way in which, using the program, testable, nonstatistical predictions can be made from causal models of correlational data.

3. OBJECTIONS TO DISCOVERY BY COMPUTER

3.1. Introduction

The TETRAD program can be thought of as a device for peering into a vast space populated by causal models rather than by stars and planets. Some people would prefer not to look. There is a line of thought that objects to any computer program that claims to aid in the discovery of scientific theories. This chapter examines the arguments for that line of thought.[9]

Some objections apply to almost any form of computer discovery or computer-aided search for theories. The objections we will consider include the following:

1. People have various kinds of special knowledge that computers do not have, and that knowledge makes people better at discovery than computers can possibly be.

2. Discovery is a form of inference and inference should proceed in accordance with the requirements of Bayesian statistics and Bayesian epistemology, but computer programs that aid in scientific discovery often do not work on strict Bayesian principles.

3. Offering computer programs that are intended to aid in the process of discovery is playing with fire. The programs are bound to be used stupidly and therefore should not be made available.

In addition, there are special objections to discovery procedures that are applied to statistical data. Such procedures must inevitably look at the data and use background knowledge together with structural criteria *and the data* to guide the search for the best explanations. Such procedures are routinely denounced as "ransacking" and "data mining," but *arguments* against the procedures are rarely given (and never given fully and explicitly). We identify four lines of argument, which we will discuss in detail in the third section of this chapter. In brief, they are

---

[9]Versions of these arguments have been given to us either orally or in private correspondence by several people, and since our response is entirely critical and depends on reconstructing terse remarks, we avoid attributions save to published statements.

1. There is a clear difference between "exploratory" procedures and "confirmatory" procedures. Exploratory procedures that examine the data to search for theories may provide theories worthy of investigation, but they do not provide any confirmation of those theories.

2. It is circular or "tautologous" to use the data to search for the best explanation of the data and then claim that the theory thus found is confirmed by that same data.

3. Using the data to discover a theory contradicts the usual frequency interpretation of test statistics that are based on the same data.

4. In the worst case, using the data to generate a theory will almost certainly lead to an erroneous theory.

The examination of this second set of arguments is considerably more technical.

3.2. The General Objections

People Know More Than Computers

Objection

Computers literally don't know what they are talking about. A computer procedure for searching for good theories must use structural criteria of some sort in its search, but we humans know a lot more than structure. We know what the variables mean, how they were obtained, whether some took their values prior to the time that others took theirs, and more. This knowledge is relevant to choosing a good statistical model, and a computer does not have it.

Comment

There are two aspects to the objection. Because we humans know things about particular causal relations, or about the impossibility of particular causal relations, it may be thought that we can locate correct alternatives faster and more accurately than any computer can. But further, any computer program that uses structural criteria in its search, whether the criteria are statistical fit, explanatory power, or whatever, will be likely to produce many absurd results, including causal hypotheses that we know cannot be correct.

Response

The use of structural criteria without the kind of knowledge we humans have of causal possibilities and impossibilites can indeed be expected to lead to many absurd conclusions. The sensible thing to do is to combine human knowledge about a domain with the computer's structural criteria. There are two ways in which human knowledge can be combined with the computer's capacity to carry out systematic search. One way is to let the computer report the results of its search using structural criteria that are sufficiently inclusive to permit many alternative solutions to a problem. Human users can then employ their knowledge to narrow down the alternatives. The other way is to make it easy for humans to convey their knowledge about the domain to the computer, and then have the computer use this knowledge and structural considerations to guide its search. One of the major ideas behind contemporary expert systems is that knowledge specific to some subject matter can be programmed into the computer, so that the machine can use that knowledge in guiding its search.

In fact, without substantive knowledge structural criteria alone may sometimes lead to absurd hypotheses. But we should not therefore reject the use of those criteria when their results are consistent with what we think we know. Structural criteria encompass all of the usual virtues of theories, including simplicity, correct predictions, explanatory power, and so forth; in the absence of complete prior knowledge, we have no better means than these for forming preferences among our theories.

The Bayesian Objection

Objection

Artificial intelligence programs for discovering statistical models are really carrying out decision procedures, but they do not act like rational Bayesian agents. Even if a program did carry out Bayesian calculations, whatever prior probability distribution and utilities the program uses may not be shared by human researchers.

Response

An artificial intelligence program might be designed to simulate a rational Bayesian agent. Programs of this sort have been developed for medical diagnosis (see Gorry *et al.* [39]). But an artificial intelligence program might also be designed to help humans behave *more like* ideally rational agents. A program might well do the second sort of thing without carrying out any explicitly Bayesian calculations.

An ideal Bayesian rational agent is logically omniscient. The agent considers every possible hypothesis, asigns it a prior probability, assigns or determines a likelihood for the evidence on each hypothesis, and forms posterior probabilities by conditionalizing on the evidence. For many reasons, humans are not ideal Bayesian agents. As L. J. Savage [88] noted, we humans are always falling short of coherence, and our struggle is always to get a little closer to it. In recent years, Bayesian statisticians have begun to consider explicit strategies for recovering from incoherence [67].

One of the most important ways that we fall short of the ideal is in failing to consider alternative hypotheses. In applying Bayesian procedures to empirical data, we may form a collection (finite or infinite) of alternative hypotheses to account for the data, in such a way that each hypothesis determines a likelihood for the data. With proper priors, the sum or integral of our priors over all alternatives in the collection is equal to one. There is usually a further catch-all hypothesis, namely that none of the hypotheses we have explicitly considered is correct. On reflection, we would rarely think that the catch-all alternative has zero prior probability, but we do not know how to use it to assign a likelihood to the evidence. That is exactly because we generally do not know what the unexamined alternatives are or what their mathematical properties may be. In the first chapter of this book we argued that this failure is one of the major limitations in sciences in which nonexperimental or quasiexperimental data are to be explained.

From a Bayesian perspective, the TETRAD program is a device for investigating a part of the catch-all hypothesis and for locating within it specific alternatives that give the evidence a reasonable likelihood, and that have the virtues of simplicity and explanatory power. These virtues can be thought of as utilities (see Kadane [55] and Hempel [46]) or as a constraint on prior probabilities (see Jeffreys [51] and Zellner [114]). Of course, a researcher might not share these utilities, or these priors, but we argue in a later chapter that they are fundamental desiderata in all sciences.

The "Fire" Objection

Objection

Even if computer procedures for generating models are, if intelligently used, valuable aids to discovery, they should nonetheless not be made available exactly because they will not be used intelligently. Automated procedures may make it easier to fit arbitrary bodies of data and to find models that appear to give good explanations for the data, even when the general modeling assumptions (linearity, for example, or absence of autocorrrelation, normality, etc.) are seriously in error. If so, they make it easier for people to obtain illusory conclusions, and they make science worse.

Response

The trouble with the argument is that it is generic, and it makes for terrible science policy. A perfectly analogous argument can be given against every technical innovation, computerized or not, that aids the enterprise of knowledge. There is nothing special in this regard about programs that aid in discovery. Regression packages make it easier for people to produce utterly inappropriate models when they neglect autocorrelation, multicollinearity, nonlinearity, etc. Estimation packages make it possible for people to assign numbers to ill-justified causal linkages, or even to confuse estimation with testing. Statistical tests make it easier for people to unjustifiably think they have established the truth of a model when it passes some statistical test of low power. Theoretical work, say Fisher's and Wishart's work on the distribution of correlations, can have similar effects. Even programs for automated statistical diagnostics can make it easier to do stupid things. If one had a package that automatically checked for linearity and made appropriate transformations, and checked for autocorrelation, distribution assumptions, etc., it would make it all the easier for people to whip up good statistical analyses with stupidly chosen variable sets.

The same is true of technical innovations outside of statistics. Every physical instrument, from the telescope to the linear accelerator, has a variety of stringent conditions for its reliable use. If the user is unsophisticated and the conditions for correct use are not met, a lot of garbage can and usually does result. Introductory physics students who repeat classical experiments with standard apparatus, for example, Millikan's oil drop experiment, rarely get the accepted results. The history of science is riddled with hypotheses advanced because of inappropriate uses of new technologies. Should we therefore regret the introduction of the telescope, the microscope, the micrometer, the camera?

Every good technical innovation expands our capacities and presents new possibilities for discovery, new domains in which inquiry can be carried out. It also presents, for the same reason, the possibility of new errors and new stupidities. There is absolutely nothing special in this regard about automated discovery procedures. The objection therefore rests on a more general policy, namely, that the possible errors of the least competent members of a community are sufficient reason to suppress the introduction of new technical developments. Fairly, and therefore generally applied, that is a policy for ending science, not for furthering it.

3.3. No Peeking

Preliminary Remarks

Many social scientists and applied statisticians believe (or at least say) that one should never, or almost never, search through a body of data to discover theories. Instead, one should somehow come up with a causal model based on "theoretical considerations." Such people believe that computer programs examining data and applying structural crtieria and background knowledge to data as they conduct a heuristic search are objectionable no matter how well they perform in practice.

It is hard to make any reasonable case for this rather radical perspective. Theoretical considerations, if they are to have any weight in guiding theory selection, must be well founded and therefore must be justified by data of some kind or other. The position seems to be that only theories generated by not looking at any data, or only theories generated by not looking at any relevant data, can be true or can claim our serious attention. There is no rational reason to believe this sort of mysticism, however strongly it may be felt. Above all, the position denies what we know and what we can demonstrate: we know that people can consider only a tiny fraction of the causal models that are consistent with prior knowledge; we know that in the practice of statistical modeling, assumptions based on theoretical considerations are rarely well justified and alternative explanations are rarely considered systematically; and we can (and will, in following chapters) demonstrate that, with computer aids, better theories can be found. Finally, we know that if close examination of data in order to search for explanations of it were prohibited, most of the natural sciences would not have developed. We would have to make do without the efforts of Copernicus, Kepler, Darwin, Cannizarro, and many, many others.

There is a more interesting and more precise kind of objection, not to computer search for theories but to certain ways of conducting that search. This line of thought insists that while relevant data may indeed be examined in the process of searching for a theory to explain it, *the data used to discover a theory must be distinct from the data used to confirm or test or argue for the theory.*

The TETRAD program, like any discovery program, looks at data and searches for a good explanation of it. The causal models found by using TETRAD on a body of data can always be tested by comparing them with another sample, a sample other than the one used in the search procedure. In the cases described in later chapters we sometimes do just that. So the program can always be used in such a way that the data used in discovery are distinct from the data used in testing. But we also believe that there is often nothing wrong with using one and the same body of data to discover a theory and to confirm it or test it. We will consider four arguments to the contrary.

Exploratory and Confirmatory Procedures

Objection

Computer searches are exploratory strategies and therefore cannot provide any confirmation of the hypotheses generated.

Response

It has become routine in the social sciences to distinguish between "exploratory" data analysis procedures and "confirmatory" data analysis procedures, or between exploratory and confirmatory uses of data analysis procedures. The TETRAD program is perhaps most naturally classified as an exploratory procedure. We wish to point out, however, that the distinction carries with it a great deal of dubious intellectual baggage.

"Exploratory" is very often used to suggest that a procedure, or an application of a procedure, is useful for suggesting hypotheses to be tested, but that it does not of itself give any reason to believe any of the hypotheses suggested. Similarly, "confirmatory" is often used to suggest that a procedure does not suggest hypotheses, but that when somehow provided with a hypothesis, the procedure may provide a reason to believe it. Procedures that amount to parameter estimation and statistical hypothesis tests based on those estimates are called confirmatory, while other procedures usually are not. Except as a misleading terminology for distinguishing statistical hypothesis tests from other procedures for drawing conclusions from data and background information, this distinction is illusory. If an "exploratory" procedure routinely turns up hypotheses that do well by statistical tests and make accurate predictions, and if the procedure rarely turns up hypotheses that do poorly by such criteria, then the fact that a particular hypothesis is turned up by the procedure provides some substantial reason to believe the hypothesis, or at least to give it more credence than those hypotheses rejected by the exploratory procedure.

The notion that "confirmatory" procedures, such as statistical hypotheses tests, provide some substantial reason to believe hypotheses *independently of exploratory procedures* is mistaken, at least in the case of linear models. On small sample sizes, tests such as chi square have low power. Unless all but a handful of alternative hypotheses have been ruled out, the fact that a model passes a statistical test provides almost no reason to give it credence, for there may well be billions of alternative models of the same data that, were they to be subjected to statistical testing, would do as well as or better than the particular model under consideration (see Chapter 1). We cannot rationally pretend that the alternatives don't exist, or that they are inconceivable or unconceived. If we have no knowledge as to whether or not better theories may be hiding among the unexamined multitudes, how can it be reasonable to give credence to the theory we happened to think of and examine statistically? But when the sample size is large, and the test has high power, the linear model is usually rejected exactly because it is, at best, an approximation. Thus, Blau and Duncan's model of the American Occupational Structure, which accounts for almost all of the correlations among its variables, is applied to a sample size in excess of 20,000 and fails various statistical tests (see Fox [27], Freedman [28]). This means that the p values of chi square statistics for linear models can only be used *comparatively*, but to do that we must discover the alternatives for comparison.

In fact, of course, we haven't either the human time or the computer time to do statistical analyses on more than a small number of alternative models. That fact makes it all the more important that statistical tests, if they are to be used, be used in conjunction with exploratory procedures that can search heuristically through enormously large numbers of possible models to discover those that will provide the best explanation of the data.

Equivocating over the Model

Objection

A procedure that searches for a good theory, using the data that the theory is supposed to explain, and then argues that the theory deserves credence because it explains that same data, is tautologous.[10]

Comment

We believe that the principal intuition behind the objection is that, in order for a model to be confirmed, it must be tested, and in order for a model to be tested something must be done that *could have* disconfirmed the model. Suppose a model is first conjectured and then the data is obtained to test it. Then, even if the data actually confirms the model, if the data *had* turned out differently it *would have* disconfirmed the model, and so something has been done that *could have* provided disconfirmation. In contrast, if a model is generated from a data set and then "tested" on that same data set, nothing has been done that could have disconfirmed the model.

Response

If the argument were sound, everyday counting procedures would be invalid. Imagine that the task is to determine the number of people in a room. We do that by counting, a procedure that involves generating hypotheses algorithmically as the data changes. We don't think of the procedure as "tautologous," and we are right not to do so even though different data would cause us to generate different hypotheses. It looks as though something is wrong with the argument.

The objection depends on an elementary logical mistake: equivocation. Let's suppose that an ideal search procedure would use data but would never yield a model in conflict with that data.[11] Now we clearly distinguish two different claims.

> I. No possible data, when given to an ideal search procedure, will result in a model that is disconfirmed by that same data.

> II. No possible data can disconfirm the model produced by an ideal search procedure that uses some particular body of data.

---

[10]See, for example, Robert Ling's review of Kenny's *Correlation and Causality* [69].

[11]In fact, there is reason to think that an ideal search procedure would <u>not</u> have this property. See Osherson *et al.* [83].

I is true, but II is false. The objection confuses the true claim, I, with the false claim, II, and the argument turns on that confusion. The mistake is to confuse the true claim that the generation procedure cannot possibly yield a model that is disconfirmed by the data used to find that model, and the false claim that nothing has been done that could have disconfirmed the model actually generated. If variables are measured and a model, call it M, is generated from the data obtained, something *has been done* that could have disconfirmed *M*: the measurements could have turned out differently, and if they had turned out differently they would have disconfirmed M. The situation is in all relevant respects exactly like the situation in which the model tested is generated without examining the data. It is true that nothing has been done that could result in *the generation of a model* that is disconfirmed by the data (at least not if the generation procedure is an ideal one). But that is not the issue; the issue is whether anything has been done that could have disconfirmed the model actually generated, in this case M, and something of that kind has been done. If the data had turned out differently, M would not have been generated, exactly because M would have been disconfirmed.

Consider counting again. If there are twelve people in a room the counting procedure will generate the hypothesis that there are twelve people in the room, and will stop with that hypothesis. The data will confirm the conclusion. If there had been only ten people in the room, the hypothesis that there are twelve would not have been generated by the counting procedure, exactly because it would have been in conflict with the facts.

Difficulties with Frequency Interpretations

Objection

If the model is found using the data, and the model is estimated and tested using that same data, then the standard errors of coefficient estimates and the p values of statistical tests may lose their usual meaning.[12]

Comment

Suppose a coefficient in a linear model is estimated by a maximum likelihood estimator. Given the sample size and the assumption that the model correctly describes an infinite population, the estimator has certain *mathematical* properties, such as its variance. Similarly, given a model, data, and a sample size, the chi

---

[12]Bentler [6] and Bentler and Lee [62] make this objection to the practice of standardizing models on the same data that are used to estimate coefficients or perform chi square tests of the models.

square statistic for that model, data, and sample size has certain mathematical properties, such as its p value. The clearest and least controversial meaning of these statistics is that they are simply mathematical relations between the stochastic model and the data set.

Frequentists give these mathematical relations a further interpretation, and it is this interpretation that is applied in the objection. Suppose we have a stochastic model, M, a data set, of size n, randomly selected from some population, and a probability value, p, for a chi square statistic calculated from the model and the data. The interpretation is that the p value of the statistic is to be understood as the long run frequency (or limiting relative frequency) with which a value that extreme would be obtained in a sequence of random samples of the same size, n, drawn from a population that is truly described by the model M. An analogous long run frequency or limiting frequency interpretation is given to the standard errors of coefficient estimates.

The point of the objection is just that if the procedure we use involves somehow estimating the model from the data, then the p values of tests and the variances of estimators *cannot* be given this frequency interpretation. For if we imagine a sequence of samples drawn from the population in which each sample is used to discover a model and calculate a chi square value and estimate coefficients, then *the model found will typically vary from sample to sample in the sequence.* At each step in the sequence we won't be estimating the same coefficients as occur in M, and we won't be determining the value of the chi square statistic for one and the same model M.

The objection can be put pictorially. The frequency interpretation of the p value of a test statistic for M for a given data set is the frequency with which we would get a more extreme value for the statistic in a sequence like the one shown in Fig. 3-1. But if the model M we generate depends on the sample data we obtain, then the procedure corresponds to the sequence shown in Fig. 3-2.

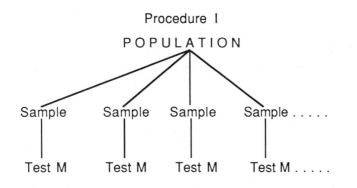

Figure 3-1: Standard frequency interpretation of a statistical test.

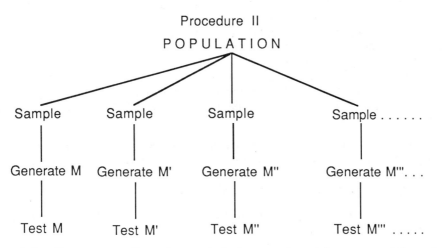

Figure 3-2: Sequence attributed to statistical tests of models generated from data.

The p value of the chi square statistic as conventionally calculated does not, in general, have anything to do with the long run frequency of values of chi square statistics in a sequence of this second kind.

Response

The argument is a complicated muddle. First, note that, except in Monte Carlo studies and the like, sequences of the sort described are almost never actually carried out. We do not do large numbers of repeated samplings of Head Start students, for example, and apply one and the same model to them or a model generating technique to them. In practice we look at no more than a handful of data sets for any collection of variables. We may, or may not, change the model we apply to later data sets based on how our initial models perform when tested on earlier data sets. We do not chose a model, draw a sample from a population, standardize the model and estimate it, choose another sample, and so on infinitely, or even for a long while. In practice we argue over alternative explanations for a few data sets and move with our statistical or algorithmic techniques from problem to problem.

So the attachment of long run frequencies to p values and standard errors is not a *description* of scientific practice. Instead it is a way of trying to *interpret* what the statistics *mean*. If you think that probabilities are mysterious but long run frequencies are not, then assigning a long run frequency to a probability claim is a way of making sense of the probability.

We don't wish to challenge the frequency interpretation of probability. But we claim it applies just as well to the p values and standard errors of models obtained by looking at the data as to models obtained by not looking at the data. We claim that for a particular model, M, obtained by examining a data set, D, the p value of a statistic calculated from M and D *can* be given a frequency interpretation just like that in the first sequence shown above. Suppose you draw a random sample D, use it to find a model M, and calculate a value for the chi square statistic. Now the p value can be interpreted as the frequency with which a value as large or larger would be obtained in a sequnce just like the first one above, except for the first trial in the sequence (Fig. 3-3).

So, if you want a frequency interpretation of the p value calculated for a model generated by looking at the data, there it is, as clearly as it is for models generated without looking at the data. Moreover, as far as the frequency interpretation of probability is concerned, Procedure I and Procedure III are indistinguishable.

Those who make the objection under discussion will very likely fuss at this point and say something like the following.

Further Objection

Every stage in the sequence associated with the frequency interpretation of a statistic obtained by a procedure must reproduce all of that procedure. If the procedure generates a model from the data, then every stage in the sequence associated with the statistic must also generate a model from the data. So Procedure II must be used, not Procedure III, and Procedure II does not give a frequency interpretation of the p values or standard errors of a fixed model, M.

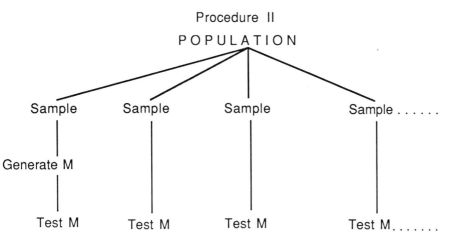

Figure 3-3: Our interpretation of a statistical test.

Further Response

The appropriate response is quite simple: why? A frequency interpretation is wanted, and one has been given in Procedure III. Moreover, it is an interpretation in which the frequency agrees with the mathematical p value. Why insist that the only appropriate frequency interpretation is the *wrong* one, namely, the second of the three sequences we have shown? We think the answer to this question is that two quite different concerns are behind the objection, and they have been confused.

Reliability

One concern is to give a frequency interpretation of the statistics. We have shown that to be a trivial matter. The second concern is with the *reliability of the procedure*, and that is a quite different and much more complicated matter. Under the Neyman-Pearson account of hypothesis testing, we may choose a significance level, such as .05, and decide to reject a model M if it yields a test statistic with a p value smaller than that significance level. The significance level tells us, under the frequency interpretation, the frequency with which we would erroneously reject M in a sequence of tests using samples drawn at random from a population correctly described by M. The significance level tells us something about the reliability of the testing procedure. It tells the probability (in the frequentists' sense) that we will reject M, given that M is in fact true. The procedure for generating the model has nothing to do with this decision theoretic account of testing the model, and it can be applied to the testing of computer-generated models just as the frequentist interpretation can be applied to the statistics for such models. It applies to the model M in Procedure III as well as to the model M in Procedure I.

But we can quite appropriately wonder about more than the reliability of a testing procedure once a model is generated. We can instead ask about the reliability of any procedure for selecting theories where the selection process may consist both of generating models and of testing them. Suppose our Procedure II uses sample data and background knowledge to generate a model (or a set of alternative models) and then computes the value of some statistic for each model and rejects models whose probability value for the statistic is too small. What is the probability that the true model will not be generated or will be generated but then rejected? What is the probability that a false model wlll be generated and not rejected? The p values and significance levels don't tell us the answers to these questions because they don't tell us anything about the probability that a procedure generates the true model.

Given a procedure that generates a model from data and a procedure that tests models, we can think of them in combination as a procedure that accepts data, generates a model, tests the model, and conjectures a generated model that passes the test. It makes sense to ask about the reliability of a combined procedure of this kind and to compare the reliabilities of different procedures. One way in which procedures can differ is with regard to how they divide and use the data. Some procedures may use all of the data in generating a model and use the same data in testing the model generated, other procedures may divide the data and use part of it for generating and another part for testing. Discovery procedures can vary in whether they produce a unique model for every data set, whether they sometimes produce several alternative models, and whether they always produce some model or other. They differ on whether they are able to make use of background knowledge other than that provided by the data sample. The usual factor analysis procedures, for example, make no use of background knowledge, whereas the TETRAD procedure requires it.

There are a great many dimensions to any comparison of procedures. Some specification must be made of the value of a correct answer, the value of an erroneous answer, and the value of producing no answer at all. Some measure of approximation must be provided and a value specified for various degrees of approximation. Some measure of information must be provided and a value specified for the informativeness of procedures that produce alternative models.

However these features of evaluation are specified, we can expect that the performance of a discovery procedure will depend on what is to be discovered, on the background knowledge available, and on the size of a random sample that is the data. We shall not attempt to specify appropriate evaluation functions for linear statistical models. In a later chapter we illustrate, however, that by using the TETRAD program, with large sample sizes and appropriate background knowledge, one can, in various circumstances, identify unknown causal connections with great reliability.

The question of reliability is not confined to computerized or computer-aided discovery procedures. People are discovery systems quite as much as computers are. Fair play in evaluating a computer procedure requires comparing it with humans. Whatever the preferred evaluation function may be, it can be applied to people as well as to computers. We can give people the same problems given to the computer and compare the results. Our own experience is that expert statisticians, social scientists, and psychologists are extremely reluctant to play John Henry, but the anecdotal evidence provided by the scientific literature and the indirect evidence provided by cognitive psychologists is that humans are not very reliable discovery systems. In any case, an automated discovery procedure cannot rationally be dismissed because it sometimes fails. *The essential question in evaluating the reliability of a fully automatic or computer-aided discovery procedure is whether the procedure is more reliable in its domain than are humans who must address the same problems without its aid.*

The Worst Case Objection

There is an objection to computer-aided construction of statistical models that does not depend on any misunderstanding. We will give it first informally and then more carefully.

Objection

An algorithmic procedure for finding models by examining the data and applying heuristic search will produce *some* model, even for data that are in fact randomly generated from independent variables. With enough variables and a small enough sample, correlations will appear just by chance even though the variables are independently distributed, and given such data an algorithmic procedure will find a causal model that accounts for the correlations even though they are in fact due to chance. Algorithmic procedures guarantee that a model will be found that appears to account for the data even if there is no true account to be given beyond the chance effects of the sampling procedure.

Comment

A little more precisely, the argument seems to have the following form.

1. Computer-aided heuristic searches for statistical models must examine the data for statistical dependencies among the variables, search for the model or models that best explain those dependencies, subject the models thus obtained to statistical tests based on the data, and output those models that survive the tests.

2. No procedure for searching for hypotheses is acceptable if there are circumstances in which it is very probable that that procedure will

yield a false conclusion.

3. For any procedure as in 1, a number r of independent random variables and a sample size n can be found such that it is very probable that a sample of size n will show k statistically significant correlations (or other statistic) among h of the r variables, for some number h and for some number k. That is, it is highly probable that at least k correlations will be sufficiently high that the probability of correlations as large as *those* occurring by chance in a sample of size n drawn from a population of values of the h random variables is less than .05, or whatever significance level is chosen.

4. In the circumstance described in 3, it is very probable that a procedure, such as described in 1, will output false hypotheses.

5. Therefore, by 4 and 2, a computer-aided heuristic search procedure is unacceptable.[13]

Response

Premise 2 is incorrect for two reasons. First, it puts all of the weight in judging a procedure on the desirability of avoiding *false* theories. We think that is desirable, to be sure, but it is at least equally important in judging a procedure to consider the desirability of finding *true* theories (see Levi [63]) or approximately true theories.

If the only criterion for comparing methods is that of avoiding commitment to a false theory, then the optimal strategy is clear: accept no theories whether they are discovered by humans, by humans with computer assistance, or by computers alone. Instead of any such strategy, we prefer to weigh the desirability of avoiding commitment to a false theory against the desirability of not overlooking commitment to true theories, or approximately true theories. Computer programs such as TETRAD help us to avoid overlooking theories that may turn out to be correct. They therefore assist us in avoiding an important kind of error, and that contribution should not be ignored in assessing the advantages and disadvantages of computer-generated theory.

Second, premise 2 assumes that a procedure ought to be judged by the *worst imaginable case*. We think procedures should be judged by the *expected* case. In the majority of cases researchers are pretty confident that the statistical dependencies they find are due to some causal structure or other, even while they may be much less confident about any particular explanation of the data. In the vast majority of cases, if the investigator were not strongly inclined to think that

---

[13]This argument is modeled on a similar argument about estimation given by Ronald Giere [33].

there is some explanation other than chance (or bad measurement design) for the patterns found in the data, a causal model would not be sought in the first place. Unless the researcher thinks there is a large probability that the dependencies in the data are spurious, there is no sufficient reason not to use the data to search for the best explanation of it. Of course, some of the correlations found may be due to chance, and that is the more likely the smaller the sample size in proportion to the number of variables considered. The investigator should certainly take account of that fact and, where appropriate, test a model on new samples.

These theoretical arguments overlook the reality of practice. In practice, many social and behavioral scientists behave much like natural scientists. Studies of really important questions are repeated, and the dependencies that demand explanation are the robust ones. In practice, researchers in the social and behavioral sciences, like their colleagues in the natural sciences, will inevitably look at the patterns in the data in search for the best explanation of it. Inevitably, alternative explanations of the same data will be offered by a series of workers, provided the questions at stake are important enough. That is the procedure in every empirical science worthy of the name. Artificial intelligence procedures only aid people in doing better what they will do, and in most cases ought to do, anyway.

In practice, TETRAD does *not* make the user overconfident. We find that people who develop models without the systematic heuristic search provided by the computer typically place too much confidence in particular models. The computer does not mislead us by generating a single, false theory when, in fact, we should withhold acceptance from all theories. Instead, the computer often warns us, when we have data that do not warrant any particular conclusion, that there are a great many different ways to explain the phenomena, none especially better than the rest, and that we are therefore not warranted in accepting any particular conclusion.

Even while we regard the last argument given against heuristic search as unsound, it does provide an important caution. Whether in astronomy or sociology, some statistical dependencies will occur by chance, and if we account for them by causal processes, then we will make a mistake. That is part of the burden of science; sometimes we are going to be wrong.[14]

---

[14]The technical worst case argument against procedures that generate theories by examining the data can be defeated by taking a sufficiently large random sample. Thus, in the case of Blau and Duncan's study of the American occupational structure, with a sample size in excess of 20,000 there is virtually no chance that the correlations and other dependencies among half a dozen variables are due to chance.

Explanation and Prediction

The strong conviction that "exploration" or "search" must be separated from confirmation or testing has a long history, but the arguments for the separation are seldom clearly formed. The conviction is almost universal in applied statistics, shared by Bayesians and more orthodox statisticians alike. Ultimately, the desire to separate the data used in discovery and in justification, in theory generation and in theory testing, probably derives from the conviction that only correct *prediction* counts as confirming a hypothesis. Explanation after the fact is discounted on the grounds that it is, or may be, *ad hoc*.

Something of the same prejudice is occasionally found in the natural sciences, but it is much less prevalent. The DENDRAL program [68] examines mass spectrograph data to find the best explanation for that data, and chemists do not find this practice objectionable. Physicists routinely reexamine old data in search of new explanations. Recently, for example, data from one of the classic tests of the general theory of relativity, the Eotvos experiment, was reexamined to argue that the principle of equivalence, which is fundamental to the theory, is false. Einstein himself argued for the general theory on the grounds that it explained data about irregularities in the motion of Mercury, irregularities that had been known for sixty years prior to the publication of the general theory in 1915 and that had been the subject of many alternative explanations. In fact it is clear that Einstein used the anomalous motion of Mercury and the equivalence principle as guides in his long search for a satisfactory relativistic theory of gravitation. Copernican astronomy was founded almost entirely on historical observations of the sun, moon, and planets. Most of these observations had been made centuries and even millenia before Copernicus wrote and had been used to obtain other theories, notably the Ptolemaic theory and its modifications. Cannizzarro's powerful argument for the (then controversial) atomic theory in 1860 was not based on any newly confirmed predictions but on a systematic review of the evidence that had been accumulated in the preceding decades and on the argument that the atomic theory provided the best explanation for patterns revealed by that data.

Whatever the rhetoric, most physical scientists act as if a good explanation can be nearly as valuable as a good prediction, and most of their science would not have emerged if their predecessors had been forbidden to examine the data in searching for theories, or if data once used to test a theory were thereafter forever tainted and useless for confirmation.

People rightly worry that a theory constructed by someone after seeing the data will be constructed specifically to account for that data. If the theory is deliberately constructed to account for the data, then the data provides no test of the theory and hence no reason to believe the theory. This worry is well founded, but misstated. The notion of "constructing a theory to account for the data" is complex. In one sense people certainly do construct theories; they make them up, piece them together, put them forward. In another sense, a theory is simply an abstract object, like sets or numbers. The abstract objects may be discovered, but discovering them isn't creating them. Theories are out there and have whatever logical relations they have with the data, whether or not anyone happens to think of them. Either a theory has the right logical relations with the actual evidence, in which case the evidence confirms it, or the theory has the wrong logical relations with the actual evidence, in which case the evidence disconfirms it. How a particular human being happened to discover the particular theory has nothing to do with the matter. The job of a computer program for discovering theories is to find the theories with the right logical relations to the evidence.

How can this understanding of confirmation and testing be reconciled with the powerful sense that some theories are unsatisfactory because they are "cooked" to account for the data? The answer is that the "right" logical relations to the evidence consist in a lot more than merely being consistent with the evidence or entailing the evidence. Cooked theories may entail the evidence but they don't entail the evidence in the right way.

The following chapters describe a conception of explanation that applies to linear causal models, and that is more robust and demanding than the requirement that the theory fit the observed statistical dependencies. The TETRAD program helps to search for theories that provide such strong explanations.

PART II

The TETRAD Program

4. CAUSAL AND STATISTICAL MODELS

4.1. Introduction

Our principal concern is with procedures for *specifying* a model or models to account for nonexperimental or quasi-experimental data. We are especially interested in procedures for specifying the causal hypotheses implicit in a model, for it is these hypotheses that are often of chief importance in practice, and reliable statistical estimation usually depends on having the correct causal structure.

Most linear models in the social and behavioral sciences have a causal interpretation, and often the causal claims within a statistical model are the principal concern and point of the investigation. Sometimes, of course, no causal interpretation is given to a model, or is appropriate. More often, the causal claims in a model are signaled by special phrases. Psychologists often mark causal relations by specifying that some variables are *dependent* and others are *independent*. Econometricians, and increasingly other social scientists, mark causal relations by specifying that some variables are *endogenous* and others are *exogenous*.

Linear causal models include a set of equations relating the variables of the model, a set of stochastic assumptions about the probability distributions of those variables, jointly and individually, and a set of causal relationships among the variables. Factor analytic models are of this sort, and so are path analysis models, structural equation models, models with random variable coefficients, and many regression models and econometric models. The strategy behind the TETRAD program is to abstract the causal structure from a statistical model, ignoring the equations and most of the statistical assumptions. We call this abstract structure a **causal model** to distinguish it from the fuller statistical model containing it. The causal model consists of a **directed graph**.

It is possible to work with a very simple mathematical structure, the directed graph, rather than with the more complex equations and distribution assumptions of a linear model, because the directed graph of hypothetical causal relations determines important statistical properties of any linear model that contains it. The theoretical basis of the TETRAD program consists of a number of new theorems about the connection between directed graphs and statistical properties of models. These theorems are described in this chapter and proved in Chapter 10 of this book. Because of these connections, in later chapters we will be able to ignore most of the usual mathematical paraphernalia of linear models and focus on graph structures.[15]

---

[15]In order to facilitate the proofs given in Chapter 10, some of the formal definitions given in that chapter differ in minor details from the more informal definitions given in this chapter.

The aim of this chapter is to explain how causal hypotheses can be represented by directed graphs, to describe the relationship between directed graphs and the usual forms of structural equation models, and to describe some of the most important statistical properties that are determined by the directed graph of causal hypotheses in a model.

Linear causal models usually contain parameters whose values are not specified. For example, a model may contain an equation that specifies that variable X is a linear function of variable Y, but the linear coefficient may not have a specified value. Such free parameters must be estimated from the correlation or covariance data of samples drawn from the population to which the model is supposed to apply. When we write of a **statistical model** we mean a model that may contain free parameters. These parameters can either be constants with an unknown value, or random variables. When we use the phrase **estimated model** we mean the result of specifying the values of all free parameters in a statistical model, using appropriate sample data. Statistical models with free parameters do not entail actual (non-zero) numerical values for the correlations or covariances of their variables, but they can entail that the population correlations or covariances must satisfy certain equations. These equations are sometimes called **overidentifying constraints**. Estimated models imply definite numerical values for the correlations or covariances of their variables, and these values can be compared with the correlations or covariances exhibited by samples drawn from the population.

4.2. Directed Graphs and Causal Models

Directed Graphs

Hypothetical causal relationships implicit in a model may be represented as a directed graph. A directed graph is simply a list of pairs of variables. The first member of a pair is assumed to be a direct cause of the second member of that pair.[16] Directed graphs can also be represented by line drawings. For six variables connected with socioeconomic status, say socioeconomic status (SS), father's education (fe), mother's education (me), father's occupation (fo), mother's occupation (mo), and family income (in), one simple causal theory can be represented by a list

$$\{ <SS,fe>, <SS,me>, <SS,in>, <SS,fo>, <SS,mo>, <fe,fo>,$$
$$<e1,fe>, <e2,fo>, <e3,me>, <e4,mo>, <e5,in> \}$$

---

[16]Variable X has a "direct" effect on variable Y in this sense provided the variation in Y in the population is due in part to a variation in X that is not mediated by any other variables that are explicit in the model.

or by a picture (Fig. 4-1).

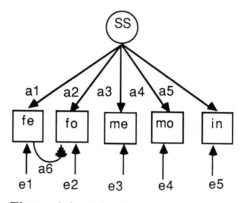

Figure 4-1: Directed graph representation.

An ordered pair of variables that is either in the list of a directed graph or is connected by an arrow in the drawing is called a **directed edge**. We can think of a directed edge pictorially as simply the arrow connecting two variables. The variables connected by the directed edges are **vertices** of the directed graph. A directed edge is said to be **into** its second vertex (the head of the arrow) and **out of** its first vertex (the tail of the arrow). If there is an edge out of x and into y then x is **adjacent** to y. The number of edges directed into a vertex is its **indegree**; the number of edges directed out of a vertex is its **outdegree**.

Paths and Treks

Sequences of directed edges that connect variables specify a hypothetical path of causal influence from one variable to the other. More exactly, we define a **path** from variable u to variable v as a sequence of directed edges u->w-> ... ->v, with all arrows running in the same direction, i.e., the second vertex of each edge in the sequence is the first vertex of the next edge in the sequence. For example, in the directed graph illustrated above, the sequence <SS,fe> <fe,fo> is a path from SS to fo, and <SS,fo> is another path from SS to fo. We will usually write such paths as SS->fe->fo, and fe->fo, respectively. A path will be said to **contain** a variable or vertex if that vertex occurs in one of the directed edges in the path. A path that contains a subpath beginning and ending in the same vertex is said to contain a **cycle** or to be **cyclic**. A path that does not contain a cycle is **acyclic** or **open**. A directed graph that contains a cyclic path is said to be cyclic; a directed graph that does not contain any cyclic path is said to be acyclic.

A path in a causal model represents a hypothetical causal influence that runs from one variable to another. Such an influence produces a correlation or covariance between the variables that are linked by the path. A model that postulates a path connecting variables that are actually correlated thus provides a means to explain the correlation.

A causal model can also explain a correlation between two variables as the result of other variables that affect both of them. The model depicted above predicts a correlation between me and fo because each of these variables is assumed to be affected by a third variable, SS. We call this sort of connection between two variables a **trek**, and we understand a path to be just one special sort of trek.

More exactly, a trek between two variables u and v is an open path from v to u, or an open path from u to v, or a pair of open paths from some variable, w, to u and to v such that the two paths have exactly one variable, w, in common. The unique variable common to both paths in an open trek is called the **source** of the trek.

For example, in the directed graph above, the pair of paths SS->fo and SS->mo is a trek between fo and mo. SS is its source. The pair of paths SS->fe->fo and SS->mo is another trek between fo and mo, and SS is again its source. The path fe->fo is a trek with fe as its source.

There are a variety of ways to introduce new treks between variables. Suppose we want to introduce a new trek between fo and me in Fig. 4-1. We could do this by adding a directed edge fo->me (Fig. 4-2-a), or a directed edge me->fo (Fig. 4-2-b), or a directed edge fe->me (Fig. 4-2-c). We can even add a new variable, call it G, and introduce the directed edges G->fo and G->me (Fig. 4-2-d), and this list is by no means exhaustive. Finally, we can include a correlation that is not accounted for by a causal model simply by postulating an unexplained correlation between the appropriate variables or between causes of those variables that are external to the causal model. Such external sources of variance are often called **error variables**. We can represent unexplained correlations of error variables by including the error variables in the directed graph and drawing an undirected line between them, as we do in Fig. 4-3. The correlated errors e2 and e3 create a new trek between fo and me, even though such connections are not explicit in the definition of "trek" just given. The calculation of treks in models with correlated errors is described in the next section.

Different ways of adding directed edges to an initial model may have differing statistical effects because the total set of treks created may be different. In Fig. 4-2-b we add me->fo to our original model and no new trek (and hence no new source of correlation) is created between fe and me. In Fig. 4-2-a we add fo->me to our model and we also create a new trek (and a new source of correlation)

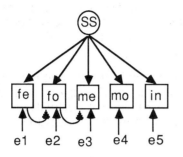

(a)

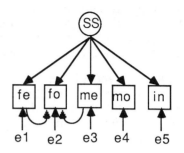

(b)

(c)

(d)

Figure 4-2: Alternative ways to add a trek.

between fe and me because of the link fe->fo->me. These are statistically inequivalent causal models. Different ways of adding directed edges and unexplained error correlations can also have differing statistical effects. In Fig. 4-3 a correlated error is introduced between fo and me. This model is also statistically inequivalent to the model of Fig. 4-2-a. Such statistical inequivalences prove to be extremely important in guiding the search for alternatives to an initial model.

The number of directed edges in a model is important statistically because each additional edge reduces the number of **degrees of freedom** of the model by one. The same is true if, instead of adding new treks, we add unexplained correlations

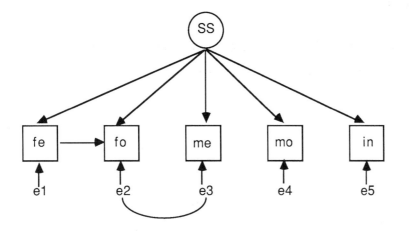

Figure 4-3: Producing a new trek by correlating error terms.

of error variables. If we add an unexplained correlation of the errors of fo and me, we do not introduce a new source of correlation between fe and me. But we do reduce by one the degrees of freedom of the model.

4.3. Statistical Models from Causal Models

Causal models form part, often a tacit part, of statistical models. To expand a causal model into a statistical model, equations must be written specifying the relations among the variables and appropriate stochastic assumptions must be made. Since the work of Simon [93, 94] considerable thought has been given to how the causal part of a model can be extracted from a set of equations and stochastic assumptions. In practice, a stylistic convention is often adhered to: writers give an affected variable on the left hand side of an equation and its direct causes on the right hand side of an equation. With this convention in mind, one can often infer the directed graph a theorist intends from the equations given. This kind of reconstruction of the causal model from the equations is not, however, the sort of reduction of causal hypotheses to properties of equation systems that Simon was after, since it depends on a stylistic convention. We are concerned with the reverse problem: Starting with a causal model, which is merely a directed graph, how are the equations of a statistical model to be obtained? For that, either of two simple process will suffice.

Method I

To get a statistical model from a directed graph simply do the following:

1. Attach a distinct parameter to each directed edge in the directed graph of the model (Fig. 4-4).

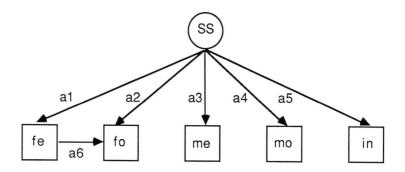

Figure 4-4: Edge labels added.

2. For each variable in the directed graph that has a causal predecessor (i.e., the variable is not of zero indegree), add an "error" variable directed into that variable but not into any other variable. Thus, the model in Fig. 4-4 becomes the model in Fig. 4-5.

3. For each variable in the model that is not of zero indegree, write an equation specifying that variable as a linear function of the variables directed into it. The parameters are the linear coefficients. Thus, we get the equations in Fig. 4-6 from the graph in Fig. 4-5.

4. Assume that any pair of variables that are *not connected by a trek* are statistically independent.

5. Specify that the linear coefficients are constants of undetermined value, or have a determinate value, or are random variables distributed independently of each other and of all other variables in the model.

6. Consistent with the above, make whatever assumption about the distribution of the random variables seems appropriate.

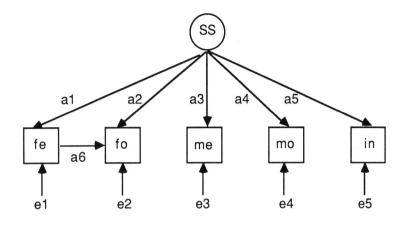

Figure 4-5: Error terms added.

$$fe = a_1 SS + e1$$

$$fo = a_2 SS + a_6 fe + e2$$

$$me = a_3 SS + e3$$

$$mo = a_4 SS + e4$$

$$in = a_5 SS + e5$$

Figure 4-6: The equations from Fig. 4-5.

Method II

The models obtained by Method I all have uncorrelated errors. Since there are no treks between the e variables, they are all assumed to be uncorrelated with one another. That assumption is unnecessary. Instead, when a full statistical model is constructed, follow steps 1 through 3 of Method I, but rather than assuming that the errors are uncorrelated, postulate a correlation of the error variables directed into the two variables.

When correlated errors are introduced into a model, the treks between variables are calculated as if a correlated error between two variables were really a new unmeasured common cause affecting both variables.

In the same way, if a model has two latent variables, and no causal connection between them is specified but it is assumed that the latent variables are correlated, the treks are computed as if the latent variables had a new common, latent cause.

Finally, consistent with these conventions, postulate that variables not connected by a trek are statistically independent. For example, suppose one has a causal model like that illustrated but with a correlated error between fe and fo rather than the directed edge from fe to fo. Then simply take the initial model (Fig. 4-7)

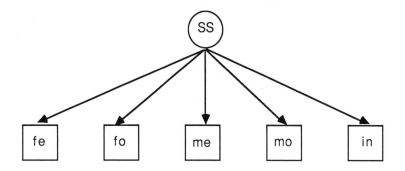

Figure 4-7: Initial model.

and proceed as in steps 1, 2 and 3 to obtain Fig. 4-8.

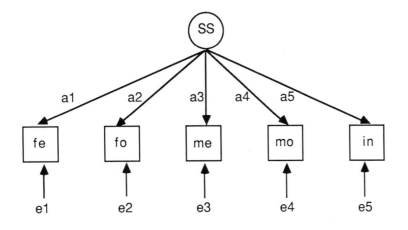

Figure 4-8: Initial model after steps 1, 2, and 3.

Finally, specify that the variables e2 and e1 are correlated. Pictorially, the final model can be represented by drawing an *undirected* line[17] connecting e2 and e1, as we do in Fig. 4-9.

The procedures in the TETRAD program assume that if a full statistical model is associated with a causal model suggested or analyzed by the program, then the statistical model can be obtained in one of the ways just described. In a later chapter we will describe how to turn TETRAD models into models suitable for estimation and statistical testing by standard packages such as LISREL and EQS.

If the linear coefficients are assumed to be constants and not random variables, then the models that result from a directed graph through the procedures just described are **structural equation models**.[18] So far as the TETRAD program is

---

[17]Some writers use an "arrow" with two heads and no tail to signify such correlations.

[18]The stochastic assumptions that usually accompany structural equation models can be understood in the following way. The structural equations are understood to apply to each member of the sample. Thus, the equations above should be indexed by i, where i denotes the ith member of the sample. The linear coefficients are not random variables and are assumed (usually contrary to fact) to be constant in the population. e_{1i} is assumed to be statistically independent of e_{1j} if i is not equal to j. Usually, e_{1i} and e_{1j} are assumed to have the same probability distribution. This applies similarly for e_{2i}, e_{2j}, etc. These assumptions characteristic of structural equation modeling are appropriate if the stochastic elements are attributed to random sampling with replacement.

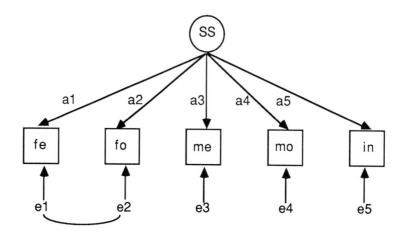

Figure 4-9: Statistical model with correlated error terms.

concerned, many of the assumptions usually made in structural equation modeling can be considerably relaxed. The program will work for models in which the linear coefficients are not constant but instead are independently distributed random variables. It applies whether or not the error distributions for different members of the sample have the same probability distribution, so that models in which the variance of the error variables is not constant (heteroscedastic models) are permitted. The variables of the model can be standardized or not.

4.4. Treks and Coordinating Path Effects

The **covariance** of two random variables, X and Y, is just the difference between the expected value of the product XY and the product of the expected value of X and the expected value of Y, that is, Exp(XY) - [Exp(X) Exp(Y)]. The **correlation** of X and Y is their covariance divided by the product of their standard deviations. We assume that the random variables always have distributions so that these statistics are well defined. The data for which causal models are to account are usually sample covariances or correlations, and it is data of this kind that the TETRAD program is meant to address.

The first job of a theory is to explain the data. In the case of linear statistical models, that usually means explaining the correlations or covariances among the measured variables in some sample. Suppose we have a statistical model, and the linear coefficients in that model are somehow specified, whether by statistical estimation, or a priori, etc.[19] The estimated statistical model does not determine unique values for the covariances of the measured variables in the population it is to describe, nor does it determine probability distributions for covariances in a sample drawn from the population.

To calculate population covariances we need to know the variance of every variable of zero indegree, including the error variables, and we need to know the covariance of any pair of variables that have, according to the model, an unexplained correlation. *These variances and covariances, together with the directed graph and the values of the linear coefficients, determine the population covariances of the measured variables according to the model.*

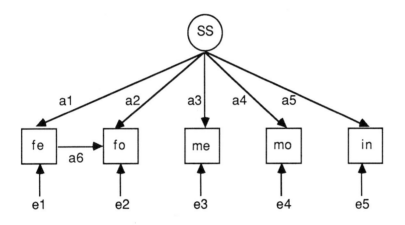

Figure 4-10: A model of socioeconomic status.

Return to the simple model we considered earlier (Fig. 4-10). One trek between fe and fo is <SS, fe>, <SS, fo> with coefficients a_1 and a_2, and the other is <fe, fo> with coefficient a_6. With any path in the directed graph of a model, we associate the product of the linear coefficients associated with the graph. Thus the path <SS, fe>, <fe, fo> is associated with the product $a_1 a_6$. The coefficient product of an acyclic path is unique up to permutation of the coefficients in the product; no two

---

[19]In the case of models with stochastic coefficients, assume the population mean value is specified.

distinct paths have the same product of coefficients. Since a trek consists of at most two paths, we can also associate each trek with a product of linear coefficients, namely, the product of all of the coefficients for any edge in each path in the trek. Thus the trek <SS, fe>, <SS, fo> has the product a_1a_2. The product of coefficients associated with any trek is unique up to permutation of the factors, and no two distinct treks have the same product of coefficients.

A **coordinating path effect** for two variables X and Y, having a trek with source S connecting X and Y is the product of the trek coefficients multiplied by the variance of S. For example, the coordinating path effect for the trek <SS, fe>, <SS, fo> in the preceding example is just $a_1a_2Var(SS)$.

For any acyclic graph, the covariance of two variables, X, Y is just the sum, over all distinct treks between X and Y, of the coordinating path effects.

The covariance of fe and fo, Cov(fe, fo), in the preceding example is just $a_1a_2Var(SS) + a_6Var(fe)$. In applying the rule, source variables that have unexplained covariances postulated by the model should simply be viewed as having a common latent cause[20] whose variance is equal to the unexplained covariance.

The population covariances a model implies are determined by the variances of its source variables, the linear coefficients, and the directed graph of causal relations postulated by the model. The probability distribution of the sample covariances is determined by these factors plus the joint distribution assumed for the variables. The directed graph itself determines very little about the covariances. In fact, all that the directed graph may imply about the values of any particular covariance is that, if the covariates are not connected by a trek, then their covariance is zero. But if we are to search for alternative models to explain the data, and the automatic part of the search uses only the data, the directed graphs of alternative models, and some distribution assumptions, then the directed graph *alone* must determine something about the population covariances. And it does. *The directed graph of a model determines patterns among the covariances of the measured variables in the population, without determining unique values for those covariances.* These patterns are overidentifying constraints.

4.5. Constraints on Correlations

---

[20]That is, if X and Y are assumed to have correlated errors, in applying this rule one treats them as though the model contained a latent variable T and directed edges T->X and T->Y whose associated coefficients are fixed at one.

Overidentifying Constraints and Directed Graphs

Before the coefficients of a statistical model are estimated or specified, the model does not imply unique values for the population covariances, but it can imply that whatever those covariances may be, they must satisfy certain conditions. Whatever the population covariances may be, if they are consistent with the model then they will satisfy these conditions no matter what values the linear coefficients may have. Conditions of this kind are called **overidentifying constraints** in the econometrics literature for the reason that when a model implies such constraints there are generally multiple ways to estimate its parameters. Blalock [7] calls these conditions **prediction equations** because they also represent implications of a statistical model that can be tested more or less directly.

Certain important kinds of overidentifying constraints are determined entirely by the directed graph of a model. In order to determine whether a statistical model implies these sorts of constraints, one need only examine the causal model embedded in it. Although there are other kinds, the two kinds of overidentfying constraints that we shall consider, which are entirely determined by the directed graph, are **vanishing partial correlations** and **tetrad equations**.

Vanishing Partial Correlations

Consider the simple example given by the causal model shown in Fig. 4-11.

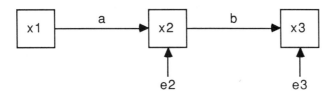

Figure 4-11: A simple path model.

Given any arbitrary numbering of a set of measured variables, the correlations of the variables can be arranged into a square, symmetric matrix whose diagonal elements are all unity. If the correlations are those that obtain in the population, the matrix is called the **population correlation matrix**. If the correlations are those in a sample, then the matrix is the **sample correlation matrix.** In the present example we can write the population correlation matrix as

$$
\begin{vmatrix} \rho_{11} & \rho_{12} & \rho_{13} \\ \rho_{21} & \rho_{22} & \rho_{23} \\ \rho_{31} & \rho_{32} & \rho_{33} \end{vmatrix} = \begin{vmatrix} 1 & a & ab \\ a & 1 & b \\ ab & b & 1 \end{vmatrix}
$$

where a and b are undetermined linear coefficients.

In this simple example the model implies a constraint on the correlation matrix. The constraint is easily obtained by considering the treks in the model. First, however, we will derive the constraint in the conventional way, by means of the partial correlation coefficient. The partial correlation of x_1 and x_3 with respect to x_2 is defined to be (see Anderson [2]):

$$
\rho_{13.2} = \frac{\rho_{13} - \rho_{12}\rho_{23}}{(1 - \rho_{12}{}^2)^{1/2} \, (1 - \rho_{23}{}^2)^{1/2}}
$$

which, in this case, is

$$
\frac{ab - ab}{(1 - a^2)^{1/2} \, (1 - b^2)^{1/2}}
$$

Thus, the model implies that

$$\rho_{13} - \rho_{12}\rho_{23} = 0$$

which is a constraint on the correlations.

Note that the derivation of this constraint did not depend on assigning any particular numerical values to the coefficients a and b. The model will imply the vanishing partial correlation *no matter what* values a and b might have.[21] We are especially interested in models that imply constraints no matter what values the non-zero linear coefficients may have. We will say in such cases that the model the constraint, **implies** or **entails** the constraint, or sometimes for emphasis that the model **strongly implies** or **strongly entails** the constraint. In cases in which estimated models determine a constraint because of particular values of the parameters, we will say that such a model **weakly implies** the constraint.

We can derive the same constraint by considering the treks in the (acyclic) graph of the model: if the variables are standardized, the correlation between two measured variables is equal to the sum, over all treks connecting the variables, of the product of the coefficients corresponding to the directed edges in the trek (see Heise [45]). Consider the graph of the model again (Fig. 4-12).

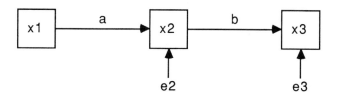

Figure 4-12: A simple path model.

In this case there is but one trek between x_1 and x_3, hence

---

[21] Unless, of course, a = b = 1, in which case the partial correlation is not defined.

$$\rho_{13} = ab = \rho_{12}\rho_{23}$$

or

$$\rho_{13} - \rho_{12}\rho_{23} = 0.$$

It turns out that this derivation does not depend on the assumption that the variables are standardized. We do not need to know or stipulate anything about the variances of the variables in order to derive the vanishing partial correlation from the directed graph. There is a general principle involved in the example.

Theorem 1: The *directed graph* of a model *alone* determines the vanishing partial correlations the model implies.

This theorem holds no matter what the graph may be. It holds for cyclic graphs as well as acyclic graphs. In Chapter 10 we prove the following theorem, which provides a condition on directed graphs that is necessary and sufficient for the implication of a vanishing partial correlation.

Theorem 2: For any directed graph, G, and any three distinct variables, x, y and z which are vertices of G, the following two conditions are equivalent:

1. Every trek between x and z contains y, and either every trek between y and z is an open path from y to z or every trek between x and y is an open path from y to x.

2. Any model for which G is the causal graph implies that $\rho_{xz} - \rho_{xy}\rho_{yz} = 0$.

This theorem means that the partial correlation constraints implied by a linear causal model can be determined entirely from its directed graph.

There are fast algorithms for determining the properties of directed graphs that are relevant to the implication of vanishing partial correlations, and the TETRAD program embodies such an algorithm. In Chapter 10 we give the algorithm and prove its adequacy.

Tetrad Equations

Tetrad equations involve products of correlations among a set of four measured variables. There are three possible inequivalent products of two correlations which involve all and only four variables. For example, if the four variables are w, x, y, and z, then the three possible correlation products are

$$\rho_{wx}\rho_{yz}$$
$$\rho_{wy}\rho_{xz}$$
$$\rho_{wz}\rho_{xy}$$

Tetrad equations say that one product of correlations (or covariances) equals another product of correlations (or covariances). There are three possible tetrad equations, any two of which are independent, in a set of four variables. They are

$$\rho_{wx}\rho_{yz} = \rho_{wy}\rho_{xz}$$
$$\rho_{wy}\rho_{xz} = \rho_{wz}\rho_{xy}$$
$$\rho_{wx}\rho_{yz} = \rho_{wz}\rho_{xy}$$

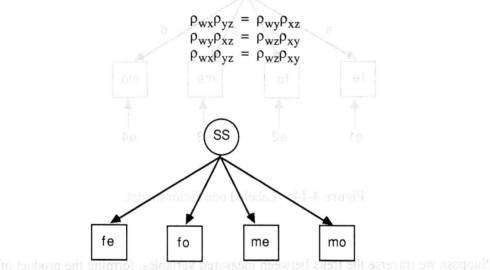

Figure 4-13: One factor model.

The model shown in Fig. 4-13 entails the tetrad equations

$$\rho_{fo,fe}\rho_{me,mo} = \rho_{fo,me}\rho_{fe,mo}$$

$$\rho_{fo,mo}\rho_{fe,me} = \rho_{fo,fe}\rho_{me,mo}$$

$$\rho_{fo,mo}\rho_{fe,me} = \rho_{fo,me}\rho_{fe,mo}$$

More complex models can entail much more complicated sets of tetrad equations.

In simplest terms, a tetrad equation is implied by a causal model if and only if the directed graph associated with the model possesses an appropriate symmetry property. Suppose we give each directed edge in Fig. 4-13 a distinct letter as a label (Fig. 4-14).

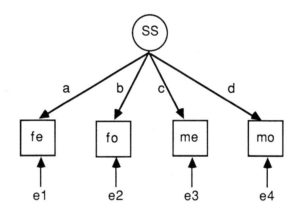

Figure 4-14: Labeled one factor model.

Suppose we traverse the treks between measured variables, forming the product of the labels of all of the directed edges we pass over. In this case there is but one trek between each pair of variables. If we follow the trek connecting fe and fo we pass across the directed edge from SS to fe, with label a, and across the directed edge from SS to fo, with label b. So we form the product of labels (ab) and, for reasons that are explained in detail in Chapter 10, we associate that product of labels with the correlation, $\rho_{fe,fo}$, of fe and fo. In the same way, we associate the correlation of me and mo with the product (cd), of fe and me with the product (ac), of fe and mo with the product (ad), and so on. This labeled graph has the following symmetry: if we multiply the label product (ab) by the label product (cd), we get the same total product that is obtained by multiplying the label product (ad) by the label product (bc):

$$(ab)\,(cd) = (ad)\,(bc)$$

On substituting the associated correlations for the respective label products, this equation becomes a tetrad equation:

$$\rho_{fe,fo}\rho_{me,mo} = \rho_{fe,mo}\rho_{fo,me}$$

In the same way, the two other tetrad equations implied by this model can be derived from examining the symmetry of label products.

Theorem 3: The tetrad equations strongly implied by a statistical model are determined entirely by the directed graph of the model.

The tetrad equations implied by a causal model are therefore also implied by all statistical models whose causal hypotheses are represented by the causal model. The causal model makes certain assumptions about the joint distribution of some variables and about the existence of moments, but does not otherwise restrict the distribution of each variable individually. How the variables are distributed does not matter; the tetrad equations are implied regardless of whether the variables are standardized or unstandardized, normally distributed or not.

In fact something much stronger than Theorem 3 holds. There exists an algorithm for deriving the tetrad equations implied by *any* acyclic directed graph.[22] The algorithm is described in Chapter 10, where its adequacy is proved.

Tetrad Equations Derived from Vanishing Partial Correlations

We have said that the implication of both vanishing partial correlations and tetrad equations is determined by the directed graph of a model, and we have said, in Theorem 2, what property of a directed graph determines whether or not that graph implies a particular vanishing partial correlation. We have noted the symmetry property that determines tetrad equations, and that property in fact gives an entirely graph theoretic means of computing the tetrad equations implied by a model. One

---

[22]We believe the algorithm is also adequate for cyclic graphs, although as of this edition we do not yet have a proof for that case.

might wonder whether there is some connection between vanishing partial correlations and tetrad equations. There is. A directed graph implies a tetrad equation if it implies that four numerators of partial correlations vanish.

Theorem 4: A directed graph, G, implies the tetrad equation

$$\rho_{ij}\rho_{kl} = \rho_{ik}\rho_{jl}$$

if for some variable, v, it implies the four conditions:

$$\rho_{ij} - \rho_{iv}\rho_{jv} = 0$$

$$\rho_{kl} - \rho_{kv}\rho_{lv} = 0$$

$$\rho_{ik} - \rho_{iv}\rho_{kv} = 0$$

$$\rho_{jl} - \rho_{jv}\rho_{lv} = 0.$$

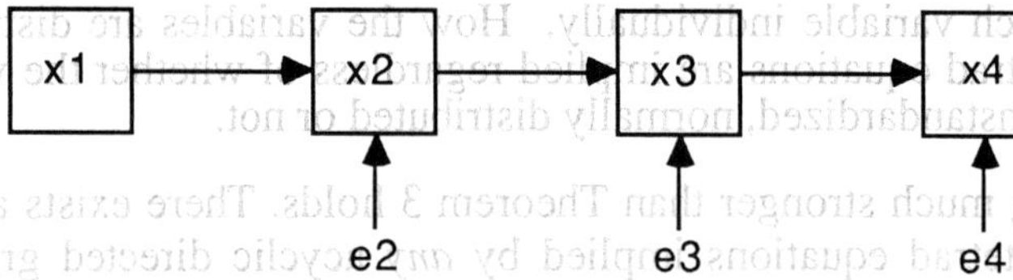

Figure 4-15: Path model.

For example, the model in Fig. 4-15 implies that

$$\rho_{13}\rho_{24} = \rho_{14}\rho_{23}$$

and the reader can verify that the numerators of the partial correlations

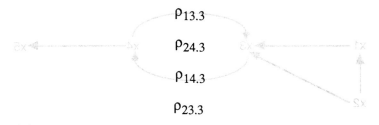

$$\rho_{13.3}$$
$$\rho_{24.3}$$
$$\rho_{14.3}$$
$$\rho_{23.3}$$

must all vanish.

Figure 4-17: A counterexample to the converse of theorem 4.

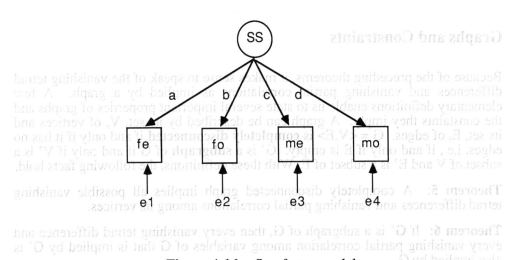

Figure 4-16: One factor model.

In the model in Fig. 4-16 all three possible tetrad equations among fe, fo, me, and mo are implied because the model implies that all of the partial correlations among these variables vanish when SS is controlled for.

The converse of this theorem is not true. A model can imply a vanishing tetrad difference without implying vanishing partial correlations that, in turn, imply the tetrad equation. For example, the model in Fig. 4-17 (in which we neglect to exhibit error terms) implies that $\rho_{15}\rho_{23} - \rho_{25}\rho_{13} = 0$, but it does not imply any corresponding set of vanishing partial correlations.

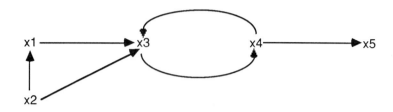

Figure 4-17: A counterexample to the converse of theorem 4.

Graphs and Constraints

Because of the preceding theorems, it makes sense to speak of the vanishing tetrad differences and vanishing partial correlations as implied by a graph. A few elementary definitions enable us to state several important properties of graphs and the constaints they imply. A graph can be described by its set, V, of vertices and its set, E, of edges. $G = <V,E>$ is **completely disconnected** if and only if it has no edges, i.e., if and only if E is empty. G' is a **subgraph** of G if and only if V' is a subset of V and E' is a subset of E. With these definitions, the following facts hold.

Theorem 5: A completely disconnected graph implies all possible vanishing tetrad differences and vanishing partial correlations among its vertices.

Theorem 6: If G' is a subgraph of G, then every vanishing tetrad difference and every vanishing partial correlation among variables of G that is implied by G' is also implied by G.

Other Constraints

There are many other forms of constraints that can be implied by linear models. For example, models with six or more measured variables can imply vanishing sextad differences and models with eight or more measured variables can imply vanishing octad differences, and so on. A model only implies higher order constraints of this kind, however, if it also implies a set of vanishing tetrad differences that also imply the higher order vanishing differences. So in a sense, these higher order constraints are nothing new.

A model may also imply higher order vanising partial correlations in which the effects of two or more variables are controlled for. TETRAD does *not* compute higher order vanishing partial correlations that may be implied by the model.

There are, in addition, constraints that are independent of tetrad and vanishing partial constraints. A model with at least five measured variables may imply **pentad** constraints, which assert that a sum of products vanishes, where each product has five correlations as factors. If a model implying pentad constraints has but one common source, then the pentad constraints will be implied as well by the tetrad equations the model implies, but other models can imply pentad constraints that are independent of vanishing tetrad differences. Under appropriate limitations, models may also imply **tetrad inequalities** and other constraints in the form of inequalities.

The existence of other constraints means that a procedure, such as TETRAD, that searches for models by attempting to explain the vanishing tetrad differences and vanishing partial correlations found in the data will tend to be too generous. It will generate models that do not explain higher order constraints that hold in the data, and it will also generate models that imply higher order constraints that do not hold in the data. We will see in Chapter 8 that TETRAD occasionally generates alternative models that perform very differently when tested statistically.

Latent Variables and Overidentifying Constraints

Nearly all causal models contain "latent" variables. Latent variables are simply any variables that occur in the model but have not been measured.[23] The most ubiquitous type of latent variables are error terms, but latent variables also often occur as common causes of several measured variables, and unlike error variables they usually carry with them some theoretical interpretation.

"Latent" does not mean "unobservable," and merely because a variable happens not to be among those measured in a study does not mean that the variable could not be measured, were we careful and clever enough. Some philosophical and methodological issues concerning latent variables will be discussed in a later chapter. For now, we wish only to explain some connections between latent variables and overidentifying constraints.

We know from Theorem 4 that a model implies a tetrad equation if it implies that all of the numerators of their partial correlations vanish when taken with respect to *some* common variable. If the converse of Theorem 4 were true, whenever we found a set of tetrad equations to hold, and also found that among the measured variables no set of vanishing partial correlations hold that imply the tetrad

---

[23]Notationally, TETRAD distinguishes between latent and measured variables by whether or not the first character in the variable's name is capitalized. If the first letter is capitalized, TETRAD interprets it as a latent variable. In our figures, we follow the same convention. We also follow a somehwat standard convention by putting measured variables in boxes, interpreted latent variables in circles, and uninterpreted error terms in nothing at all.

equation, then we could conclude that the tetrad equations could only be explained by a model that introduces a latent variable. We know from the model shown in Fig. 4-17 that the converse of Theorem 4 is *not* true. We have, however, found no case in which a model *without cycles* implies a tetrad equation unless it also implies a set of vanishing partial correlations implying that tetrad equation. Our experience is not proof that such models do not exist, but we suggest the following two heuristics:

1. If a set of tetrad equations hold among measured variables, and no vanishing partial correlations hold among the measured variables that imply the tetrad equations, and no cyclic model without latent variables is acceptable, then *ceteris paribus* a model with latent variables provides the best explanation of the data.

2. If a set of vanishing partial correlations among a set of measured variables hold in the data and imply tetrad equations that also hold, then do *not* introduce a latent variable as a common cause of the measured variables unless there is good substantive reason to do so.

4.6. Correlated Errors are not Equivalent to Direct Effects

Part of the power of the TETRAD program lies in its ability to use overidentifying constraints to discriminate among circumstances in which X causes Y, Y causes X, or X and Y have correlated errors. Models with direct causal effects between their measured variables may have quite different statistical properties than do models in which the direct effects are replaced by correlated errors. That is because the statistical implications of a causal model are determined by its set of treks, and directed edges can create very different treks than those created by correlated errors. Since this aspect of causal models, although simple enough, is sometimes misunderstood, we will give a more formal demonstration.

Two examples of linear causal models are given in Figs. 4-18 and 4-19. Structurally, they are typical of many measurement models in sociology, psychometrics, and social psychology.

The equations for Model 1 (Fig. 4-18) are

$$x1 = a_1F + e1$$

$$x2 = a_2F + e2$$

$$x3 = a_3F + e3$$

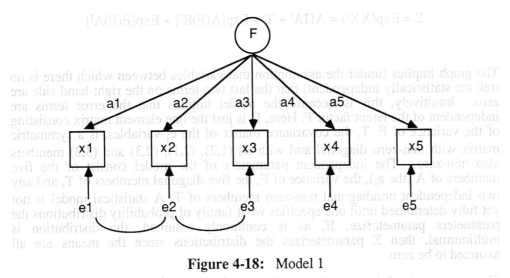

Figure 4-18: Model 1

$$x4 = a_4 F + e4$$

$$x5 = a_5 F + e5$$

or in matrix form

$$X = A(F) + E$$

Here, X is the column vector of the x_i, A is the column vector of the a_i, F is the matrix whose one element is F, and E is the column vector of e_i. To get the correlation matrix for this model we multiply each side of the matrix equation by its transpose and take the expectation value of both sides of the resulting matrix equation.[24]

The result is

---

[24]We assume that the means of all variables are zero and that F has unit variance.

$$\Sigma = \mathrm{Exp}(XX^t) = A\Pi A^t + T + \mathrm{Exp}[A(F)E^t] + \mathrm{Exp}[E(F)A^t]$$

The graph implies (under the assumption that variables between which there is no trek are statistically independent) that the last two terms on the right-hand side are zero. Intuitively, this is because the model implies that the error terms are independent of the latent factor F. Here, Π is just the one element matrix consisting of the variance of F. T, the covariance matrix of the e_i variables, is a symmetric matrix with non-zero diagonal and with its (1,2), (2,1), (2,3) and (3,2) members also non-zero. The independent parameters of the model consist of the five members of A (the a_i), the variance of F, the five diagonal members of T, and any two independent nondiagonal non-zero members of T. A statistical model is not yet fully determined until one specifies what family of probability distributions the parameters parameterize. If, as is commonly assumed, the distribution is multinormal, then Σ parameterizes the distributions since the means are all assumed to be zero.

The components of the preceding matrix equation assert that

$$\rho_{ij} = a_i a_j$$

Elementary algebra then shows that this model entails that

$$\rho_{13}\rho_{45} = \rho_{14}\rho_{35} = \rho_{15}\rho_{34}$$

We recognize these equations as three tetrad equations.

Consider a second model, shown in Fig. 4-19. The equations for this model are

$$x1 = a_1 F + e1$$

$$x2 - ax1 = a_2 F + e2$$

$$x3 - bx2 = a_3 F + e3$$

$$x4 = a_4 F + e4$$

$$x5 = a_5 F + e5$$

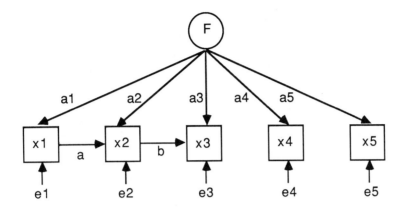

Figure 4-19: Model 2.

In matrix form these equations are

$$BX = A(F) + E$$

or, equivalently,

$$X = B^{-1}A(F) + B^{-1}E$$

where X is a column vector of the x_i variables, A is the column matrix of the a_i, E is the column vector of the variables e_i, and

$$B = \begin{vmatrix} 1 & 0 & 0 & 0 & 0 \\ -a & 1 & 0 & 0 & 0 \\ 0 & -b & 1 & 0 & 0 \\ 0 & 0 & 0 & 1 & 0 \\ 0 & 0 & 0 & 0 & 1 \end{vmatrix}$$

The matrix B^{-1} looks like B except that -a is replaced by a, -b is replaced by b, and the (3,1) element is not zero but ab.

The covariance matrix is again obtained by multiplying both sides of the matrix equation by their respective transposes and taking expectation values. This gives

$$\Sigma = Exp(XX^t)$$

$$= B^{-1}A\Pi A^t B^{-1t} + B^{-1}TB^{-1t} + Exp[B^{-1}E(F)A^t B^{-1t}] + Exp[B^{-1}A(F)E^t B^{-1t}]$$

where Π is the variance matrix of F and T is the covariance matrix of the e_i variables. The last two terms on the right vanish. That is, again, because there is no trek between any e_i variable and F. Therefore F and each e_i must be statistically independent, which implies, since all variables have zero means, that the expected value of the product of F and e_i is zero for all i. For the same reason the expected value of the product of any two distinct e_i variables is zero. All of the off-diagonal elements of T are therefore zero.

Examining the components of the covariance matrix, we find that the equation

$$\rho_{13}\rho_{45} = \rho_{14}\rho_{35}$$

is not implied, which proves that the two models imply different constraints on the covariance matrix and are, therefore, inequivalent.

4.7. Statistical Issues, Briefly Considered

The parameters of a model must be estimated from sample data, and sample data must be used to perform statistical tests of a model. The TETRAD program does not do statistical estimation of parameters and performs only statistical tests for vanishing tetrad differences and vanishing partial correlations. It performs no tests of models or of the significance of parameter estimates. TETRAD is a program for helping in model specification, not for estimating parameters and performing statistical tests of models. Thus the program is best used in conjunction with a statistical package that will perform these analyses. There are several packages of this kind, some of them virtually indistinguishable save for ease of use or speed of processing.

Different statistical procedures are favored in different social science disciplines, often for reasons that are unclear. Econometricians tend to prefer least squares estimates of parameters, perhaps because they so often consider regression models. For more complex models, multistage least squares procedures are often used in econometrics. In other social sciences, full information maximum likelihood estimators are more commonly used. These procedures have been automated in the LISREL computer program and in the recently released EQS computer program. In later chapters we will estimate parameters using the EQS program.

Hypothesis tests are also performed in different ways in different social science disciplines. There are, for example, various tests of the assumption of linearity but they are rarely performed in many social science disciplines in which linear models are used. A specific model can only be tested provided the model implies some constraint on the variance/covariance matrix. Regression models do not, and so the tests performed on them are usually only tests of the estimated regression coefficients. In psychology, a "null hypothesis" is often constructed contradicting the hypothesis of interest and the null hypothesis is then tested. This procedure has been rightly criticized by many authors (see Oakes [81]). In social sciences outside of econometrics, models are often subjected to chi square tests in conjunction with maximum likelihood estimates of parameters. An especially clear discussion of these tests can be found in Fox [27]. These tests compute a statistic that, on the assumption that the variable distribution is multinormal, is asymptotically distributed as chi square with the number of degrees of freedom equal to the number of variances and covariances among the measured variables minus the number of free parameters (including variances) of the model. Chi square statistics of this kind are computed by both the LISREL and EQS programs.

In applying TETRAD, we routinely assess the models found using full information maximum likelood estimation. We view the probabilities of test statistics, or p values as they are sometimes called, as *likelihoods*. Likelihoods are simply probabilities conditional on hypotheses, and probabilities can be compared. The probability of the chi square statistic for some model and data set is a measure both of fit and simplicity, for it takes into consideration both the residuals and the number of free parameters used in producing those residuals. Hypotheses can be compared by the ratio of the likelihoods they give to the same test statistic on the same data. Of course, that is not all there is, or should be, to the comparison of competing hypotheses, but it is a consideration, and we will use it repeatedly.

The use of statistical tests has a decision theoretic foundation in Neyman-Pearson theory, and the most devoted adherents of the tradition reject any theory comparisons that are not framed as hypothesis tests. They would, in particular, reject the comparison of alternative models in terms of likelihoods, simplicity, or explanatory power. The Neyman-Pearson decision theory is rarely strictly applied, but when it is, it does not permit anything but the *rejection* of theories. The acceptance of a theory, however tentatively, cannot be justified on Neyman-Pearson grounds, save in those rare cases in which every alternative theory has been rejected. Nor does the decision theory provide any judgements about which of several *false* theories is the *better approximation*. But in all of science, including social science, the principal job is not to reject false theories but to find the better approximations and reject the worse approximations.

In practice, in most applications of linear modeling, we can be fairly confident that every model we will consider is false. The almost universal experience is that as sample sizes increase, testable linear models fail powerful statistical tests. The task is not to find a *true* linear model but to find the models that are the best linear approximations to the truth, and to assess whether that approximation is good enough to serve in practice. In such contexts, there is little point to decision procedures whose function is to reject false theories.

There is, to our knowledge, no formal account of the connection between properties of sample statistics, on the one hand, and the approximate truth of models, on the other. In the absence of such an account, we use the p values, simplicity, and explanatory power to assess models, and where we can we test models by means of nonstatistical predictions.[*]

---

[*]Added in proof. We have discovered that the converse of Theorem 4 is false even in the acyclic case, as the following example shows. The graph {<x1,x3>, <x2,x3>, <x3,x4>, <x5,x4>, <x5,x3>} (where we have neglected to include the error variables attached to each dependent variable) implies the tetrad equation $\rho_{x1,x3}\rho_{x2,x4} = \rho_{x1,x4}\rho_{x2,x3}$. However, there is no variable m in the graph such that $\rho_{13.m} = \rho_{24.m} = \rho_{14.m} = \rho_{23.m} = 0$. In chapter 8, in the study of longitudinal data with SAT scores, the heuristic based upon the assumption that the converse to Theorem 4 is true in the acyclic case is used to justify the introduction of a latent variable. While the justification is faulty, it remains true that it is necessary to introduce a latent variable in order to explain the observed pattern of tetrad equations in that case.

5. THE STRUCTURE AND METHOD OF TETRAD

The TETRAD program helps to search for good models of correlation or covariance data. This chapter describes the methodological principles behind TETRAD, how they are realized in the program, and how these principles can be used with the program in searching for good causal models. It lists the output the program provides, describes some of the calculations that go into the output, and illustrates how the output can be used to find good causal models. It also compares TETRAD's search strategy with other search strategies. More detailed mathematical characterizations of the fundamental algorithms of the program, and proofs of their adequacy, are given in chapter 10 of this book. Several cases illustrating the use of the program on empirical and simulated data are described in later chapters.

5.1. The Methodological Principles That Underlie TETRAD

The Inference Problem

Suppose we have a set of covariances or correlations and an initial linear causal model to account for them. The initial model may contain latent variables, but it is otherwise very simple in the sense that it postulates very few direct causal connections in order to account for the measured correlations. More technically, let us suppose that the initial model contains one and only one trek for each measured non-zero covariance. If the model is estimated from the correlations or covariances and tested, say, by a chi square test, it may do very poorly and may, in fact, be rejected by conventional standards. Even so, suppose we have reason to think that the model is plausible and that it may well be true but incomplete. There may be other causal connections among the variables, there may be correlated errors, or there may be omitted unmeasured variables that have an effect on several of the measured or unmeasured variables. If the initial model yields a chi square value with zero probability, but we think its positive causal claims are nonetheless plausible, then the problem is to find the "best" elaborations of the initial model.

But what does "best" mean? No one has a complete answer to that question, but we propose a mixture of considerations about scientific explanation.

> Other things being equal, the best models are those that imply patterns or constraints judged to hold in the population, that do not imply patterns judged not to hold in the population, and that are as simple as possible.

93

For brevity, we will sometimes say that constraints that are judged, on the basis of a sample, to hold in the population are constraints that *hold in the data.*

Implying Constraints That Hold in the Data

By **Spearman's principle** we mean the following.

Other things being equal, prefer those models that, for all values of their free parameters, entail the constraints judged to hold in the population.

This is a principle stated *ceteris paribus*; it can be defeated if one has reason to think that a constraint on the correlation matrix is satisfied by chance, if some model that violates the principle has other extraordinary virtues, or if one has reason to think that the general assumptions of linear modeling are inappropriate to the case. The reason we call this Spearman's principle are given in Chapter 9.

Spearman's principle can be justified in several ways. One is through its historical role in the natural sciences. The principle antedates Spearman by millenia. It was a fundamental principle used in ancient planetary theory. It was used by Kepler to argue for Copernican Astronomy and by Eddinton to argue for the General Theory of Relativity. It plays a major role in assessing explanations in contemporary partical physics and cosmology.

Spearman's principle can also be grounded on the following observation. If a linear causal model implies a constraint only for particular values of its linear coefficients, then the set of values of the coefficients for which the constraint holds is usually a set of measure zero. Given any "natural" probability measure in the values of the coefficients, the values for which the constraint holds will have zero probability. By contrast, if a model strongly implies a constraint, then the model implies the constraint for all values of its linear coefficients.

Not Implying Constraints That Do Not Hold in the Data

By **Thurstone's principle**, we mean the following.

Other things being equal, a model should not imply constraints that are not supported by the sample data.

We call this idea Thurstone's principle, although we mean no historical attribution, because it is derived from a principle that is fundamental to factor analysis. In factor analysis, one reduces the difference between predicted and observed correlations (the residuals) by introducing additional causal structure. The heuristic we use to reduce the residuals is to avoid implying constraints that are not supported by the data. Thurstone's principle is one of the most elementary and uncontroversial requirements imposed on theories.

The Simplicity Principle

Nearly every methodologist, whether philosopher, statistician, or scientist, has emphasized the importance of the virtue of simplicity. It is surprising that something so widely admired should be so difficult to characterize, but there are no satisfactory general accounts of the notion of simplicity that apply to the variety of scientific contexts in which the notion is used. In the special case of causal models, we understand simpler models to be those that posit fewer causal connections. In effect, we suppose an initial bias against causal connections and require that a case be made for any causal claims. This requirement has nothing to do with whether the data are experimental or nonexperimental; in fact, it is because of this bias that good evidence and arguments are demanded for controversial causal claims, whether about the efficacy of a drug or the effects of pornography.

The Principles Conflict

In practice, the three principles interact and conflict. Spearman's principle will tend to be satisfied by simple models, since such models imply a great many constraints. But constraints are seldom *exactly* satisfied in any sample, and thus, on the average, the fewer constraints implied, the better Thurstone's principle will be realized. Modifying a model to account for more and more of the empirical covariances generally means adding more and more free parameters thus increasing the complexity of the model and losing degrees of freedom. The TETRAD program provides information about how modifications to an initial model affect both Spearman's and Thurstone's principles. In effect, the user is free to judge how the explanatory principles are to be weighted.

5.2. How the Methodological Principles Are Realized in TETRAD

The Constraints That TETRAD Calculates

To satisfy Spearman's or Thurstone's principle strictly, we would have to search for the models that imply all of the constraints that are judged to hold in virtue of the sample correlations. In practice, we cannot do that. First, we do not know how to test for all forms of constraints, and second we do not have fast algorithms for computing all forms of constraints implied by an arbitrary model. Evidently, what is required is some *heuristic* procedure for searching and testing the vast space of elaborations of the initial model.

Our strategy is to look only at constraints of two special kinds: vanishing tetrad differences and vanishing partial correlations. These constraints are numerous enough that they help to discriminate between alternative elaborations of an initial model, they are rapidly computable implications of models, and they have statistical tests available for them. Further, these two kinds of constraints have nice *inheritance* properties that can be used in building up the best models from the initial model. Adding directed edges or correlated errors never increases the number of vanishing tetrad differences and vanishing partials that are implied by a model. Thus if at any stage a model does not adequately meet Spearman's criterion, no further elaboration of that model will either, and we can avoid considering all such elaborations.

Comparing Models

TETRAD will, upon request, print a table listing every tetrad or vanishing partial equation that is implied by a model and every equation that holds to within a user-set significance level. Each time a model implies an equation judged to hold in the population, the model satisfies Spearman's principle for that equation. TETRAD automatically calculates the number of equations that hold at a particular significance level, the number of those equations that are implied by the model (the number explained), and the number of equations that are judged to hold but are *not* implied. According to Spearman's principle, other things being equal we prefer models that explain a greater number of equations that are judged to hold in the population.

If a model implies an equation that is judged not to hold in the population, then the model *violates* Thurstone's principle for that equation. TETRAD automatically calculates the number of equations a model implies that do not hold to within a user-set significance level. Some equations violate Thurstone's principle more severely than others, i.e., they have larger residuals than others, so it is not only the *number* of equations that violate Thurstone's principle that matters but the *total residual*. TETRAD automatically sums the residuals of all the equations implied by a model and reports that number as the **Total Tetrad Residual** (TTR) for tetrad constraints and as the **Total Partial Residual** (TPR) for vanishing partial correlation constraints. According to Thurstone's principle, other things being equal we prefer models that have the *lowest* TTR and the *lowest* TPR.

Comparing Elaborations of a Model

The information TETRAD gives is addressed to the inference problem we sketched above. Starting with a simple model, what are its best elaborations?

In order to help the user compare elaborations of a model, TETRAD supplies information on the effect each elaboration has on the model's ability to satisfy Spearman's principle and Thurstone's Priniciple. If an initial model implies an equation that holds in the data, but the addition of an edge (or correlated error) would result in a model that no longer implies that equation, adding the edge causes the model to violate Spearman's principle for that equation. If a model implies an equation that would no longer be implied when an edge is added to the model, we say that the edge **defeats** that equation. TETRAD supplies a measure of the amount of damage to Spearman's principle each elaboration causes: **I(H-I)**. Mnemonically, this expression stands for the *I*ncrease in the number of equations that *H*old but that are not *I*mplied. Other things being equal, we prefer the elaboration that has the *lowest* I(H-I) value.

Symmetrically, if an elaboration defeats an equation that is judged not to hold in the data, then that elaboration prevents the model from violating Thurstone's principle for that equation. The model previously implied an equation considered false, but after the elaboration it does not imply that equation. TETRAD supplies two measures of how much each elaboration helps a model to satisfy Thurstone's principle. It calculates **D(I-H)**, the *D*ecrease in the number of equations that are *I*mplied that do not *H*old, and it calculates an elaboration's **Rttr**, or the *R*eduction in the *t*otal *t*etrad *r*esidual that would result from the elaboration. Other things being equal, we prefer the elaboration that has the *highest* Rttr value and the *highest* D(I-H) value.

5.3. Search Strategies for Finding Good Causal Models

The three principles suggest a strategy for model specification. Beginning with a very simple model, determine how it fares by Spearman's and Thurstone's criteria (number of equations explained and the TTR, respectively). Then, step by step, examine increasingly complex elaborations of the initial model and determine how they behave. Stop elaborating as soon as it is judged that a model satisfies Spearman's and Thurstone's principles sufficiently well. In this way, unnecessarily complex models will not be considered. The steps in the search look like a tree diagram (Fig. 5-1). Here, M represents the initial model, the asterisks immediately below it represent models that add one directed edge or correlated error to M, the next level of asterisks represent models that add two edges or correlated errors to M, and so on. The idea is that one first searches for the best additions at the first level below M and ignores all additions at that level that are not among the best. One then considers all daughters of each of the best first level additions and sees which among them are best, and so on. This sort of procedure is known as a

Figure 5-1: Search tree.

breadth-first search. Notice that after the search through each level is completed, if the search is to continue then every daughter of the best nodes must be generated and evaluated. That means that to carry out the search we must have rapid ways to evaluate the effects of every possible addition to any model.

The breadth-first search strategy can be used with the TETRAD program, and we illustrate it in several cases in later chapters.

5.4. A Sketch of the TETRAD Program

TETRAD's Output

The TETRAD program operates in two modes. One mode provides the user with information to conduct a breadth-first search, one edge at a time, as described in the previous section. The other, more automatic mode, conducts a search that does not necessarily proceed one edge at a time, but which may consider several simultaneous additions to an initial model. The two modes can be used together.

TETRAD requires the user to provide the computer with a directed graph, representing an initial causal model, and a set of variances and covariances, or correlations, for the measured variables in the model. In addition the user can set a significance level to be used in testing constraints. With that input, the user can obtain any or all of the following information:

1. A list of all tetrad equations and vanishing partial correlations among measured variables that *pass a statistical test* at a level of significance specified by the user, as well as the p value of each constraint.

2. A list of all vanishing tetrad differences and vanishing partial correlations *implied* by the model given to the program, together with the p values of these constraints for the sample data provided.

3. A count of how many tetrad equations and vanishing partial correlations hold at a specified significance level, of how many of these are explained (i.e., implied, by the model given to the program), of how many constraints are implied by the model but do not hold (I-H), and of how many that hold are not implied (H-I).

4. The sum, over all tetrad equations implied by the model, of (absolute values of) the tetrad differences found in the sample (*TTR value*), and the sum, over all vanishing partial correlations implied by the model, of (absolute values of) the partial correlations found in the data (*TPR value*).

5. Two tables, the *Rttr chart* and *Rtpr chart*, that list, for each possible directed edge or correlated error that may be added, the effects of adding that edge or correlated error to the initial model. The information includes I(H-I), D(I-H), Rttr (or Rptr), and Pi (see Section 5.4).

6. For each possible addition of an edge or correlated error, a list of the tetrad equations or vanishing partials that are implied by the initial model but are no longer implied if the addition is made, and the probabilities of the corresponding residuals found in the sample (on the hypothesis that the differences vanish in the population). This option is called the **Compare** function.

7. A crude index of fit, the **Pi** value, for any model that is an elaboration of a basemodel specified by the user (see Section 5.4).

8. Sets of suggested elaborations to a simple initial model, found by TETRAD's automatic search procedure.

We illustrate how these pieces of information can be used to find good causal models in Section 5.5. First, however, some further explanation is needed of the information computed by the program.

Tetrad Residuals

For full statistical models with specified values for all parameters, we measure the difference between a correlation value implied by the model and the observed correlation by the *residual*. The residual is a function of the difference between a predicted correlation value and the observed correlation. The degree to which a tetrad equation implied by a model agrees with observed correlations can be measured in a similar way, but its calculation does not require that the model be estimated.

Consider, for example, the model Fig. 5-2.

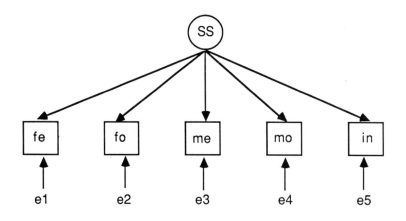

Figure 5-2: Directed graph representation.

This model implies that:

$$\rho_{fo,me}\rho_{fe,mo} = \rho_{fo,mo}\rho_{me,fe}$$

If these variables stand for father's education, father's occupation, mother's education, mother's occupation, and family income for members of some population, we do not expect that sample correlations will exactly satisfy this equation even if the model is correct. Suppose the observed correlations among these four variables, estimated from the sample, are

$$\sigma_{fo,me} = .433$$

$$\sigma_{fe,mo} = .381$$

$$\sigma_{fo,mo} = .521$$

$$\sigma_{me,fe} = .394$$

The tetrad equation implied by the model can be written equivalently as a vanishing tetrad difference:

$$\rho_{fo,me}\rho_{fe,mo} - \rho_{fo,mo}\rho_{me,fe} = 0$$

How much the observation differs from the implication can be measured by the positive square root of

$$(\sigma_{fo,me}\sigma_{fe,\,mo} - \sigma_{fo,mo}\sigma_{me,fe})^2$$

With the numbers just given, this quantity, which we call the *tetrad residual* is

$$[((.433)(.381) - (.521)(.391))^2]^{1/2} = .0387$$

One measure of how well a full statistical model with specified values for all of its parameters fits the data is the sum of the residuals of all correlations or covariances. Similarly, one measure of how well a causal model fits the data is the sum of the tetrad residuals of all the tetrad equations the model implies. As we said above, this quantity is the **Total Tetrad Residual** or *TTR*.

Partial Correlation Residuals

In the same way, we can consider the vanishing partial correlations that a model strongly implies and compare them with the actual partial correlations found in the sample data. For each vanishing partial implied by a model, we call the corresponding absolute value of the sample partial correlation the *partial correlation residual* or *PR*. Just as with the sum of the tetrad residuals, we can sum the PR values for each partial correlation that must vanish in the population if the causal model is correct. We abbreviate this sum as *TPR*.

The TTR and TPR values are the heuristic measures we use for how well Thurstone's principle is satisfied by a model. The lower these values are, the better the principle is satisfied.

The Statistical Procedures

Testing for Vanishing Tetrad Differences

For each foursome of measured variables in a data set, there are three possible tetrad equations which may or may not hold. For n variables, the number of possible tetrad equations is therefore three times the number of ways of choosing 4 from n. The TETRAD program tests for each possible tetrad equation. The test is based on Wishart's formula for the variance of the sampling distribution of a tetrad difference. Consider four variables, x_1-x_4. Let D be the determinant of the sample variance-covariance matrix for the foursome of variables such that the (i,j) member of D is the covariance of x_i and x_j. Let D_{12} be the upper left corner two-dimensional subdeterminant of D, and D_{34} the bottom right corner subdeterminant. N is the sample size. The formula for the sampling variance of the tetrad difference

$$T = Cov(x_1x_3) \; Cov(x_2x_4) - Cov(x_1x_4) \; Cov(x_2x_3)$$

is given by

$$(N-2) \; VAR(T) = D_{12}D_{34}(N+1)/(N-1) - D$$

Other cases are obtained by permutation of indices. The distribution of the tetrad difference for correlations follows the same formula. The TETRAD program converts covariance tetrad differences to correlation tetrad differences in order to facilitate comparison of the tetrad residuals for different foursomes of variables.

TETRAD uses Wishart's formula to perform an asymptotic test for each possible tetrad equation. As the sample size grows without bound, the distribution of a tetrad difference converges in probability to a normal distribution (see Anderson [2]). The program compares the tetrad difference found in the data with a normal distribution having variance given by Wishart's formula and having mean zero.

Aside from its asymptotic character, there are several disadvantages to this test. The test is performed on each tetrad equation as though it were independent of the others. For many reasons, this assumption is almost never correct. The result is that in Monte Carlo studies, for example, we find that true tetrad equations are rejected by the test more frequently than the significance level would suggest. One might view the set of tetrad equations as a collection of *contrasts* (see Scheffe' and Miller [89, 80]) and seek simultaneous confidence intervals for all of the tetrad equations implied by a model as well as a test of the entire set of tetrad equations so implied. Such an approach poses a new and difficult statistical problem for each model, however, and we know of no general method for solving it or for computing such confidence intervals. In this case it is better to do what can be done, even if some error is introduced thereby. We regard the procedure as an example of Simon's "satisficing."

Another disadvantage of the tetrad difference statistic is that it is not very powerful when the correlations are small. The product of two small numbers is small, and the difference of such products (when the signs are the same) is smaller still. In Monte Carlo studies we have found that the statistic tends to be too generous in accepting tetrad equations when the sample sizes are small (below 300, for example) and the correlations are less than .3.

Testing for Vanishing Partial Correlations

For partial correlations, there is a well-known sampling distribution which can be transformed to a normal distribution using Fisher's z statistic (see Anderson [2]). TETRAD tests for vanishing partial correlations using this statistic.

As with vanishing tetrad differences, the vanishing partial correlations will not generally be independent, and in testing all of the vanishing partial correlations implied by a model, the proportion of partials that vanish in the population but fail the statistical test may differ from the significance value of the test. We accept this limitation for the same reasons as in the case of the test for vanishing tetrad differences.

It should be emphasized that the hypotheses TETRAD tests are not the usual hypotheses of a "null effect." When testing null hypotheses, an investigator is often interested in rejecting the hypotheses and thereby establishing that some effect of interest is significant. (The weakness of such tests has been discussed by

Meehl [78].) In such cases, increasing the significance level makes it more likely that the null hypothesis will be rejected and therefore *weakens* the test of the hypothesis of interest. In contrast, when testing the hypothesis that a tetrad difference vanishes, one is usually interested in the case in which the hypothesis is *not* rejected. Increasing the significance level makes it more likely that the hypothesis of a vanishing tetrad difference will be rejected and therefore *strengthens* the test of this hypothesis. We will often test hypotheses at very high significance levels.

Determining the Constraints Implied by a Model

Given a data set and an initial model, the TETRAD program will compute all of the tetrad equations implied by the model. It will do the same for vanishing partial correlations and it will report the sample tetrad difference and sample partial correlation for each constraint that is entailed by the model. The procedure is rigorous for acyclic graphs, and we conjecture that it is correct for cyclic graphs as well.

The procedures the program uses to compute the implied vanishing partial correlations are applications of the theorems in Chapter 4. The algorithms are described in more detail, and their adequacy proven, in Chapter 10.

Indices of Fit

Many indices of fit have been proposed in the literature on structural equation modeling. Bentler and Bonett proposed a "normed fit index" [5]. Let M_0 be a model that can be obtained from any of the models to be compared by fixing parameters. M_0 is thus more restrictive than any of the models to be compared. For example, M_0 might be the "null" model that fixes all structural parameters at zero. Let F be any fitting statistic one pleases. Let F_0 be the value of F for M_0 estimated from a sample covariance matrix S. In general, F_0 will be worse (i.e., larger) than the F value for any of the models to be compared. F_0 provides a standard, or unit, for how bad a model can be, and each of the models to be compared can be measured for fit by a fraction of F_0. For any model M_t, Bentler and Bonett propose the index of fit

$$\Delta_{0t} = (F_0 - F_t)/F_0$$

The index takes values between 0 and 1, and bigger is better, other things being equal.

The point of the normed index of fit is easily seen with a least squares loss function for F. In that case F is the sum of squares of residuals. F_0 is simply the sum of squares of S, and Δ_{0t} is simply unity minus the squared sum of residuals of M_t as a fraction of the squared sum of residuals of S. The analogy with the notion of "percentage of variance explained" in analysis of variance is suggestive. A model can give a test statistic with a very low probability even though it explains a very large proportion of the the sum of squares of S.

Nothing about the normed fit index requires that the function F be one for which a sampling distribution and appropriate statistical tests are available. Thus a normed fit index can be calculated for the sum of tetrad residuals. A natural choice for M_0 is a model that implies every possible tetrad equation among the measured variables. A single-factor model, in which each measured variable is an indicator of one latent factor such that there are no directed or undirected edges connecting measured variables or their error terms, is a model that implies every possible tetrad equation among the measured variables. A model represented by a completely disconnected graph also implies every possible tetrad equation and every possible vanishing partial correlation equation.

TETRAD provides all of the information necessary to calculate a normed fit index using tetrad residuals.

James *et al.* [50] have objected that the normed fit index does not take into account the number of free parameters in a model. They propose instead the index

$$\Pi_{0k} = (d_k/d_0)[(F_0 - F_k)/F_0]$$

where d_k and d_0 are the degrees of freedom of the models M_k and M_0 respectively. The objection is not entirely fair, since Bentler and Bonett do not claim that normed fit ratios are by themselves a sufficient basis for preference among models, any more than the probability of a chi square statistic is such a basis. But James *et al.* are surely correct that there is more to good explanation than simply reducing the proportion of the residuals unaccounted for and that parsimony is part of what makes for a good explanation.

These indices have, for two reasons, considerable arbitrariness. First, any sufficiently constrained model can be taken for M_0 and different choices will lead to different values for the indices. The model specifying that all variables are independent is a fairly natural choice for M_0. Second, there is no natural or privileged measure of how much extra residual is worth tolerating for the gain of a degree of freedom. The Π index assumes such a measure, but it is fairly arbitrary. The Π index is, in principle, objectionable since it gives the worst possible value (zero) to any model which specifies that all variables are statistically independent, even when the data are, in fact, generated by such a structure. In practice, we are rarely interested in such models, and the objection does not much matter. For all the arbitrariness, it seems a substantial improvement to prefer models with greater Π values than to base preferences solely on likelihoods or on Bentler and Bonnett's index of fit.[25]

TETRAD uses a surrogate for Π. The **Pi** value calculated by the program is based on the total tetrad residual, TTR, rather than on any usual fitting statistic. Otherwise, the principles are the same. The choice of a model M_0 in the TETRAD program is equally arbitrary, and we let the user make it. TETRAD's default for M_0 is the model with one common latent factor for all measured variables. This model is chosen because it implies every possible tetrad equation and, therefore, no model can have a higher TTR value. The user is free to choose any other model for M_0. The program must be given the TTR value for M_0, and it must be able to calculate the degrees of freedom of M_0. For TETRAD to calculate the degrees of freedom, it must know the number of edges in M_0 and the number of linear coefficients that have fixed *a priori* values. No Pi value is calculated using partial correlations.

There is no simple connection between the residuals matrix and the sum of the tetrad residuals, although as the sum of squared residuals approaches zero, the sum of tetrad residuals must also vanish. For a fixed sample, the sum of tetrad residuals, TTR, can be changed only by altering the model and the set of constraints implied. Changes in the model can, in principle, reduce the TTR without reducing the sum of squares of residuals, although typically when one statistic is reduced, the other will be reduced. TETRAD uses the tetrad residuals rather than any of the usual fitting statistics because the TTR is a rapidly computable indicator that is minimally dependent on distribution assumptions.

TETRAD's Automatic Search Procedure

The search for alternative models using the TETRAD's Rttr chart can be rather prolonged and can require a lot of work on the part of the user. TETRAD has an automatic search procedure that can considerably shorten the search time required. The procedure is limited to models with latent variables.

The automatic search procedure does not search for additional edges or correlated errors. Instead it searches for *treks* to be added to the initial model. It does not search one trek at a time but instead considers the effects of the simultaneous addition of a *set* of treks. The output of the search is a *set of suggested trek additions* to the original model. The program may suggest several alternative sets

[25]Alternative fit indices are computed by the LISREL program, although the LISREL VI manual offers no argument for the particular indices chosen.

of trek additions. The user must then use his or her judgment both to decide how many of these treks to add and to decide how to realize them as a combination of directed edges or correlated errors. The Rttr chart can be of considerable help in this regard.

The automatic search procedure actually carries out repeated searches as many times as the user requests. The suggested treks depend on which tetrad equations are judged to hold in the population, and that depends on the significance value chosen. In general, increasing values of the significance levels will result in the judgment that fewer tetrad equations hold, and that in turn will lead the search procedure either to suggest more treks or to add more sets of suggested trek additions.

How the Automatic Search is Conducted

TETRAD's search for suggested sets of trek additions carries out a strategy that insists on maximizing Spearman's principle and, consistent with that restriction, tries to maximize Thurstone's principle and Simplicitly. For any set of tetrad equations judged to hold in the population, and any initial model, M, there are sets of trek additions to M that will imply every correct tetrad equation implied by M, and insofar as is possible consistent with that restriction, will not imply any tetrad equations that do not hold in the population. TETRAD's "Suggested Sets" are just these sets of trek additions to the initial model.

The TETRAD procedure for determining the sets of treks with the properties described is heuristic, not rigorous. In some cases the program will suggest a trek that, in fact, prevents the implication of a tetrad equation that is implied by the initial model and that holds at the specified significance level.

Simple initial models usually imply a lot of tetrad equations, some of which hold at a given significance level and some of which do not. If everything implied holds, then no addition to the initial model can be made that prevents the implication of false tetrad constraints. As the significance level is increased, fewer and fewer tetrad equations will hold, and so more of the constraints implied by the initial model will be judged false and larger numbers of trek additions are possible. The program increases the significance level from 0.0 until some tetrad equations implied by the initial model do not hold. Then the program finds all of the sets of simultaneous trek additions that will not prevent the implication of any constraint that holds but will prevent the implication (insofar as possible) of constraints that do not hold. The significance level is then increased again until some tetrad equations implied by the initial model and holding at the previous significance level no longer hold, and the search is conducted again. This process is repreated for as many iterations as the user requests. Two or three significance levels are usually enough.

A more detailed description of TETRAD's search algorithm is given in Chapter 10.

Limitations of the Procedure

The Suggested Sets of trek additions are really intended for the analysis of multiple indicators and may go badly astray for other kinds of initial models. The procedure has several requirements, and the conditions should be kept in mind when using the program.

1. The procedure is heuristic, not rigorous.

2. The initial model must be of a simple form. It must not have cycles, and it must not have directed edges either from measured variables to other measured variables or from measured variables to latent variables. Every measured variable must depend on one and only one latent variable. Every latent variable must be connected (but not necessarily connected by a trek) with every other latent variable. We call the graphs of models meeting these conditions **skeletal**.

3. The procedure assumes that any treks to be introduced between latent and measured variables are introduced as directed edges from the latent variable to the measured variable. In the output, suggested treks between latent variables and measured variables are denoted by directed edges, for example by "T->x1."

TETRAD will provide suggested sets of trek additions for models that are not skeletal, but it will give a warning that the model is improper.

5.5. How to Use TETRAD's Output

To briefly illustrate how TETRAD's output is used, we describe a case that will be examined in much greater detail in Chapter 8. Recall the summary of TETRAD's output given above:

1. A list of all tetrad equations and vanishing partial correlations among measured variables that *pass a statistical test* at a level of significance specified by the user, as well as the p value of each constraint.

2. A list of all vanishing tetrad differences and vanishing partial

correlations *implied* by the model given to the program, together with the p values of these constraints for the sample data provided.

3. A count of how many tetrad equations and vanishing partial correlations hold at a specified significance level, of how many of these are explained, i.e., implied, by the model given to the program, of how many constraints are implied by the model but do not hold (I-H), and of how many that hold are not implied (H-I).

4. The sum, over all tetrad equations implied by the model, of (absolute values of) the tetrad differences found in the sample (*TTR value*), and the sum, over all vanishing partial correlations implied by the model, of (absolute values of) the partial correlations found in the data (*TPR value*).

5. Two tables, the *Rttr chart* and *Rtpr chart*, that list, for each possible directed edge or correlated error that may be added, the effects of adding that edge or correlated error to the initial model. The information includes I(H-I), D(I-H), Rttr (or Rptr), and Pi (see Section 5.4).

6. For each possible addition of an edge or correlated error, a list of the tetrad equations or vanishing partials that are implied by the initial model but are no longer implied if the addition is made, and the probabilities of the corresponding residuals found in the sample (on the hypothesis that the differences vanish in the population). This option is called the "Compare" function.

7. A crude index of fit, the *Pi* value, for any model that is an elaboration of a basemodel specified by the user.

8. Sets of suggested elaborations to a simple initial model found by TETRAD's automatic search procedure.

We will show each element of TETRAD's output in turn. The data are from M. Kohn's National Survey, reported in his *Class and Conformity* [60]. They concern the answers to five questions on a much larger questionaire. A factor analysis suggested that the responses to these questions are due to a single common factor, which Kohn took to be an Authoritarian-Conservative (AC) personality trait (from 3101 white, non-farm males).

The initial measurement model is pictured in Fig. 5-3. Here, q1-q5 stand for the indicators and e1-e5 their disturbance terms. In the studies described by Kohn, the subjects were presented with a number of statements, and they were to indicate how strongly they agreed or disagreed. The questions were scored on a five category scale from "strongly disagree" to "strongly agree."

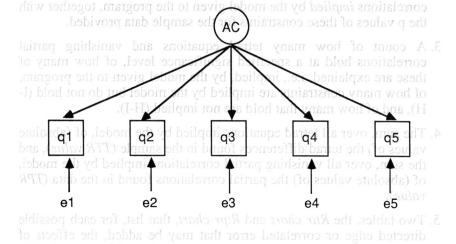

Figure 5-3: Initial Authoritarian-Conservatism measurement model.

We will begin with the one-factor model, and search for the best elaborations of it. The elaborations may be either directed edges, indicating that the answers given to some questions have direct effects on the answers given to other questions, or they may be correlated errors. First, we give the initial model and the data to TETRAD and we ask for information concerning how well the model satisfies Spearman's and Thurstone's principles. Figure 5-4[26] lists every tetrad equation that could possibly hold in the data, specifies the absolute value of the tetrad difference for that equation in the sample data, informs us whether or not the equation is implied by the model, informs us whether or not it passes a statistical test at an unusual significance level (.5), and gives us the p value of the tetrad difference in the sample on the hypothesis that the tetrad difference vanishes in the population. The reason for the significance level chosen will be explained in Chapter 8.

This kind of table covers items 1 and 2 in the list of TETRAD's output. The table

---

[26]In TETRAD's output, we abbreviate the expression

$$\rho_{i,j}\,\rho_{k,l} = \rho_{i,k}\,\rho_{j,l}$$

with

$$ij, kl = ik, jl$$

The graph analyzed in this example is:
AC->q1 AC->q2 AC->q3 AC->q4 AC->q5

The significance level is: 0.5000

The sample size is: 3101

Tetrad Equation	Residual	Impld.	Held	P(diff.)
q1 q2, q3 q4 = q1 q3, q2 q4	0.0068	y		0.3185
q1 q2, q4 q3 = q1 q4, q2 q3	0.0019	y	y	0.8099
q1 q3, q4 q2 = q1 q4, q3 q2	0.0087	y		0.2241
q1 q2, q3 q5 = q1 q3, q2 q5	0.0255	y		0.0000
q1 q2, q5 q3 = q1 q5, q2 q3	0.0295	y		0.0000
q1 q3, q5 q2 = q1 q5, q3 q2	0.0039	y	y	0.5163
q1 q2, q4 q5 = q1 q4, q2 q5	0.0160	y		0.0464
q1 q2, q5 q4 = q1 q5, q2 q4	0.0007	y	y	0.9193
q1 q4, q5 q2 = q1 q5, q4 q2	0.0167	y		0.0285
q1 q3, q4 q5 = q1 q4, q3 q5	0.0382	y		0.0000
q1 q3, q5 q4 = q1 q5, q3 q4	0.0051	y		0.3811
q1 q4, q5 q3 = q1 q5, q4 q3	0.0331	y		0.0000
q2 q3, q4 q5 = q2 q4, q3 q5	0.0204	y		0.0016
q2 q3, q5 q4 = q2 q5, q3 q4	0.0070	y		0.2063
q2 q4, q5 q3 = q2 q5, q4 q3	0.0134	y		0.0418

Figure 5-4: Statistical information for the AC skeleton.

shows, at a glance, that all possible tetrad equations are implied by the model and that only three of them hold at a significance level of .5.

To have TETRAD automatically determine how well this model satisfies Spearman's and Thurstone's principles, we ask for standard output and get the information in Fig. 5-5 which comprises items 3 and 4 in the list of output elements. The measures of how well this model satisfies Spearman's principle for tetrad constraints, the number of equations explained, and the (H-I) value, are perfect. This is to be expected of a model that implies every possible equation. It also trivially satisfies Spearman's principle for partial correlation constraints, as there are no vanishing partial correlations in the data at this significance level.

The graph analyzed in this example is:
AC->q1 AC->q2 AC->q3 AC->q4 AC->q5

The significance level is: 0.5000

The sample size is: 3101

The Total Tetrad Residual, or TTR, is: 0.22699

I-H, the total number of equations implied by the model
that do not hold in the data, is: 12

H-I, the total number of equations that hold in the data but
are not implied by the model, is: 0

The number of equations that hold in the data is 3

The number of equations explained by the model is 3

The Total Partial Residual, or TPR, is: 0.00000

PI-PH, the total number of equations implied by the model
that do not hold in the data, is: 0

PH-PI, the total number of equations that hold in the data but
are not implied by the model, is: 0

The number of equations that hold in the data is 0

The number of equations explained by the model is 0

Figure 5-5: Standard results.

Because of this we will not bother requesting any of TETRAD's output that concerns partial correlation constraints. Adding elaborations to a model that implies no partial correlation constraints cannot make it imply them.

The model does not satisfy Thurstone's principle for every tetrad constraint. (I-H) is 12, which means that there are 12 equations implied by the model which do not hold at a significance level of .5. The other measure of how well a model satisfies Thurstone's principle is the TTR. For this initial model it is .2269. In itself this number tells us little. What is important is how much of this TTR can be eliminated by elaborations of the model.

Now, we turn to the task of finding good elaborations to this model. Figure 5-6, the Rttr Chart, gives us a list of each possible addition of a directed edge or correlated error. For each such addition, we are given the Rttr value, i.e., how much each elaboration of the initial model reduces the TTR value of the initial model. We are also given D(I-H), i.e., how many equations that are implied by the initial model, but do not hold (at the .5 significance level), are no longer implied if the addition is made. We are also given I(H-I), the difference between the initial model and the modified model with regard to how many equations hold in the data at the specified significance level but are not implied.

Recall that the best elaborations are those that have the *highest* Rttr value, the *highest* D(I-H) value, and the *lowest* I(H-I) value.

The Rttr chart suggests that q3->q5, q5->q3, or q3 C q5 are the best single elaborations of the initial model. Any one of them does more than any other elaboration to reduce the TTR value and is, thus, best by our heuristic for Thurstone 's principle. Further, none of these elaborations will prevent the model from implying any tetrad equation that holds at the specified significance level and was implied by the initial model, i.e., their I(H-I) = 0. No alternative modifications do better. Thus, these elaborations are also best by Spearman's principle.

Notice that edges and correlated errors involving the pair q1-q4 seem second best. *One cannot conclude from this fact that directed edges or correlated errors connecting q1-q4 should be introduced at the second level of search.* Once q3->q5, q5->q3, or q3 C q5 has been added to the initial model, the q1-q4 elaborations may no longer be the best at the second level. To find the best further additions, we would consider the initial model with q3->q5 added, the initial model with q5->q3 added, and the initial model with q3 C q5 added. We would run all of these models through TETRAD again, asking for the Rttr charts. Figure 5-7 shows an Rttr chart for the initial model with q3->q5 added. Notice that after q3->q5 has been added, q1-q4 is no longer the elaboration that most reduces the TTR. Edges q5->q2, q2->q3, and q3->q2 are now the best according to Thurstone's principle. According to Spearman's principle, however, q1->q4 is better than any of these edges. Its I(H-I) value is only 1 while the other edges have an I(H-I) value of 2. To see exactly what effect adding either of these edges has, we can use TETRAD's Compare option, which is item 6 in the list of TETRAD's output. We input the skeleton + q3->q5 and ask for Compare first on the edge q1->q4 and then on the edge q5->q2 (Fig. 5-8).

From these charts we can see that the elaboration q5->q2 defeats (i.e., prevents the implication of) a superset of the equations that q1->q4 defeats. The two extra equations that q5->q2 defeats are

Edge	Rttr	D(I-H)	I(H-I)
q1->q2	0.080	4	2
q2->q1	0.080	4	2
q1 C q2	0.080	4	2
q1->q3	0.088	5	1
q3->q1	0.088	5	1
q1 C q3	0.088	5	1
q1->q4	0.115	5	1
q4->q1	0.115	5	1
q1 C q4	0.115	5	1
q1->q5	0.089	4	2
q5->q1	0.089	4	2
q1 C q5	0.089	4	2
q2->q3	0.071	4	2
q3->q2	0.071	4	2
q2 C q3	0.071	4	2
q2->q4	0.067	5	1
q4->q2	0.067	5	1
q2 C q4	0.067	5	1
q2->q5	0.083	5	1
q5->q2	0.083	5	1
q2 C q5	0.083	5	1
q3->q4	0.067	5	1
q4->q3	0.067	5	1
q3 C q4	0.067	5	1
q3->q5	0.160	6	0
q5->q3	0.160	6	0
q3 C q5	0.160	6	0
q4->q5	0.087	5	1
q5->q4	0.087	5	1
q4 C q5	0.087	5	1

Figure 5-6: Rttr chart for AC skeleton at .5.

The graph analyzed in this example is:
q3->q5 AC->q1 AC->q2 AC->q3 AC->q4 AC->q5

The significance level is: 0.5000

Edge	Rttr	D(I-H)	I(H-I)	Pi
q1->q2	0.025	2	2	0.490
q2->q1	0.025	2	2	0.490
q1 C q2	0.025	2	2	0.490
q1->q3	0.042	4	2	0.534
q3->q1	0.042	4	2	0.534
q1 C q3	0.025	3	1	0.488
q1->q4	0.043	3	1	0.538
q4->q1	0.043	3	1	0.538
q1 C q4	0.043	3	1	0.538
q1->q5	0.026	2	2	0.493
q5->q1	0.042	4	2	0.534
q1 C q5	0.026	2	2	0.493
q2->q3	0.054	4	2	0.567
q3->q2	0.054	4	2	0.567
q2 C q3	0.022	2	2	0.480
q2->q4	0.033	3	1	0.510
q4->q2	0.033	3	1	0.510
q2 C q4	0.033	3	1	0.510
q2->q5	0.044	3	1	0.538
q5->q2	0.054	4	2	0.567
q2 C q5	0.044	3	1	0.538
q3->q4	0.038	4	2	0.522
q4->q3	0.038	4	2	0.522
q3 C q4	0.021	3	1	0.478
q4->q5	0.029	3	1	0.499
q5->q4	0.038	4	2	0.522
q4 C q5	0.029	3	1	0.499

Figure 5-7: Rttr chart for AC skeleton plus q3->q5.

The graph analyzed in this example is:
q3->q5 AC->q1 AC->q2 AC->q3 AC->q4 AC->q5

Edge added: q1->q4

Tetrad Equation	Residual	Impld.	Held	P(diff.)
q1 q2, q4 q3 = q1 q4, q2 q3	0.0019		y	0.8099
q1 q3, q4 q2 = q1 q4, q3 q2	0.0087			0.2241
q1 q4, q5 q2 = q1 q5, q4 q2	0.0167			0.0285
q1 q2, q4 q5 = q1 q4, q2 q5	0.0160			0.0464

Rttr: 0.043   D(I-H):   D(H-I): 1

The graph analyzed in this example is:
q3->q5 AC->q1 AC->q2 AC->q3 AC->q4 AC->q5

Edge added: q5->q2

Tetrad Equation	Residual	Impld.	Held	P(diff.)
q1 q2, q4 q3 = q1 q4, q2 q3	0.0019		y	0.8099
q1 q3, q4 q2 = q1 q4, q3 q2	0.0087			0.2241
q1 q3, q5 q2 = q1 q5, q3 q2	0.0039		y	0.5163
q1 q4, q5 q2 = q1 q5, q4 q2	0.0167			0.0285
q1 q2, q4 q5 = q1 q4, q2 q5	0.0160			0.0464
q2 q3, q5 q4 = q2 q5, q3 q4	0.0070			0.2063

Rttr: 0.054   D(I-H): 4   D(H-I): 2

Figure 5-8: Compare's output for edges q1->q4 and q5->q2.

Tetrad Equation	Residual	Impld.	Held	P(diff.)
q1 q3, q5 q2 = q1 q5, q3 q2	0.0039		y	0.5163
q2 q3, q5 q4 = q2 q5, q3 q4	0.0070			0.2063

It is difficult to decide whether defeating the implication of these two equations is desirable. One of them holds fairly closely, so defeating it would violate Spearman's principle. On the other hand, not defeating the equation that has $p = .2063$ would violate Thurstone's principle (at a significance level of .5). The decision should be made according to how the user weights the two principles.

Item 7 in the list of output elements is Pi. Pi can give a rough indicator of how to balance Thurstone's principle with simplicity. The more we elaborate a model, the fewer constraints it implies and, thus, the more it satisfies Thurstone's principle. More complicated models have fewer degrees of freedom, however, and a model's performance on a statistical test depends on its number of degrees of freedom. At a certain point elaborations help Thurstone's principle but hurt a model's performance on a statistical test. Our Pi measure attempts to give the user some idea of when this point has been reached. Look at Fig. 5-5 again. The model input will serve as the base model. Pi values for a base model are undefined even though we output 0 for their value. In Fig. 5-7 the model input is the skeleton plus the edge q3->q5. The Pi value for this model is .56348. What concerns us is whether the Pi value of further elaborations will be comparable to .56348 or higher. In the Rttr chart shown in Fig. 5-7, Pi values are listed for each candidate elaboration. These are the Pi values of the model input plus the elaboration shown in the Rttr chart. The edge q5->q2, for example, has a Pi value of .567 in the Rttr chart. This indicates that the skeleton + q3->q5 + q5->q2 has a Pi value of .567, which is higher than the skeleton + q3->q5. This suggests that q5->q2 is certainly a worthwhile elaboration. The Pi measure is only a crude guide, and we have found cases where adding an edge that decreases the Pi value still brings up the p value of the model.

In this case we would continue to search for a third elaboration. Continuing in this way we could form a search tree. A full search tree using the Rttr chart can become quite large, even if one uses substantive assumptions and strong structural criteria to prune the tree at each level. The second level of a medium-sized model can easily contain as many as twenty nodes, which means that to obtain the next level, the TETRAD program would have to be run twenty times. Since a run of the program can take several minutes, this search would be a tedious business if the investigator had to stay at the computer, running case after case. This task can be avoided by running TETRAD in *batch mode*. In batch mode the user simply creates an input file for each case and a command file that calls the TETRAD program, gives the program the appropriate commands, and names the input files and output files to be used. Batch files for a score of cases can be set up in a few minutes.

Finally, we illustrate TETRAD's automatic search for suggested elaborations on Kohn's initial model. One command to the TETRAD program produces the information in Fig. 5-9. There are a few simple heuristics we use with the suggested sets of trek additions.

1. We add the treks suggested at the lowest significance level first, in all possible ways (consistent with substantive restrictions). Thus, in this

The graph analyzed in this example is:
AC->q1 AC->q2 AC->q3 AC->q4 AC->q5

Sets of suggested treks at significance level = 0.0418

{q3-q5 }

Sets of suggested treks at significance level = 0.5163

{q1-q3 q2-q5 q3-q5 }

Sets of suggested treks at significance level = 0.8099

{q1-q4 q2-q5 q3-q4 q3-q5 }
{q1-q3 q2-q5 q3-q4 q3-q5 }
{q1-q4 q2-q3 q3-q4 q3-q5 }
{q1-q3 q2-q3 q2-q5 q3-q4 }
{q1-q4 q2-q3 q2-q5 q3-q4 }
{q2-q3 q2-q5 q3-q4 q3-q5 }
{q1-q3 q2-q3 q2-q5 q3-q5 }
{q1-q3 q1-q4 q2-q3 q3-q5 }
{q1-q3 q1-q4 q2-q5 q3-q5 }
{q1-q3 q1-q4 q3-q4 q3-q5 }
{q1-q3 q1-q4 q2-q3 q2-q5 }
{q1-q3 q1-q4 q2-q3 q3-q4 }

Figure 5-9: TETRAD's results on the Authoritarian-Conservatism skeleton.

case we would add q5->q3 or q3->q5, just as we did using the Rttr search strategy.

2. When a set of treks is added simultaneously, they may interact to form further treks that have not been suggested with the same set or even at the same signfiicance level. Thus, q5->q3 and q2->q5 together form a trek connecting q2-q3. In general, realizations of treks that form further treks will further reduce the TTR value of the modified model, but they will also cause a loss in the ability to

explain tetrad equations, and the user must judge whether the gain outweighs the loss. Our rule of thumb is that we prefer implementations of suggested treks at a given level which create further treks not suggested at that level only if all treks implied by a modification are suggested at the next significance level of suggested sets. Thus, for example, we would consider q1->q3, q5->q3, q2->q5, even though a q2-q3 trek is created because the set

$$\{q1\text{-}q3 \ q2\text{-}q3 \ q2\text{-}q5 \ q3\text{-}q5 \ \}$$

is suggested at the next level of significance.

5.6. TETRAD and Other Search Procedures

Several procedures have been proposed for searching for alternative linear causal models, given an initial model. Anything that works is to be applauded, but we believe TETRAD has some considerable advantages. Alternative procedures include the following:

1. *Examination of Residuals*

One strategy is to locate the correlation with the largest residual and free a structural parameter associated with a causal connection between the measured variables thus correlated. Costner and Schoenberg [18] have shown that the strategy is, as one might expect, often misleading. For example, if a model implies several tetrad equations that are not even approximately satisfied in the data, the addition of an edge or set of edges connecting variables whose residual correlations are not maximal may be the most efficient way to modify the model so that the false constraints are not implied. A closely related strategy examines normed residuals; the residuals are assumed to be normally distributed and are represented in units of the variance of the distribution.

2. *Partial derivatives of a fitting statistic*

Byron [13] and, in a modified form, Sorbom [101] have proposed a strategy that is now embodied in the LISREL programs. The strategy is to treat a statistic as a function, for given sample correlations, of the fixed parameters of the model and to consider the partial derivatives of the function with respect to each parameter. For example, the partial derivatives may be evaluated at the maximum likelihood estimate of the parameters. The parameter with the largest squared partial derivative (and appropriate second derivative) is freed. The LISREL VI program contains "modification indices," which are the ratios of these first derivatives and corresponding second derivatives, and the program will, if desired, free parameters one after another according to the size of their modification indices. In other words, LISREL VI conducts a beam search through the space of alternative models. Sorbom noted that the strategy may be misleading because it is applied sequentially, one parameter at a time, and also because a large change in a parameter with a small partial derivative may produce a better fit than a small change in a parameter with a larger partial derivative. In Chapter 8 we will see examples, such as the Wheaton data on alienation, in which the strategy does seem to pass by the best models. Costner and Herting [19] have explored the limitations of the strategy, and suggested that it is not reliable for detecting connections between indicators of a common latent variable. They also point out that it may lead to errors if it is *not* applied one parameter at a time.

Any strategy for finding good alternatives to an initial model is bound to be heuristic, and that means that it is bound to fail in some circumstances. There are practical and structural reasons, however, why the nested model search conducted by the LISREL program is especially inadequate, and since the program is widely used, they deserve to be mentioned.

Consider the tree of increasingly less constrained models described in an earlier section. The LISREL search strategy starts with an initial, presumably simple model as does the TETRAD strategy. But LISREL determines at each stage a *unique* model at the next level. That means that the LISREL procedure considers only a single path through the tree of alternative models. Searches of this kind are called **beam searches** in the artificial intelligence literature. For the reasons mentioned above, the decision at each stage as to which is the best parameter to free may be unreliable, and this fragility is compounded by the beam search. A second difficulty with the LISREL procedure is that it gives *no weight* to preserving the ability of the initial model to explain constraints satisfied by the data. Spearman's principle has no role in the search. A third difficulty has to do with stopping the search. The LISREL search strategy stops when the chi square difference between a model obtained at stage n of the search and the next model, obtained at stage n+1, is not statistically significant. The trouble is that models which are elaborations of the n+1 model, and which are never considered by the LISREL search, may be very significant and may have chi square differences (when compared with the nth stage model) that are very significant. For example, we will later describe a study of alienation for which, starting with an initial model that has a chi square p value of zero, LISREL finds an elaborated model with a chi square p value of .335. The LISREL procedure adds two free parameters to the initial model and then stops. But with TETRAD we find a further elaboration of the LISREL model, freeing two more parameters, that has a chi square p value of .99. Together, the two further modifications found with TETRAD make a statistically significant difference in the fit. A fourth practical difficulty with the LISREL procedure is that the LISREL formalism derives from factor analysis, and because of those origins the formalism does not permit direct causal relations between measured variables. That means that if one represents a causal model in the most straightforward way in LISREL, the search procedure will not discriminate between directed edges and correlated errors between measured variables. The result is that one cannot detect the direction of omitted directed edges between measured variables, as one can with TETRAD. This limitation can be overcome in principle by the artifice of using dummy theoretical variables for measured variables, but in practice the strategem makes the representation of the models more cumbersome and may often fail to be used. Using the TETRAD program it is straightforward to find many plausible models that exhibit much better fit than those produced by LISREL's beam search.

3. *Testing Submodels*

For multiple indicator models, Costner and Schoenberg described a mixed strategy for specifying revisions. Part of the strategy amounted to eliminating tetrad residuals by examining two factor submodels, each with two indicators, and adding directed edges (and appropriate free parameters) to such submodels when they fail chi square tests. The modified submodels do not entail a tetrad equation implied by the unmodified submodel and, thus, the modification eliminates a tetrad residual. Costner and Schoenberg did not propose carrying out an analogous procedure, however, for other kinds of submodels.

4. *Exploratory Factor Analysis*

Exploratory Factor analysis is a procedure for finding an initial model rather than a procedure for revising or elaborating a model (although factor rotation procedures, varimax, for example, might be thought of as model revision procedures). Factor analysis has the advantage that, save for interpretation of the factors, it is fully automatic. It has several disadvantages not shared by the TETRAD program.

1. Factor analysis imposes stong *a priori* limitations on possible causal structures. Measured variables cannot have effects on other measured variables, or on latent variables.

2. Factor analysis does not explore alternative causal structures for the latent factors introduced.

3. Factor analysis does not incorporate any of the user's prior knowledge about the causal processes that generate the data.

4. Factor analysis recognizes Thurstone's principle, and in some forms it recognizes a principle of simplicity, but it does not recognize Spearman's principle.

Factor analysis can be used in conjunction with the TETRAD program to suggest an initial model. The study of Kohn's data illustrates such a use of factor analysis.

5.7. Future Developments

The program we have described in this chapter, and whose use we will illustrate in succeeding chapters, has a variety of unfortunate limitations. Most of these limitations can be remedied, and our research has already begun to address them.

1. TETRAD requires a complete initial model. But often a researcher's *reliable* prior knowledge is more fragmentary. Often, too, a researcher has prior knowledge as to what causal relations *do not* occur, and TETRAD makes no use of this knowledge. Future versions will permit the user to enter whatever causal knowledge, positive or negative, is available about a domain. That knowledge will be used to automatically construct a variety of initial models, including both models with and without latent variables.

2. TETRAD fails to consider classes of constraints that are computable, testable, and highly informative. A future program will consider such constraints.

3. TETRAD's automatic procedure for producing elaborations of an initial model does not rigorously maximize Spearman's principle, and does not work well for models without latent variables. A rigorous algorithm is in fact available (but too demanding for small personal computers). The alternative search procedure using the Rttr chart, which with TETRAD must be carried out more or less by hand, can be fully automated.

4. TETRAD's output requires skill and experience to interpret properly. Future programs will not require such interpretation and will output completely specified causal models.

5. TETRAD does not give maximum likelihood estimates of the coefficients in the models it considers, nor does it give the p values of statistical tests of the models. A future program will automatically call the EQS program to obtain such information for every suggested causal model.

We believe that it is feasible to more fully automate the search for causal models, and we believe that would be a good thing. A more automatic program would make it easier for researchers to discover whether or not they have overlooked plausible alternative explanations of their data, would help to focus subsequent empirical research, and would provide a caution against jumping to causal conclusions.

6. WHAT TETRAD CAN DO

In the preceding chapters we have claimed a lot for the TETRAD program, and some readers may well be skeptical. We claim that researchers with TETRAD will do better science than researchers without it. That is a difficult claim to substantiate, and much of the remainder of this book describes the evidence for our confidence. To give the reader a sense of what can be done with the program, in this chapter we present a number of problems that are easily solved with TETRAD's help. The answers to the problems, and the methods used to find those answers, are given in later chapters. Using the demonstration program that accompanies this book, the reader can repeat our procedures. The answers to problems 1, 2, and 6 are given in Chapter 8; the answers to questions 3, 4, and 5 are given in Chapter 7.

For now, however, we ask the reader simply to consider the following question: can the problems be solved *without* using the TETRAD program? We urge the reader to use whatever techniques he or she may favor to attempt to solve the problems and see if those techniques do as well as the TETRAD program.

In real science the answers are not in the back of the book, and sometimes there are no answers at all. Some data sets simply cannot be modeled adequately by any remotely plausible linear theory, and some data sets can be accounted for about equally well by a vast collection of alternative linear causal models.

Heuristic search can be of help in these circumstances too, although none of the problems of this chapter show how. On real data sets, TETRAD sometimes yields results that suggest that no linear model will adequately explain the data. In other cases, the program gives results that suggest that too many linear models will explain the data.

6.1. Alienation

To do this problem one must use LISREL or EQS or some other program that provides maximum likelihood estimates and chi square tests.

Joreskog and Sorbom [52] discuss two models of data on alienation taken from a study done by Wheaton *et al.* [111]. The models are used to illustrate the operation of the LISREL programs. Their first model, pictured in Fig. 6-1, has a chi square probability (with 6 degrees of freedom) of zero. Joreskog and Sorbom amend this model by freeing two parameters and arrive at the model, shown in Fig. 6-2, with 4 degrees of freedom and p = .335, n = 932. The variance-covariance matrix for this problem (Table 6-1), with obvious abbreviations, is taken from the User's Manual to LISREL IV [52].

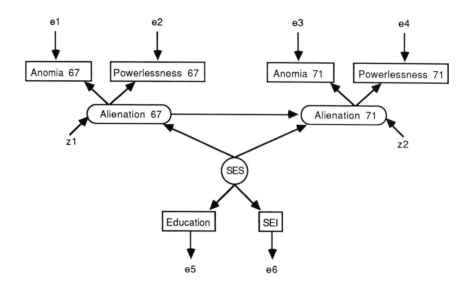

Figure 6-1: Alienation: original model.

Here are two problems:

Problem 1: Find a model that frees 3 parameters in the original model (and thus has 3 degrees of freedom) and gives a chi square statistic with probability greater than .8.

Problem 2: Find a model, distinct from that in problem 1, that frees 3 parameters in the the original model and gives a chi square statistic with probability greater than .9.

6.2. A Problem Using Simulated Data

In the studies in this section and the next, we generated data from a known model using SYSTAT BASIC. We produced data for the exogenous variables with a pseudo-random-number generator distributed normally with mean 0 and variance 1. All other variables are linear combinations of their respective immediate ancestors in the directed graph of the model. The linear coefficients were also chosen at random, although their values for each particular model are nonstochastic constants.

For this problem we generated correlational data from a model that is an

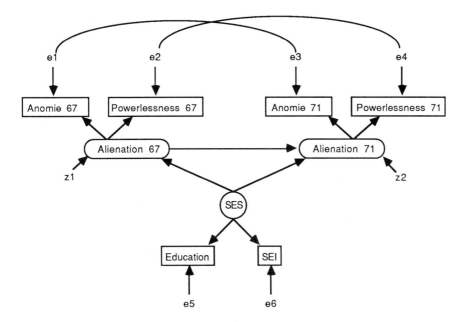

Figure 6-2: Alienation: amended model.

	A6	P6	A7	P7	ED	SE
A6	11.834					
P6	6.947	9.634				
A7	6.819	5.091	12.532			
P7	4.783	5.028	7.495	9.986		
ED	-3.839	-3.889	-3.841	-3.625	9.610	
SE	21.899	-18.831	-21.748	-18.775	35.522	450.288

Table 6-1: Covariance data for the Alienation study.

elaboration of Fig. 6-3. T1 and T2 are to be interpreted as unmeasured latent variables, and e1-e7 as unmeasured error terms. T1 and e1-e7 are distributed

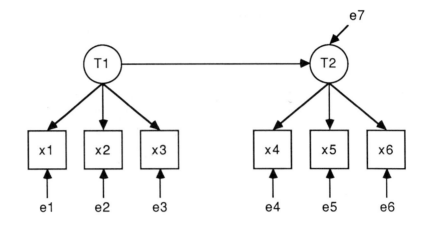

Figure 6-3: Generating skeleton.

normally with mean 0 and variance 1. x1-x6 are our measured variables. The sample size is 5000. The correlation matrix is shown in Table 6-2.

	x1	x2	x3	x4	x5
x2	0.25120				
x3	0.49724	0.30191			
x4	0.36036	0.20448	0.42635		
x5	0.32524	0.51905	0.38348	0.48400	
x6	0.23871	0.12966	0.27900	0.44256	0.47144

Table 6-2: Correlation data, n = 5000.

Two edges that were in the model that generated the data have been removed from Fig. 6-3. The omitted edges are either directed edges from latent to measured variables, directed edges from measured to measured variables, or correlated error terms. The true model has no more than one edge or correlated error between each pair of variables.

Problem 3: Find the two missing edges. You do not have to give a single answer. The fewer alternative answers however, the better, as long as the correct answer is among the alternatives.

The space of possible answers to this problem contains 2190 members.

TETRAD correctly picks out one edge uniquely. It narrows the choices for the second edge to six; running these six models through the EQS program, and picking those that have significant p values for their chi square statistics leaves three models, including the correct answer.

6.3. Causal Order from Correlations

Monte Carlo Data: Study 1

The three models pictured in Fig. 6-4 all imply different overidentifying constraints. Specifically, they all imply different sets of tetrad equations. We generated five data sets for this problem. For each of the five data sets, we randomly selected a model from the three in Fig. 6-4 and then generated data with $n = 2000$ in the same way we have described above. The problem is as follows.

Problem 4: For each of the five data sets below, determine whether model a, model b, or model c generated the data.

The chance of randomly choosing the correct sequence of models is 1 in 243. In five minutes a TETRAD user identified the sequence perfectly.

Data Set 1, Study 1					
	x1	x2	x3	x4	x5
x2	0.70895				
x3	0.70653	0.61196			
x4	0.77571	0.67201	0.87201		
x5	0.75803	0.65612	0.63334	0.84425	
x6	0.69713	0.59854	0.58938	0.78916	0.87428

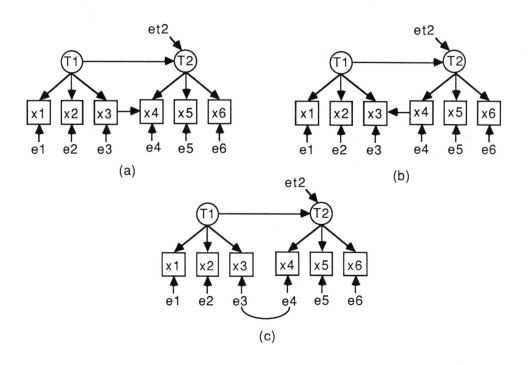

(a)

(b)

(c)

Figure 6-4: Three elaborations of the generating skeleton.

Data Set 2, Study 1				
	x1	x2	x3	x4	x5
x2 0.73218				
x3 0.71264	0.61605			
x4 0.65140	0.56910	0.88900		
x5 0.75321	0.65899	0.64722	0.82760	
x6 0.69263	0.60523	0.60106	0.76872	0.87026

Data Set 3, Study 1				
	x1	x2	x3	x4	x5
x2 0.72900				
x3 0.70424	0.61704			
x4 0.65653	0.57492	0.90401		
x5 0.76259	0.66237	0.66115	0.66115	
x6 0.71318	0.62563	0.63339	0.78092	0.87924

Data Set 4, Study 1				
	x1	x2	x3	x4	x5
x2 0.73119				
x3 0.77805	0.68057			
x4 0.68019	0.60167	0.92926		
x5 0.76382	0.67034	0.85745	0.84872	
x6 0.70363	0.62473	0.79043	0.79385	0.87863

Data Set 5, Study 1				
	x1	x2	x3	x4	x5
x2 0.74892				
x3 0.70336	0.62088			
x4 0.65350	0.56444	0.89529		
x5 0.75899	0.65678	0.63346	0.81258	
x6 0.71367	0.60912	0.58985	0.75083	0.86361

Monte Carlo Data: Study 2

Problem 4 was relatively easy because the only pair of variables with an ambiguous source of extra correlation was x3 and x4. In this problem we remove that constraint. We generated five data sets from a random elaboration of the skeleton shown in Fig. 6-3. The possible elaborations are not restricted to causal connections between x3 and x4. Any indicator of T1 may be connected with (or have correlated errors with) any indicator of T2. Thus, *one* member of the set, shown in Fig. 6-5, of alternative elaborations of the model in Fig. 6-3 comprises the possibilities for each data set.

```
x1->x4   x4->x1   e1<->e4
x1->x5   x5->x1   e1<->e5
x1->x6   x6->x1   e1<->e6
x2->x4   x4->x2   e2<->e4
x2->x5   x5->x2   e2<->e5
x2->x6   x6->x2   e2<->e6
x3->x4   x4->x3   e3<->e4
x3->x5   x5->x3   e3<->e5
x3->x6   x6->x3   e3<->e6
```

Figure 6-5: Possible elaboration for Monte Carlo II.

Problem 5: Identify the correct elaboration of the model in Fig. 6-3 in each of the five data sets shown below.

The chance of choosing the correct sequence by chance is less than 1 in 14,000,000. A TETRAD user correctly identified every member in the sequence and, exclusive of creating the data files, the entire process required only about five minutes.

Data Set 1, Study 2				
x1	x2	x3	x4	x5
x2 0.70137				
x3 0.54959	0.58843			
x4 0.77796	0.54506	0.41529		
x5 0.76528	0.53461	0.41923	0.76241	
x6 0.92669	0.55317	0.43270	0.79971	0.77696

Data Set 2, Study 2				
	x1	x2	x3	x4	x5
x2	0.73537				
x3	0.56398	0.57400			
x4	0.52982	0.54909	0.40887		
x5	0.51391	0.54306	0.40730	0.77331	
x6	0.72118	0.89617	0.56778	0.75928	0.74619

Data Set 3, Study 2				
	x1	x2	x3	x4	x5
x2	0.71903				
x3	0.51791	0.55951			
x4	0.50208	0.53428	0.39059		
x5	0.72145	0.90772	0.54715	0.72531	
x6	0.51754	0.54350	0.36724	0.80703	0.73396

Data Set 4, Study 2				
	x1	x2	x3	x4	x5
x2	0.71301				
x3	0.57291	0.59103			
x4	0.78770	0.51065	0.40642		
x5	0.50273	0.52626	0.38593	0.72558	
x6	0.53287	0.56519	0.41803	0.76173	0.77435

Data Set 5, Study 2					
	x1	x2	x3	x4	x5
x2	0.70716				
x3	0.50878	0.56222			
x4	0.52308	0.50910	0.37597		
x5	0.50341	0.50189	0.38013	0.74525	
x6	0.48956	0.49444	0.77257	0.73827	0.73473

6.4. Kohn's Study and Temporal Order among Interview Questions

Kohn's *Class and Conformity* [60] describes several large survey studies that investigate the relationships between social class, attitudes, and personality structure. One section of his book explores the relations between social class and a variety of latent factors, one of which is an "Authoritarian-Conservatism" (hereafter abbreviated "AC ") personality trait.

The measured variables for AC are answers to interview questions, measured with a five category scale from "strongly disagree" to "strongly agree." Five of the questions are

1. The most important thing to teach children is absolute obedience to their parents.

2. In this complicated world, the only way to know what to do is to rely on leaders and experts.

3. No decent man can respect a woman who had sexual relations before marriage.

4. Any good leader should be strict with people under him in order to gain their respect.

5. It's wrong to do things differently from the way our forefathers did.

The correlations among these five variables are shown in Table 6-3. The initial measurement model is pictured in Fig. 6-6. Note carefully that *the numbering of the questions is not necessarily the order in which the questions were asked on Kohn's questionaire.* There are five questions, and the number of distinct possible

	q1	q2	q3	q4	q5
q1	1.0				
q2	0.7161	1.0			
q3	0.4505	0.3356	1.0		
q4	0.7746	0.5012	0.3525	1.0	
q5	0.4263	0.3421	0.3149	0.3014	1.0

Table 6-3: Correlation matrix for the Authoritarian trait indicators.

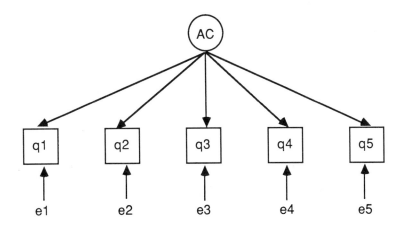

Figure 6-6: Initial Authoritarian-Conservatism measurement model.

orderings of them is 5! or 120.

Problem 6: Find the order in which the five questions were asked on Kohn's survey.

Again, a unique answer is not required, but the smaller the set of alternatives, the better. With TETRAD, the number of alternatives was reduced from 120 to 40 possibilities, and the true ordering of the questions was among the forty.

7. SIMULATION STUDIES

In Chapter 6 we posed a number of problems in which data were generated from a known linear model. The reader was given the data, the sample size, and *part* of the model used to generate the data. The problem was to find the remainder of the model. Here, we are interested in exhibiting how TETRAD handles these problems.

7.1. A Simulated Case

Problem 3 of Chapter 6 gives the reader data and a fragment of the model that generated the data. The problem is to find the missing causal connections. In this section we show how, using TETRAD and EQS, that determination can be made almost uniquely. This study, unlike the other simulation studies in this chapter, was not done blind, but the results are sufficiently unambiguous that we are confident that similar results could be obtained in blind studies.

The model from which the data (n = 5000) were generated is

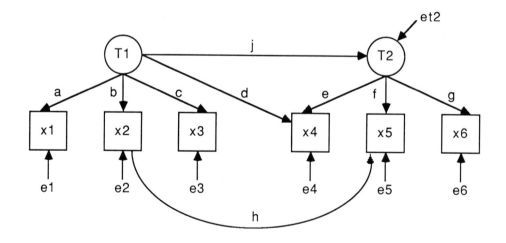

Figure 7-1: Model that generated the data.

134

where: T1, e1-e6, and et2 are distributed N(0,1); a = .865; b = .458; c = 1.217; d = .398; e = .567; f = .854; g = .772; h = .593; j = .626;

The correlations generated from this model, and a skeleton that does not include the edges T2->x4 and x2->x5 were given as problem 3 in Chapter 6.

The TETRAD Analysis

The skeleton in problem 3 from Chapter 6 is shown in Fig. 7-2.

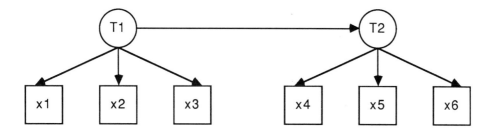

Figure 7-2: Skeleton.

Giving this skeleton to TETRAD along with the correlations, we ask for sets of suggested edges (Fig. 7-3). The first unit of suggested sets contains enough sets, each of them large enough, that we need not worry about a second unit.

```
The covariance file used for this run is named:  sim.dat
The graph file used for this run is named:  sim.g
The name of this output file is:  sim.o1

The graph analyzed in this example is:
 T1->x1 T1->x2 T1->x3 T1->T2 T2->x4 T2->x5 T2->x6

The sample size is:  5000

Sets of suggested treks at significance level = 0.0000
---------------------------------------------------------------

{ x2-x5 x4-x5 x4-x6 }
{ x2-x5 x4-x5 x5-x6 }
{ x2-x5 x4-x6 x5-x6 }
{ x2-x5 x4-x5 T1->x4 }
{ x2-x5 x4-x6 T1->x4 }
{ x2-x5 x4-x5 T1->x5 }
{ x2-x5 x5-x6 T1->x5 }
{ x2-x5 x4-x6 T1->x6 }
{ x2-x5 x5-x6 T1->x6 }
{ x2-x5 T1->x4 T1->x5 }
{ x2-x5 T1->x4 T1->x6 }
{ x2-x5 T1->x5 T1->x6 }


The Total Tetrad Residual, or TTR, is:  1.37366
```

Figure 7-3: Suggested sets for the skeleton.

The sets all contain the trek x2-x5, so we expect it to be in the original model and to do well in an Rttr chart. Treks in these sets are suggested at a significance level of .000, which means that all tetrad equations implied by the initial model and having a p value greater than zero are also implied by any model that adds a suggested set of treks (and only those treks).

We now ask for an Rttr chart with the default significance level of .05 (Fig. 7-4). x2->x5 is by far the best edge. We proceed to add it and request another Rttr chart. After eliminating inferior candidates, we arrive at six possible edges. The results for these are shown in Fig. 7-5.

The graph analyzed in this example is:
T1->x1 T1->x2 T1->x3 T1->T2
T2->x4 T2->x5 T2->x6

The significance level is: 0.0500

Edge	Rttr	D(I-H)	I(H-I)
x2->x5	1.182	12	0
x5->x2	1.088	8	4
x2 C x5	1.062	8	0
x4->x5	0.383	6	0
x5->x4	0.383	6	0
x4 C x5	0.383	6	0
x4->x6	0.420	6	0
x6->x4	0.420	6	0
x4 C x6	0.420	6	0
T1->x4	0.344	6	0
x5->x6	0.344	6	0
x6->x5	0.344	6	0
x5 C x6	0.344	6	0
T1->x5	0.420	6	0
T1->x6	0.383	6	0

Figure 7-4: Rttr chart for the skeleton at .05.

Goodness of Fit Results

Our best candidate models are the six from the Rttr chart in Fig. 7-5. Running these models through EQS, we get the results given in Table 7-1. Only three of these models have acceptable chi square values, and they include the correct model.

This example does not constitute a real test of the TETRAD program, since we knew the correct answer. We are confident that an experienced user would do

The graph analyzed in this example is:
x2->x5 T1->x1 T1->x2 T1->x3 T1->T2
T2->x4 T2->x5 T2->x6

Edge	Rttr	D(I-H)	I(H-I)
x4->x5	0.154	3	0
x4 C x5	0.154	3	0
T1->x4	0.154	3	0
x6->x5	0.154	3	0
x5 C x6	0.154	3	0
T1->x6	0.154	3	0

The Total Tetrad Residual, or TTR, is: 0.19182

Figure 7-5: Rttr chart for the skeleton plus x2->x5.

Edge Additions To Skeleton	TTR	$p(X^2)$
Skeleton	0.229	<.001
1) x2->x5, x4->x5	0.038	<.001
2) x2->x5, x4 C x5	0.038	<.001
3) x2->x5, T1->x4	0.038	0.842
4) x2->x5, x6->x5	0.038	0.842
5) x2->x5, x6 C x5	0.038	0.842
6) x2->x5, T1->x6	0.038	<.001

Table 7-1: Goodness of fit results.

equally well blind with similar problems. When multiple edges are missing the

TETRAD program will, if the initial model is correct and the sample sizes are large, often reduce the number of alternative models to a handful, including the correct model, but it will not usually produce the correct model uniquely.

7.2. Distinguishing Correlation from Causation

The following problem has five parts. First, consider the three models in Fig. 7-6.

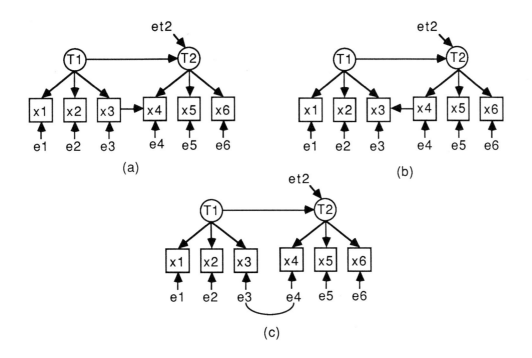

Figure 7-6: Models a, b, and c.

Each of these models is an elaboration of the *skeletal* model in Fig. 7-7. In Chapter 6, we generated five data sets. For each data set, we randomly selected a model from the three elaborations of the skeletal model and then generated data with n = 2000. The problem was as follows:

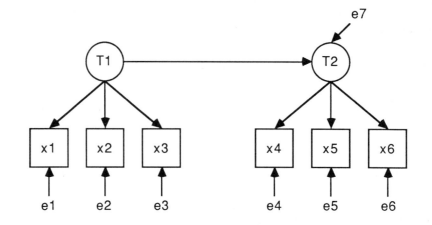

Figure 7-7: Skeletal causal model.

Problem 4: For each of the five data sets below[27], determine whether model a, model b, or model c generated the data.

The TETRAD strategy for solving these problems is easy. We give the common skeletal graph and the data set to TETRAD. We then ask for the Rttr chart at a significance level of .05. We choose this level because the sample size is large, and we know that all of the normality assumptions implicit in our statistical tests are strictly satisfied, and becuase the Suggested Sets feature of the program already suggests additions at this significance level. The Rttr chart tells us how much each possible directed edge or correlated error will reduce the TTR value of the initial model and gives us the value of I(H-I) for each possible addition. I(H-I), it will be recalled, is the increase in the number of equations that hold but are not implied.

For each data set, we choose the edge or correlated error with I(H-I) = 0 that has the highest Rttr value. It should be emphasized that the results given below were obtained by a user who did not know the correct answers beforehand. The TETRAD output for the first data set is shown below. For the readers convenience, we have identified our choice of the missing edge or correlate errors with double asterisks. For data sets 2-5 we simply list our choices.

---

[27]See page 127.

Edge	Rttr	D(I-H)	I(H-I)
x1->x2	0.328	2	4
x2->x1	0.328	2	4
x1 C x2	0.328	2	4
x1->x3	0.166	1	5
x3->x1	0.166	1	5
x1 C x3	0.166	1	5
x1->x4	1.311	9	3
x4->x1	0.662	5	7
x1 C x4	0.635	5	3
x1->x5	0.628	4	8
x5->x1	0.437	3	9
x1 C x5	0.282	2	6
x1->x6	0.635	4	8
x6->x1	0.432	3	9
x1 C x6	0.274	2	6
T2->x1	0.170	1	5
x2->x3	0.170	1	5
x3->x2	0.170	1	5
x2 C x3	0.170	1	5
x2->x4	1.263	9	3
x4->x2	0.593	5	7
x2 C x4	0.569	5	3
x2->x5	0.607	4	8
x5->x2	0.405	3	9
x2 C x5	0.254	2	6
x2->x6	0.609	4	8
x6->x2	0.401	3	9
x2 C x6	0.244	2	6
T2->x2	0.166	1	5

x3->x4	1.718	12	0 **
x4->x3	1.440	8	4
x3 C x4	1.397	8	0
x3->x5	0.791	5	7
x5->x3	0.918	5	7
x3 C x5	0.619	3	5
x3->x6	0.761	5	7
x6->x3	0.881	5	7
x3 C x6	0.567	3	5
T2->x3	0.328	2	4
x4->x5	0.460	3	3
x5->x4	0.460	3	3
x4 C x5	0.460	3	3
x4->x6	0.435	3	3
x6->x4	0.435	3	3
x4 C x6	0.435	3	3
T1->x4	0.846	6	0
x5->x6	0.846	6	0
x6->x5	0.846	6	0
x5 C x6	0.846	6	0
T1->x5	0.435	3	3
T1->x6	0.460	3	3

Our guess is that the edge x3->x4 is missing from the skeleton. We list all our guesses in Table 7-2 below. In each case, the answer chosen is correct.

7.3. Locating Connected Variables

The problems so far were relatively easy because we knew that the omitted edge or correlated error connected x3 and x4. Recall that the second set of Monte Carlo studies in Chapter 6 was more difficult, in principle, because we were not told in advance which pair of variables were connected. But in practice, one problem is

Data Set	Missing Edge or Correlated Error
1	x3->x4
2	x3 C x4
3	x3 C x4
4	x4->x3
5	x3 C x4

Table 7-2: Our guesses for problem 4.

quite as easy as the other with the TETRAD program.

We generated five data sets from a random elaboration of the skeleton shown in Fig. 7-7. The possible elaborations are not restricted to causal connections between x3 and x4. Any indicator of T1 may be causally connected with or have correlated errors with any indicator of T2. Thus, the set (Fig. 7-8) of alternative elaborations of the model in Fig. 7-7 comprises the possibilities for each data set.

```
x1->x4   x4->x1   e1<->e4
x1->x5   x5->x1   e1<->e5
x1->x6   x6->x1   e1<->e6
x2->x4   x4->x2   e2<->e4
x2->x5   x5->x2   e2<->e5
x2->x6   x6->x2   e2<->e6
x3->x4   x4->x3   e3<->e4
x3->x5   x5->x3   e3<->e5
x3->x6   x6->x3   e3<->e6
```

Figure 7-8: Alternative elaborations for problem 5.

Recall problem 5 in Chapter 6.

Problem 5: Identify the correct elaboration of the model in Fig. 7-7 in each of the five data sets below.[28]

Our procedure is exactly as in problem 4. We give the TETRAD output for the first data set, and then we simply list our guess for each of data set.

Edge	Rttr	D(I-H)	I(H-I)	
x1->x2	0.573	3	3	
x2->x1	0.573	3	3	
x1 C x2	0.573	3	3	
x1->x3	0.565	3	3	
x3->x1	0.565	3	3	
x1 C x3	0.565	3	3	
x1->x4	0.593	5	7	
x4->x1	1.362	9	3	
x1 C x4	0.567	5	3	
x1->x5	0.582	5	7	
x5->x1	1.362	9	3	
x1 C x5	0.554	5	3	
x1->x6	0.952	8	4	
x6->x1	1.569	12	0	**
x1 C x6	0.932	8	0	
T2->x1	1.120	6	0	
x2->x3	1.120	6	0	
x3->x2	1.120	6	0	
x2 C x3	1.120	6	0	
x2->x4	0.391	3	9	
x4->x2	0.659	4	8	
x2 C x4	0.261	2	6	

---

[28]See page 130.

x2->x5	0.367	3	9
x5->x2	0.655	4	8
x2 C x5	0.247	2	6
x2->x6	0.612	5	7
x6->x2	0.726	5	7
x2 C x6	0.403	3	5
T2->x2	0.565	3	3
x3->x4	0.380	3	9
x4->x3	0.663	4	8
x3 C x4	0.265	2	6
x3->x5	0.360	3	9
x5->x3	0.664	4	8
x3 C x5	0.247	2	6
x3->x6	0.571	5	7
x6->x3	0.698	5	7
x3 C x6	0.367	3	5
T2->x3	0.573	3	3
x4->x5	0.217	2	4
x5->x4	0.217	2	4
x4 C x5	0.217	2	4
x4->x6	0.131	1	5
x6->x4	0.131	1	5
x4 C x6	0.131	1	5
T1->x4	0.136	1	5
x5->x6	0.136	1	5
x6->x5	0.136	1	5
x5 C x6	0.136	1	5
T1->x5	0.131	1	5
T1->x6	0.217	2	4

The missing edge is x6->x1. We list all our guesses for problem 5 in Table 7-3.

Data Set	Missing Edge or Correlated Error
1	x6->x1
2	x2->x6
3	x2->x5
4	x1 C x4
5	x3 C x6

Table 7-3: Our guesses for problem 5.

In each of these cases TETRAD was able to give us a unique and correct answer because the modeling assumptions were strictly realized, the sample size was large, and only one additional edge or correlated error was required. In cases in which several edges or correlated errors must be inferred from an initial model and data, the program will not usually fix upon a single alternative, but it will serve to dramatically reduce the possibilities.

8. CASE STUDIES

8.1. Introduction

This chapter describes the application of TETRAD to a number of cases. The data sets we discuss are empirical rather than simulated and have been considered by several other authors. Wheaton's study on alienation, for example, has been discussed by Joreskog and Sorbom, in the LISREL manual and elsewhere, and by Bentler in the EQS manual; data from summer Head Start have been considered by a number of authors, and so have the data from Kohn's National Survey. The empirical cases have been deliberately chosen to permit the reader to compare the results found with, and without, TETRAD's aid. They, and the studies done with simulated data, are also intended to illustrate the use of search heuristics with the TETRAD program. All but one of the empirical data sets we discuss can be analyzed with the version of TETRAD on the disk accompanying this book.

The discussions of the procedures used in these cases are deliberately repetitive. We hope that repetition will promote more familiarity than contempt.

The case studies illustrate several important points:

1. For empirical data, TETRAD can help find plausible models that have been overlooked by unaided workers and that do well on a chi square test.

2. TETRAD can help search for alternative skeletal models. In particular it can help the user to decide whether or not latent variables ought to be introduced to account for the data.

3. Assuming an initial model, TETRAD can help the user discriminate between correlated errors and direct connections between variables, and can even discriminate between alternative causal directions for direct connections.

4. The program makes it easy to take advantage of the user's prior knowledge in the search for adequate models. In fact, effective use of the program requires such knowledge to eliminate hypotheses that do well by TETRAD's criteria but make no causal sense.

5. TETRAD allows the user to carry out a much more thorough search for alternative models than can be done by hand or with the aid of LISREL's beam search.

8.2. Industrial and Political Development

In 1973, H. Costner and R. Schoenberg proposed a method for identifying misspecifications in multiple indicator models. Their procedure is like the TETRAD procedure in several important respects. Costner and Schoenberg illustrated their technique with a model of data for industrial and political development (Fig. 8-1).

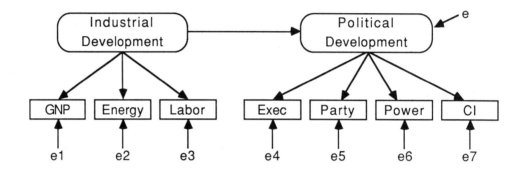

Figure 8-1: Costner and Schoenberg's initial model.

In this model, GNP is gross national product, Energy is the logarithm of total energy consumption in megawatt hours per capita, Labor is a labor force diversification index, Exec is an index of executive functioning, Party is an index of political party organization, Power is an index of power diversification, and CI is the Cutright Index of political representation.

Using their revision procedure, Costner and Schoenberg arrive at a modification of the initial model (Fig. 8-2). The revised model has a chi square statistic with p = .053 and 11 degrees of freedom. The fit is marginal. One might want to know if there are good alternatives to this model or if the fit can be improved by adding further connections. To answer these questions we use TETRAD, starting with Costner and Schoenberg's initial causal model. We have included the Costner and Schoenberg data set on the TETRAD disk. The file name is cs.dat. We urge the user to follow the analysis below with TETRAD and then experiment with the program by trying other lines of search.

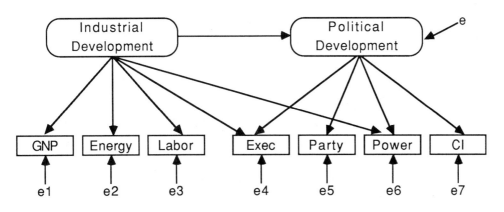

Figure 8-2: Costner and Schoenberg's revised model.

The TETRAD Analysis

We will do two searches, first with the Suggested Sets procedure, then with the Rttr chart. We begin with the skeletal causal model shown in Fig. 8-3. The abbreviation scheme we use is shown below.

$$
\begin{array}{lcl}
\text{Industrial Development} & = & \text{ID} \\
\text{Political Development} & = & \text{PD} \\
\text{GNP} & = & \text{gp} \\
\text{Energy} & = & \text{en} \\
\text{Labor} & = & \text{la} \\
\text{Exec} & = & \text{ex} \\
\text{Party} & = & \text{pa} \\
\text{Power} & = & \text{po} \\
\text{Cutright Index} & = & \text{ci}
\end{array}
$$

We create a covariance file which we show in Fig. 8-4. The first line of a covariance file contains the sample size. Each remaining line contains a covariance (or correlation) or variance and then a variable pair. The same variable name is given twice in each line in which a variance occurs. We also create a graph file, which we show in Fig. 8-5. Each line of the graph file contains an edge

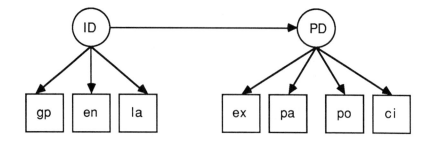

Figure 8-3: Costner and Schoenberg skeleton.

in the graph. Latent variables are capitalized and measured variables are in lower case.

Using the Sets of Suggested Treks

We proceed to use TETRAD's run format on this data file, requesting two units of suggested sets. TETRAD's output is shown in Fig. 8-6. Notice that the first of the suggested sets is precisely the one that Costner and Schoenberg locate with their procedure. Adding those edges to the skeleton and asking for standard results, we can find the TTR of the revised model. Table 8-1 shows the TTR, degrees of freedom, and chi square and its associated probability for the skeleton and the model Costner and Schoenberg suggest.[29]

Notice the difference in the TTR of the skeleton and Costner and Schoenberg's revision. The TTR, recall, is just the sum of the tetrad residuals of all of the tetrad equations implied by the model.

The goodness of fit of a model is negatively correlated with the TTR. Adding edges to a model prevents the model from implying certain tetrad equations, and the effect of adding an edge depends on which equations are no longer implied by the modified model. If the equations that are no longer implied have large tetrad residuals, the TTR will be substantially reduced. If those equations have small residuals, explanatory power will be lost without much reduction in the TTR value. Some edges will reduce the TTR substantially but will also prevent the model from explaining equations that hold closely in the data. The user is free to weight these

---

[29]We used EQS/PC to compute the chi square and its associated probability. We fixed at 1 a coefficient for one indicator of each latent construct.

```
115
1.0   gp   gp
1.0   en   en
1.0   la   la
1.0   ex   ex
1.0   pa   pa
1.0   po   po
1.0   ci   ci
0.95  gp   en
0.83  gp   la
0.66  gp   ex
0.56  gp   pa
0.45  gp   po
0.67  gp   ci
0.83  en   la
0.70  en   ex
0.54  en   pa
0.38  en   po
0.66  en   ci
0.62  la   ex
0.54  la   pa
0.38  la   po
0.61  la   ci
0.47  ex   pa
0.45  ex   po
0.60  ex   ci
0.64  pa   po
0.64  pa   ci
0.67  po   ci
```

Figure 8-4: Costner and Schoenberg data file.

factors as he or she wishes.

In its sets of suggested trek additions, however, TETRAD puts priority on preventing the loss of explanatory power over reducing the TTR. For this case that weighting is for the most part too severe. ID->ex and ID->po are good suggestions, and they are also the edges occurring in the suggested sets which most reduce the TTR value. But there are a number of edges not occurring in the suggested sets that reduce the TTR even more and lose little in explanatory power. This conclusion can be drawn immediately from an examination of the Rttr chart for the original model.

```
ID    PD
ID    gp
ID    en
ID    la
PD    ex
PD    pa
PD    po
PD    ci
```

Figure 8-5: Graph file for the skeleton.

Using the Rttr Chart

The Rttr chart provides powerful information in a general way. Given *any* acyclic linear model, it informs the user of the exact effect the addition of any single edge has on this model's TTR, its D(I-H), its I(H-I), and its Pi value. The chief disadvantage is that it gives this information only for *single* edge additions. Thus, it is not generally appropriate to find two edges which look promising in an Rttr chart and to conclude that both should be added. The two edges may interact in a way not anticipated, they may defeat the same equations and be redundant, and so forth.

The most effective way to use just the Rttr chart is to perform a treelike search, in which each node of the tree is a graph which results from the addition of a single edge to its "parent" graph. Start with a plausible initial model at the root of the tree, run TETRAD, and ask for suggested sets to find a significance level to use (see below). Then run TETRAD to obtain an Rttr chart for the initial model at that significance level. From this chart pick a set of the best individual edges to add. Add these edges to the initial model one at a time to form the first level of the tree. Run TETRAD on each graph in the first level to obtain an Rttr chart for each of them. Pick the best members from the Rttr chart for each node and form a second level, etc. Any path down the tree gives a series of nested models. The only difficulty is in knowing at what point adding edges will no longer help improve a model's fit. TETRAD's Pi value may sometimes be useful in making this decision.

The program for Suggested Sets of trek additions finds its significance levels automatically. The Rttr chart does not. The Rttr chart requires the specification of a significance level which is used to decide whether or not a tetrad equation "holds" in the population. The set of tetrad equations that "hold" is then used to discriminate among the explanatory powers of alternative one edge or one

```
The graph analyzed in this example is:
ID->gp ID->en ID->la ID->PD
PD->ex PD->pa PD->po PD->ci

The sample size is: 115

Sets of suggested treks at significance level = 0.5316
-------------------------------------------------------

{ ID->ex ID->po }
{ ex-po pa-ci ID->po }
{ ex-po ID->ex pa-ci }


Sets of suggested treks at significance level = 0.6027
-------------------------------------------------------

{ ex-po ID->ex pa-po pa-ci }
{ ex-po ID->ex pa-ci po-ci }
{ ex-po ID->ex pa-po po-ci }
{ ex-po pa-po pa-ci po-ci }
{ pa-po pa-ci po-ci ID->po }
{ ex-po pa-po pa-ci ID->po }
{ ex-po pa-ci po-ci ID->po }
{ ex-po ID->ex pa-po ID->po }
{ ID->ex pa-po pa-ci ID->po }
{ ID->ex pa-po po-ci ID->po }
{ ex-po ID->ex po-ci ID->po }
{ ID->ex pa-ci po-ci ID->po }

The Total Tetrad Residual, or TTR, is:  5.29850
```

Figure 8-6: Initial output.

correlated error additions to the initial model. The default value of the significance level is the conventional .05, but generally users should select *unconventional* values for the significance level, especially when the sample size is not large. One is not making a real decision as to which tetrad equations literally hold in the population; in all likelihood, none of them does. One is instead trying to find those patterns or constraints that are well approximated. The most important thing in selecting a significance value is to find a level that will efficiently discriminate among alternative models.

Edge Additions	TTR	X^2	$p(X^2)$
None(skeleton)	5.298	52.1	<0.001
ID->po, ID->ex	1.149	19.5	0.053

Table 8-1: Statistical results for the models Costner and Schoenberg consider.

Our recommendation is the following:

Run the suggested sets procedure before running the Rttr chart. Find the significance levels at which sets of trek additions are first suggested. Choose that value, or higher values, as the significance level for the Rttr chart.

In this case we use the significance level of the second unit of suggested sets of trek additions, .532. Asking for an Rttr chart for the skeleton at a significance level of .532, we obtain the results in Fig. 8-7.

We have included only those edges not in the suggested sets that seem especially promising. There are a number of edges that considerably reduce the TTR value without extracting a high cost in explanatory power, and many of the treks in the second unit of suggested sets of trek additions are not among the best of these. From the information in the Rttr chart, we expect that additions to the skeleton included in the suggested sets, with the exception of ID->po and ID->ex, will not substantially improve the fit of the model, and the expectation is confirmed by the findings summarized in table 8-2. These models are only marginally significant. We can do better by seeking revisions with the help of the Rttr chart.

The Search

Adding edges to a model reduces the TTR but also reduces the degrees of freedom. After a certain number of additions, the reduction in the TTR is no longer large enough to offset the loss in simplicity and explanatory power. In adding two edges, Costner and Schoenberg have substantially lowered the TTR, but their revision still has a TTR of 1.149. Pi helps indicate if adding another edge might improve the fit still further. We illustrate a full treelike search below.

We start with the skeleton and request a full Rttr chart with the significance level set at .532. The Pi values are calculated using the skeleton as a base model. Already screened results were shown in Fig. 8-7. We construct the tree shown in Fig. 8-8. Each edge and correlated error is shown along with the TTR and Pi value of the model that results from its addition. We now run TETRAD on each of the

Edge	Rttr	D(I-H)	I(H-I)

Not in a suggested set

Edge	Rttr	D(I-H)	I(H-I)
gp->ex	3.178	24	2
gp->po	2.693	25	1
en->ex	3.186	24	2
en->po	2.697	25	1
la->ex	3.111	22	4
la->po	2.593	24	2

In a suggested set

Edge	Rttr	D(I-H)	I(H-I)
ex->po	1.422	14	0
po->ex	1.422	14	0
ex C po	1.422	14	0
ID->ex	2.920	18	0
pa->po	2.003	13	1
po->pa	2.003	13	1
pa C po	2.003	13	1
pa->ci	1.553	14	0
ci->pa	1.553	14	0
pa C ci	1.553	14	0
po->ci	1.617	13	1
ci->po	1.617	13	1
po C ci	1.617	13	1
ID->po	2.407	18	0

The Total Tetrad Residual, or TTR, is: 5.29850

Figure 8-7: Rttr chart at .532.

eight models occupying a node in the first level of the tree and request an Rttr chart for each. We also ask TETRAD to give us Pi values for the models on the first level and to indicate in the Rttr charts the Pi values of models that are elaborations

Model (Additions to Skeleton)	$p(X^2)$
1) ID->po, ID->ex	0.053
2) ID->po, po->ex	0.037
3) ID->po, po->ex, ci C po	0.049
4) ID->ex, ex->po, pa C po, ci C po	0.037
5) ID->ex, ID->po, pa->po.	0.054
6) ID->ex, ID->po, po C ci	0.056

Table 8-2: The best models from the suggested sets.

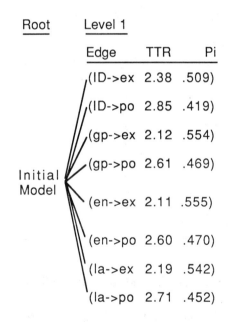

Figure 8-8: Tree with first level added.

of the first level. To illustrate, we show part of the Rttr chart and standard results for the most promising model on level one, the skeleton plus the edge en->ex, in Fig. 8-9.

Edge	Rttr	D(I-H)	I(H-I)	Pi
gp->ex	0.091	2	2	0.523
ID->po	1.231	4	0	0.705
gp->po	1.452	0	1	0.741
en->po	1.426	9	1	0.737
la->po	1.386	9	2	0.730
ex->po	1.426	9	1	0.737

The Total Tetrad Residual, or the TTR is: 2.11220

The Pi value for the model is: 0.55510

I-H, the total number of equations implied by the model that do not hold in the data, is: 32

H-I, the total number of equations that hold in the data but are not implied by the model, is: 3

The number of equations that hold in the data is 14

The number of equations explained by the model is 11

Figure 8-9: Rttr chart for skeleton plus en->ex.

We include the edge gp->ex in this chart to illustrate that it may be unwise to add both of two edges that do well in the same Rttr chart. Look again at Fig. 8-7. Edges gp->ex and en->ex both look extremely promising. After we add en->ex, however, the Rttr chart shows that gp->ex is not a good further addition. En->ex and gp->ex are almost entirely redundant.

We illustrate how to form the second level of the tree by showing the level under en->ex, the most promising node (Fig. 8-10). If we add the edge gp->po, the resulting model has a Pi value of .741. The Pi value is increasing rapidly, and the models with two additions still explain most of the equations that hold, so

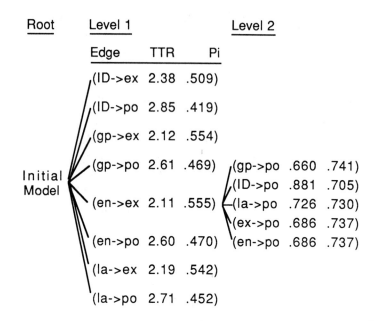

Figure 8-10: Tree with part of second level added.

searching for a third addition seems certainly worthwhile. We add each of the five edges in turn and ask TETRAD for an Rttr chart. We show part of our third level under the additions gp->po and en->po in Fig. 8-11. The Pi values of the third level are leveling off and, in some cases, decreasing. This suggests that searching at the fourth level might be fruitless.

Proceeding in this way for the entire tree, we arrive at 20 distinct models that reduce the TTR to between approximately .2 and .3 and add only three edges to the skeleton. We then run all twenty models through EQS/PC[30], getting parameter estimates and goodness of fit results. The results are in Table 8-3.

[30]See Chapter 11 for help in running twenty models in batch format.

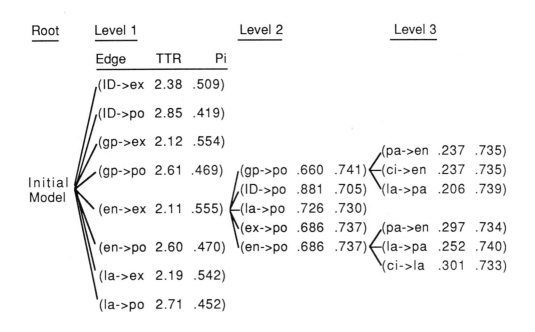

Figure 8-11: Tree with part of third level added.

Goodness of Fit Results

Note that in several cases there are models that are almost indistinguishable by TETRAD's measures but that perform quite differently on a chi square test. There are four models that have large p values $[p(X^2) > .4]$ and a number that are well above the .05 cutoff. The skeleton for this model implies constraints that may be violated in the data and are not considered by the TETRAD program. Of models that appear indistinguishable by TETRAD's measures but behave quite differently on chi square tests, some may imply false higher order constraints not implied by others.

Notice that all four models that do extremely well involve direct connections between en-po and en-ex. Also notice that the only models that have $p(X^2) < .001$ include neither of these connections. Of the two, en-po seems more important. No model that involves en-po is insignificant at the .05 level, while models that involve en-ex but not en-po have $.01 < p(X^2) < .05$.

Additions to Skeleton	TTR	Equations Explained	$p(X^2)$
1) en->po, gp->ex, la->pa	.146	7	0.0551
2) en->po, gp->ex, en->pa	.220	6	0.1189
3) en->po, gp->ex, po->pa	.220	6	0.1002
4) en->po, la->pa, en->ex	.202	6	0.4792
5) en->po, la->pa, po->ex	.202	6	0.4085
6) en->po, la->ex, ex->pa	.223	5	0.1108
7) en->ex, la->po, pa->la	.198	4	0.0246
8) en->ex, la->po, ci->la	.198	4	0.0161
9) gp->ex, pa->po, en->pa	.220	6	<0.001
10) gp->ex, gp->po, la->pa	.220	6	<0.001
11) en->po, en->ex, gp->pa	.270	5	0.5752
12) en->po, en->ex, ci->la	.241	4	0.5198
13) en->po, la->ex, pa->en	.213	3	0.1234
14) ID->po, en->ex, ex->gp	.358	5	0.1222
15) ID->po, en->ex, pa->en	.328	5	0.1526
16) en->ex, pa->po, la->pa	.272	5	0.0438
17) en->ex, pa->po, en->pa	.286	6	0.0211
18) en->ex, pa->po, ex->pa	.286	6	0.0096
19) gp->ex, gp->po, la->pa	.209	6	<0.001
20) en->po, la->ex, la->pa	.220	6	0.0819

Table 8-3: Goodness of fit results from the Rttr search.

Testing TETRAD's Suggestions About Causal Order

This series of models also offers support for a hypothesis concerning the causal order between en-po and en-ex. The Rttr chart distinguishes three possible connections among a pair of variables. Notice that every model we located with the Rttr tree search specifies the en-po connection as en->po and the ex-en connection as en->ex.

To test TETRAD's prediction about this ordering we ran a number of variants of the ordering through EQS. We exhibit the results in Table 8-4.

Additions to Skeleton	$p(X^2)$
1) en->po, en->ex	0.5504
2) po->en, en->ex	0.0336
3) en->po, ex->en	0.1434
4) po->en, ex->en	< 0.001
5) en C po, en C ex, ex C po	0.0015
6) T->en, T->ex, T->po	0.0015
7) ID->po, en->po, en->ex	0.6082
8) ID->po, po->en, ex->en	0.0477
9) ID->ex, en->po, en->ex	0.6004
10) ID->ex, po->en, en->ex	0.0931
11) ID->ex, ID->po, PD->en	0.2940

Table 8-4: Causal order comparisons.

The results are unambiguous. In every case in which two models differ with respect to a causal ordering, the model that accords with TETRAD's suggestion does markedly better on a chi square test.

Finally, we exhibit, in the table below all the models we located with TETRAD's help, their TTR value, the number of equations which hold at a significance level of .532 that the models explain, and the p value of the chi square statistic for each model. The models are ordered by the probability of their statistic.

All Models Located with TETRAD			
Model	TTR	Equations Explained	$p(X^2)$
1) en->po, en->ex, ID->po	.686	10	0.6082
2) en->po, en->ex, ID->ex	.686	10	0.6004
3) en->po, en->ex, gp->pa	.270	5	0.5752
4) en->po, en->ex, pa->en	.246	4	0.5680
5) en->po, en->ex	.686	10	0.5504
6) en->po, en->ex, ci->la	.251	4	0.5198
7) en->po, en->ex, la->pa	.202	6	0.4792
8) en->po, la->pa, po->ex	.202	6	0.4085
9) ID->po, ID->ex, PD->en	.560	5	0.2940
10) ID->po, en->ex, pa->en	.328	5	0.1526
11) ex->en, en->po			0.1434
12) en->po, la->ex, pa->en	.213	3	0.1234
13) ID->po, en->ex, ex->gp	.358	5	0.1222
14) en->po, gp->ex, en->pa	.220	6	0.1189
15) en->po, la->ex, ex->pa	.223	5	0.1108
16) en->po, gp->ex, po->pa	.220	6	0.1002
17) ID->po, po->en, ex->en	1.670	8	0.0931
18) en->po, la->ex, la->pa	.222	5	0.0819
19) en->po, gp->ex, la->pa	.146	7	0.0551
20) ID->ex, ID->po	1.149	11	0.0530
21) ID->ex, po->en, ex->en	1.364	8	0.0477
22) en->ex, pa->po, la->pa	.272	5	0.0438
23) en->ex, po->en			0.0336
24) en->ex, la->po, pa->la	.198	4	0.0246
25) en->ex, pa->po, en->pa	.286	6	0.0211
26) en->ex, la->po, ci->la	.198	4	0.0161
27) T->ex, T->en, T->po, T->ID, T->PD	.565	8	0.0145

All Models Located with TETRAD			
Model	TTR	Equations Explained	$p(X^2)$
28) en->ex, gp->po, pa->en	.237	4	0.0135
29) en->ex, gp->po, la->pa	.206	5	0.0133
30) en->ex, gp->po, ci->en	.237	4	0.0108
31) en->ex, pa->po, ex->pa	.286	6	0.0096
32) T->ex, T->en, T->po	2.345	7	0.0015
33) ex C en, en C po, ex C po	2.345	7	0.0015
34) gp->ex, pa->po, en->pa	.220	6	<0.001
35) ex->en, po->en			<0.001
36) gp->ex, gp->po, la->pa	.220	6	<0.001
37) gp->ex, gp->po, la->pa	.209	6	<0.001
38) Skeleton	5.300	13	0.000

Conclusion

It is no surprise that TETRAD's suggested sets yield Costner and Schoenberg's model immediately. The procedure by which Costner and Schoenberg obtained the model shares many features of the TETRAD algorithms and heuristics. But to justify the assumptions of the model, we need either substantive knowledge or grounds for thinking that no other plausible model explains the data as well. We have explored only a single skeleton, but in combination with EQS, TETRAD has provided a rather full sense of the possibilities available within the boundaries of that initial hypothesis. It may be of some surprise, however, that TETRAD helps us to locate a series of plausible models that are not extensions of Costner and Schoenberg's model, that all include en->po and en->ex, and that all have a much higher chi square probability than Costner and Schoenberg's model. It may also be a surprise that the data so unambiguously choose a particular causal order among a particular pair of indicator variables.

One value of locating these alternatives is that they force substantive issues to the forefront, and they clarify which substantive issues are most urgent in theory assessment. If one wishes to defend a particular causal analysis of the data, say Costner and Schoenberg's model, then one is obliged to give good reasons for preferring that explanation to the many alternatives that seem statistically satisfactory. One might, for example, argue that the measured variables in this case are indices and, therefore, cannot enter into direct causal relations with one another. (It might be argued to the contrary that causal relations among indices are acceptable surrogates for causal relations among the variables aggregated by the indices). Or one might turn to other kinds of data, or to other samples, to make a case for one set of hypotheses against another. Costner and Schoenberg's model, for example, predicts that increases in per capita energy consumption will have no effect on power diversification or executive functioning. The best alternative models predict they will have such an effect.

This case illustrates that TETRAD's procedures are heuristic, not infallible, and says something about how good they are as rules of thumb. Sometimes models that are dramatic improvements when judged by statistical tests are models that slightly decrease rather than increase the Pi value. That is not surprising, given the rather arbitrary character of the measure. Sometimes models with very low TTR values do poorly when compared statistically with models having slightly higher TTR values. That is because models can imply constraints other than tetrad equations, and the TETRAD program does not, in its present version, take account of such constraints. Typically, however, TETRAD's indicators are strongly correlated with statistical indicators.

The procedure we have described may seem elaborate. In fact, it takes much longer to describe than to carry out. The entire TETRAD analysis took about half a day. The EQS runs took somewhat longer. A more thorough search would repeat the analysis on alternative skeletons. In particular, we could consider skeletons in which the measured variables are clustered differently. Costner and Schoenberg's model, with the PD->en addition, contains eight distinct skeletons. All of them could be thoroughly analyzed with TETRAD in the course of a weekend, with more time required for statistical analysis of the most promising, distinct elaborations. In view of the time, effort, and cost that goes into data collection, a few days spent analyzing alternative models does not seem excessive.

8.3. Measuring the Authoritarian Personality

Kohn [60] describes several large studies that investigate the relationships among social class, attitudes, and personality structure. In one section of his book Kohn explores the relations between social class and a variety of latent factors, one of which is an "Authoritarian-Conservatism" personality trait. We are concerned here only with the measurement model for this latent factor.

Items on interview schedules used in social psychology are often interpreted as indicators of a common attitude or character trait that is not directly measured. Latent factors of this type may be extracted by factor analysis or the indicators may be chosen at the outset to reflect a common trait. After the correlations among the item responses due to this common factor are extracted, the item residuals are often still correlated, and these correlations are usually taken to indicate that the item responses have other common determinants besides the latent factor they are designed, or thought, to measure. The correlated residuals are often assessed statistically by treating them as the result of correlated errors in item responses without any further interpretation.

Thus Kohn extracted an "Authoritarianism-Conservatism" factor from his well-known National Survey data. Miller *et al.* [80] extracted an analogous factor from a parallel study of Polish men. Miller *et al.* isolate five "core" items, answers to interview questions, that are indicators of authoritarian personality in both national groups. Correlation data for these five indicators are available in an article by Schoenberg and Richtand [90] that demonstrates a quick maximum likelihood estimation program. The initial measurement model is pictured in Fig. 8-12. Here, q1-q5 stand for the indicators and e1-e5 are their disturbance terms.

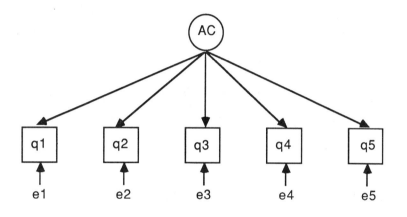

Figure 8-12: Initial Authoritarian-Conservatism measurement model.

In the studies described by Kohn, over 3000 subjects were presented with a number of statements. The subjects were to indicate how strongly they agreed or disagreed with these statements. The questions were scored with a five category scale from "strongly disagree" to "strongly agree." The five questions Schoenberg and Richtand list and their correlations were described in section 6.4 (page 132).

Miller *et al.* note that there are correlated residuals and, while suggesting various alternative accounts of their source, treat them statistically as correlated errors. Schoenberg and Richtand do the same. We suggest that such correlated residuals may indicate an "anchoring" effect among answers to the interview questions, analogous to that described by Kahneman and Tversky [56] and by Campbell *et al.* [14].

Anchoring

An anchoring effect occurs when the subject uses the results of some mental process to serve as a starting point for another, moving from the anchor instead of starting from scratch. Kahneman and Tversky proposed such an effect to explain systematic performance errors in an experiment involving sequential multiplication tasks performed under strong time constraints. They found that subjects estimated the final product within a predictable interval of the product of the first two or three numbers. Extending these results, they found anchoring effects in a wide range of mental tasks.

A similar effect may operate in questionaires and mental tests. It seems plausible that anchoring takes place in answering the kind of questions Kohn's study employs. Whether the subject wants to appear consistent or answers one question with a perspective or mood already created by a previous answer, the answer to an earlier question might well affect the answer to a later one. On this assumption, we consider the hypothesis that a correlated residual between answers to interview questions is due to a *causal relation between the indicator variables*. That is, if two indicators have residual correlation not explained by the common factor already postulated, the excess correlation is due to a causal relation among the indicators, not to an unexplained correlation among their error terms.

Miller's Respecification

To interpret the residuals for items in both the Kohn study and the parallel Polish study, Miller *et al*. use a method that has become common in the study of measurement models. They find a maximum likelihod estimate of the factor loadings and locate the parameter (fixed at zero in the model) such that the partial derivative of the maximum likelihood fitting function is the largest for that parameter. They consider only parameters representing error correlations. They free the chosen parameter, reestimate the modified model, and find its chi square value. If the difference of chi square values between the original model and the revision is significant, the added correlation is retained. The procedure is repeated until the suggested correlations are no longer statistically significant. In this way Miller *et al*. obtain the model for the five core indicators shown in Fig. 8-13. Schoenberg and Richtand make an identical revision, and when the factor loading of the first indicator is fixed at unity they find the probability of the chi square statistic to be .585.

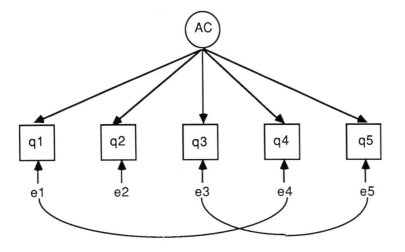

Figure 8-13: Miller's revised model.

The TETRAD Analysis

In this case, our search for alternative elaborations of the initial model (Fig. 8-14) uses only TETRAD's suggested sets.

Using the Suggested Sets

We ask TETRAD for 3 units of sets of suggested sets, using the datafile anchor.dat, which is included on the TETRAD disk. The results are shown in Fig. 8-15. Notice that TETRAD's first suggestion is the introduction of a trek between q3-q5, two of the variables that Miller *et al.* correlate. The addition of this trek does not prevent the implication of any equation that is significant at the .05 level, thus it entails virtually no loss in explanatory power. No other pairs are included in a set until the significance level is above .5, so we will use .5 as a significance level in asking for the Rttr chart below. First, however, we pursue the suggestions TETRAD gives.

Prima facie, the second suggested set

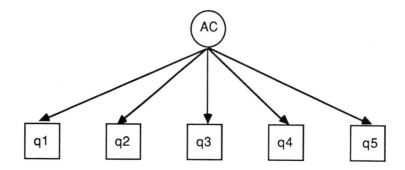

Figure 8-14: Authoritarian-Conservatism skeleton.

$$\{ \text{q1-q3 q2-q5 q3-q5} \}$$

has a number of possible orderings. In accord with our theoretical considerations about anchoring, however, we only consider direct causal relationships between indicators, and this constraint makes it impossible to order the three pairs that occur in this set without creating a further trek in addition to those suggested.

For example, if we order edges between q2-q5 and q3-q5 as in Fig. 8-16, then a new trek between q2-q3 is produced. If instead we add edges as in Fig. 8-17, then no new trek is created between q2 and q3. But notice that in Fig. 8-17 [and in Fig. 8-16 (c)], an additional edge connecting q1-q3 will also create a trek between q1 and q5.

The question is, do we want to introduce a trek between q2-q3, between q1-q5, both, or neither? Looking at the next level of suggested sets, we notice that there is no set with q1-q5, but there are sets with q2-q3 in them. Using TETRAD's Compare command we find that the introduction of a new trek between q1-q5, q4-q5, q1-q2, or q2-q4 will prevent the implication of an equation that holds at a significance level greater than .91. Combinations of edges that produce these treks are to be avoided. There is a set with q2-q3 in the third level of suggested sets that is also a superset of the one suggested set in the second level, namely,

$$\{ \text{q1-q3 q2-q3 q2-q5 q3-q5} \}$$

The graph analyzed in this example is:
AC->q1 AC->q2 AC->q3 AC->q4 AC->q5

The sample size is: 3101

Sets of suggested treks at significance level = 0.0418

{ q3-q5 }

Sets of suggested treks at significance level = 0.5163

{ q1-q3 q2-q5 q3-q5 }

Sets of suggested treks at significance level = 0.8099

{ q1-q4 q2-q5 q3-q4 q3-q5 }
{ q1-q3 q2-q5 q3-q4 q3-q5 }
{ q1-q4 q2-q3 q3-q4 q3-q5 }
{ q1-q3 q2-q3 q2-q5 q3-q4 }
{ q1-q4 q2-q3 q2-q5 q3-q4 }
{ q2-q3 q2-q5 q3-q4 q3-q5 }
{ q1-q3 q2-q3 q2-q5 q3-q5 }
{ q1-q3 q1-q4 q2-q3 q3-q5 }
{ q1-q3 q1-q4 q2-q5 q3-q5 }
{ q1-q3 q1-q4 q3-q4 q3-q5 }
{ q1-q3 q1-q4 q2-q3 q2-q5 }
{ q1-q3 q1-q4 q2-q3 q3-q4 }

Figure 8-15: TETRAD's results on the Authoritarian-Conservatism skeleton.

If we directly connect the three pairs that occur in the set from the second level to produce all and only the four treks in the above set, we are constrained to two possible orderings of the causal connections. Any other ordering would introduce a trek between q1-q5 or fail to produce a trek between q2-q3. The permissible hypotheses are these:

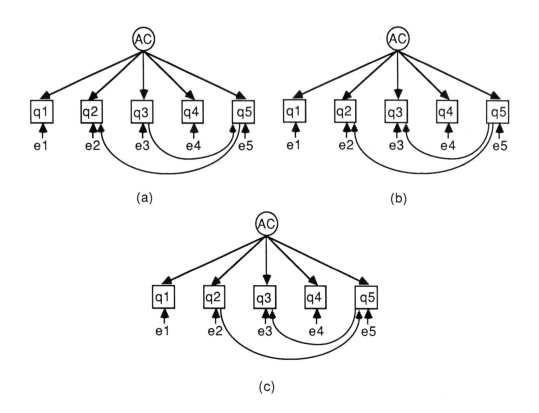

(a)   (b)

(c)

Figure 8-16: Edges that link to produce a trek between q2-q3.

1) q1->q3, q2->q5, q5->q3

2) q1->q3, q5->q2, q5->q3

Either of these additions, or subsets of them, should do well on a chi square test. They also contain information relevant to predicting the order in which the interview questions were asked. We cover that topic below.

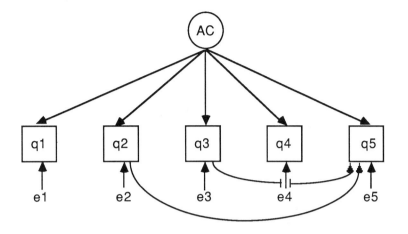

Figure 8-17: An ordering that produces no new trek between q2-q3.

Goodness of Fit Results

Running the models we have discussed through EQS, we obtain the results shown in Table 8-5.

Predicting Temporal Order

The TETRAD analysis was carried out with a pilot version of the TETRAD program before we knew the order in which the questions were asked in Kohn's survey. The results of the analysis imply predictions about that order. Earlier questions can have causal effects on later questions but not vice versa.

The two models found with TETRAD constrain the order of questions 1, 2, 3, and 5. For four questions there are twenty four possible orders in which the questions might have been asked. Assuming that one of the models found with TETRAD is correct, only eight of the twenty four orderings are possible (Fig. 8-18). The hypothesis that the actual ordering of the questions was one of these has a prior probability of 1/3.

These predictions were made before we knew the actual ordering of the questions. In fact, it was because we realized that the TETRAD program and our heuristics had yielded conclusions about causal order contrary to the numbering of the

Additions to Skeleton	$p(X^2)$
None (Skeleton)	<.001
Miller's Revision	
1) q3 C q5, q1 C q4	0.585
From the Suggested Sets	
2) q5->q3, q5->q2	0.666
3) q5->q3, q2->q5, q1->q3	0.994
4) q5->q3, q5->q2, q1->q3	0.994

Table 8-5: Goodness of fit results.

$$1 - 5 - 3 - 2$$
$$5 - 1 - 3 - 2$$
$$1 - 5 - 2 - 3$$
$$5 - 1 - 2 - 3$$
$$5 - 2 - 1 - 3$$
$$1 - 2 - 5 - 3$$
$$2 - 1 - 5 - 3$$
$$2 - 5 - 1 - 3$$

Figure 8-18: Possible orderings for questions 1, 2, 3, and 5.

questions in Schoenberg and Richtand's report[31] that we understood that the program was, in fact, making claims about the order in which the questions were asked.

The actual order of the questions on the National Survey is

$$2 - 1 - 4 - 5 - 3$$

_____

[31]Nothing Schoenberg and Richtand say suggests that the numbering used in their report was the same as the ordering for the initial study reported by Kohn.

which is one of the possible orderings of the five questions allowed by our prediction.

Conclusion

The data support an interpretation of the correlated residuals as direct causal effects between indicator variables. Not only do our best models do extremely well on a standard statistical test, they also yield a correct prediction about the order of the interview questions.

8.4. Alternatives to Regression Models

Regression models are among the most common linear statistical theories applied to nonexperimental data. They are often applied to "demonstrate" the effect of one or more "independent" variables on a "dependent" variable. The terminology implies strong causal assumptions, and in many cases the implication is deliberate. Graphically, regression models may have one or several source variables, which may or may not be correlated, and they contain directed edges from each source variable to the "dependent" variable:

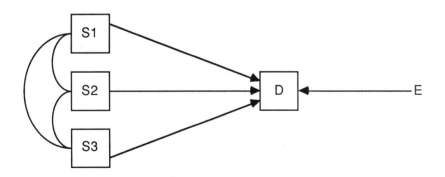

Figure 8-19: Graph of a regression model.

Although presuppositions of regression models, such as the linearity of the dependencies or normality, can be tested, the models imply no constraints on the correlations and so cannot be tested more directly. Estimates of the regression coefficients are usually accompanied by t tests in which the null hypothesis is that some regression coefficient is zero. These tests are, however, no more than tests of the existence of a particular causal edge *on the assumption* that the remainder of the regression model is correct. Unlike chi square tests of overidentified models, t tests are not tests of the regression model as a whole; t tests represent a kind of "bootstrap" test, not in the statistician's sense but in a more general sense (see Glymour [35]). Part of the theory is assumed in testing one hypothesis within the theory; in turn, the hypothesis tested is assumed in testing other hypotheses in the part of the theory that were presupposed in the first test. The result is a kind of circularity which is not vicious but, often, not very powerful either. The bootstrap style t tests of regression models do not succeed in eliminating the possibility that there are other theories that will better explain the data.

Because regression models are not testable as a whole, one cannot make a case for such a model based on the fact that it has passed a statistical test that is powerful against other alternative causal hypotheses. And for the same reason, because regression models do not imply constraints on the correlation matrix, one cannot make a case for a regression model on the grounds that it explains such constraints. It is therefore very difficult to argue that a regression model provides the best explanation of the data, unless prior knowledge guarantees that the implicit causal assumptions are correct. When the variables are indexed by different times, as in econometric time series, that is sometimes possible. More often, however, regression models contain causal assumptions that are not established by prior knowledge, and there is no excuse for failing to consider alternative causal explanations of the data. When there are strong constraints that show up in the sample data, and there are alternative causal theories that can explain those contraints, can pass statistical tests, and are consistent with our prior knowledge, then the alternative causal models may very well be preferable to the regression model. TETRAD can be used to help find such alternatives.

The Dependency Theory Example

Timberlake and Williams [108] claim that foreign investment in Third World or "peripheral" nations causes the exclusion of various groups from the political process within a peripheral country. Put more simply, foreign investment promotes dictatorships and oligarchies. They also claim that "foreign investment penetration increases government repression in noncore countries" (p. 144). It is clear that such theses, if true, have important policy implications. Timberlake and Williams try to support their first claim by means of a simple regression model. Their more complicated argument for the second thesis depends on the correctness of the regression model they propose. We will concentrate on their regression model and its alternatives.

Timberlake and Williams develop measures of political exclusion (po), foreign investment penetration (fi), energy development (en), civil liberties (cv), population (po), and government sanctions and political protests over two time spans (1968-72 and 1973-77), They correlate these measures for 72 "non core" countries. All of the variables, save population, have substantial positive or negative correlations with one another, with absolute values ranging from .123 to .864. It should be noted that their investment data concern a period preceding the increase in petrodollars loaned to Third World countries following the dramatic OPEC increases in oil prices.

A straightforward embarrassment to the theory is that political exclusion is *negatively* correlated with foreign investment penetration, and foreign investment penetration is *positively* correlated with civil liberties and negatively correlated with government sanctions. Everything appears to be just the opposite of what the theory requires. The gravamen of the Timberlake and Williams argument is that these correlations are misleading, and when other appropriate variables are controlled for, the effects are reversed.

To sustain their first hypothesis, they regress the political exclusion variable on foreign investment penetration together with energy development and civil liberties (measured on a scale whose increasing values measure decreases in civil liberties) (Fig. 8-20).

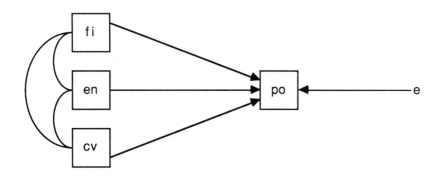

Figure 8-20: Timberlake and William's first hypothesis.

They find a statistically significant positive regression coefficient for foreign investment penetration and conclude that their first hypothesis is supported.

Timberlake and Williams thus claim to have found evidence that foreign investment in Third World nations causes governments to be unrepresentative and undemocratic. Their conclusion implies that the development of democracy and human rights would have been furthered in the early 1970s if international corporations, private banks, and other organizations based in industrial countries had not invested in Third World nations. But what evidence has the regression analysis actually provided?

The analysis *assumes* that political exclusion is the effect of the absence of civil liberties, of energy development, and of foreign investment. It further assumes that these causes act independently, that their effects are additive, and that nothing else has an effect on any of the independent variables and on political exclusion. No particular reasons are given for these assumptions, and one might have thought otherwise. For example, one might have thought that unrepresentative government causes an absence of civil liberties, or each causes the other. Nothing has been done to show that the regression model and its accompaying causal assumptions are correct. There really is no argument for the regression model, or for the more particular thesis that foreign investment promotes political exclusion, other than the bootstrap tests provided by the t tests of linear coefficients.

The TETRAD Analysis

There are some puzzling features of the data, which we might expect a good theory to explain. For example, there are in the data some relations among the correlations that hold much more exactly than we expect by chance. Using TETRAD we find that the following relations hold almost exactly in the sample data:

$$\text{A)} \quad \rho_{po,fi} - \rho_{po,en}\rho_{en,fi} = 0$$

$$\text{B)} \quad \rho_{en,cv} - \rho_{en,po}\rho_{po,cv} = 0$$

Actually, in the sample, the differences on the left in equations A and B are not quite zero. We can test these equations by asking the following: if there were an infinite population in which equations A and B held exactly, and we drew a random sample of size 72 (the number of noncore nations in the study), how likely would we be to get in that sample differences that are as large as those we find? If the answer is a very small probability, we can argue that the sample provides no evidence that the constraints A and B are other than artifacts. But in fact we find just the reverse. We find, again using TETRAD, that if the constraints A and B hold, then the probability of obtaining a difference at least as large as that found in the sample for equation A is .868, and the probability of obtaining a difference at least as large as that found in the sample for equation B is .800. These numbers help convince us that A and B are real constraints on the measured variables, and should, if possible, be explained.

These equations are interesting exactly *because they are the kind of relationship among correlations that can be explained by causal structure*. The first equation can be explained by supposing that the only effects of political exclusion on foreign investment, or of foreign investment on political exclusion, or of any third factor on both political exclusion and foreign investment, are mediated by per capita energy consumption; one variable affects another only through its effect on energy consumption. More visually, the first equation will be explained provided the causal connections between political exclusion and foreign investment are as illustrated in Fig. 8-21.

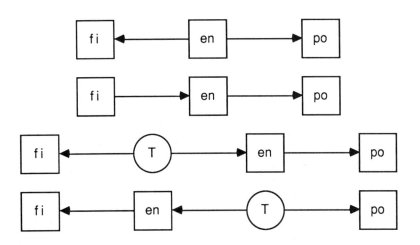

Figure 8-21: Causal explanations of equation A.

In the same way, the second equation, B, can be explained by supposing that any correlations between energy consumption and absence of civil liberties are due to the effects of political exclusion, e.g., if increases in per capita energy consumption cause an increase in civil liberties, they do so because of their direct effect on totalitarianism.

Timberlake and Williams' model does not provide any causal explanation of relations A and B, but it is easy to find assumptions that do explain these patterns, and explain them rather neatly. We exhibit some alternative explanations in Fig. 8-22. T signifies a latent common cause. The causal hypotheses in all alternatives, under the assumption of linearity, imply that both A and B hold in the population, *no matter what the values of the linear coefficients may be.*

There is also a plausible nonrecursive model that explains equation A but not equation B, namely,

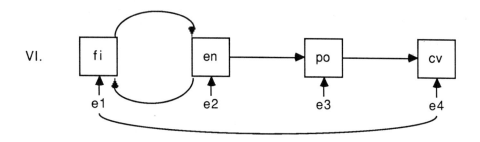

We have used the EQS program to estimate and test Model I. All linear coefficients are very significant. The coefficient giving the dependence of fi on en is positive; the coefficient giving the dependence of po on en is negative, and the coefficient giving the dependence of cv on po is positive. The p value for the chi square statistic with 2 degrees of freedom is .94.

If one accepts Model I, then the conclusion is that foreign investment in peripheral nations neither promotes nor inhibits the development of democracy and civil liberties, but raising the energy consumption per capita promotes both foreign investment and more representative government and, through representative government, increases respect for civil liberties. On this data, and given the alternatives, we would not argue that Model I should be accepted. We do claim that it, and very likely the other alternatives suggested here, is preferable to Timberlake and Williams' regression model.

8.5. Introducing Latent Variables: Longitudinal Data with SAT Scores

TETRAD is designed to search for elaborations of an initial model, but the program can also help to decide between alternative initial causal models. We

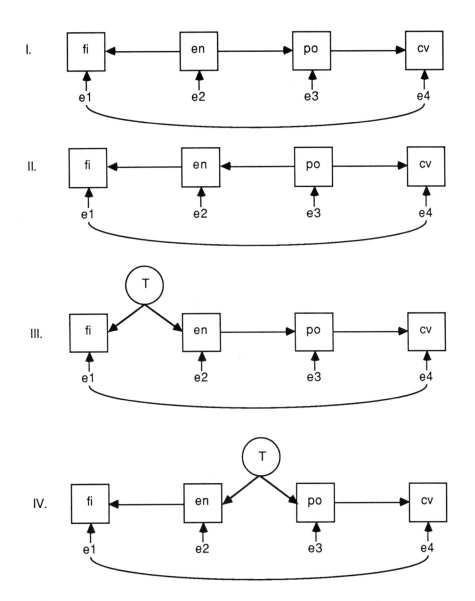

Figure 8-22: Alternatives to the regression model.

know from an earlier chapter that tetrad equations can be derived from vanishing numerators of partial correlations, and we have suggested the following heuristic:

If the tetrad equations found to hold in the sample are all implied by vanishing partial correlations found to hold in the sample, then, ceteris paribus, do not introduce latent variables to account for the correlations. But, ceteris paribus, if the tetrad equations found to hold in the sample are not all implied by vanishing partial correlations found to hold in the sample, then, provided no cyclic model in the measured variables is plausible, do introduce latent variables to account for the correlations.

In the second case, the latent variables should be introduced in such a way that the model implies the tetrad equations found to hold, and does so because the structure of the model is such that measured correlations must vanish when partialed on one or another latent variable.

An Example

Consider data from a longitudinal study of the performances of 799 schoolgirls on the Scholastic Aptitute Test. The same cohort of students took the test in the fifth, seventh, ninth and eleventh grades (see Joreskog [53]). The variance/covariance matrix is included on the TETRAD disks in a file named "sat.dat". The matrix is shown in Table 8-6.

	q5	q7	q9	q11
q5	67.951			
q7	71.01	141.578		
q9	85.966	134.748	249.748	
q11	97.153	151.068	218.757	300.669

Table 8-6: Variance/covariance matrix for SAT scores.

Using the TETRAD program we compute, for each possible vanishing tetrad difference and for each possible vanishing partial correlation, the probability of the sample difference on the hypothesis that the population difference is zero. The relevant output is shown in Fig. 8-23.

Because of the time ordering of the variables, no cyclic model without latent variables is reasonable. The heuristic tells us that an adequate linear model for this

Tetrad Equation	Residual	P(diff.)
q5 q7, q9 q1 = q5 q9, q7 q1	0.0953	0.0000
q5 q7, q1 q9 = q5 q1, q7 q9	0.0917	0.0000
q5 q9, q1 q7 = q5 q1, q9 q7	0.0036	0.7580

Partial	Residual	P(diff.)
q5 q7. q9	0.4806	0.0000
q5 q7. q1	0.4542	0.0000
q5 q9. q7	0.2931	0.0000
q5 q9. q1	0.2655	0.0000
q5 q1. q7	0.3177	0.0000
q5 q1. q9	0.3379	0.0000
q7 q9. q5	0.4595	0.0000
q7 q9. q1	0.3208	0.0000
q7 q1. q5	0.4742	0.0000
q7 q1. q9	0.3819	0.0000
q9 q1. q5	0.6347	0.0000
q9 q1. q7	0.5763	0.0000

Figure 8-23: Statistical output for SAT data.

data should contain a latent variable. If, for example, we instead attempt to model the data by supposing that each measurement is a direct cause of the succeeding measurement (e.g., Fig. 8-24),

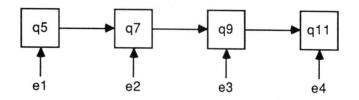

Figure 8-24: Path model.

then the model implies the third tetrad equation, and no other vanishing tetrad differences, but it also implies several vanishing partial correlations, for example, that q5 and q11 vanish when partialed on q9. If the model is modified to avoid these incorrect constraints, for example by correlating the error terms or by introducing further direct effects between earlier and later measurements, then the third tetrad equation is no longer implied.

If we attribute the correlations to the action of a latent variable or variables, then no vanishing partial correlations will be implied. Unless the latent structure is chosen carefully, however, the wrong tetrad constraints will be implied. For example, if the data are explained by postulating a single latent variable ("test taking ability", etc.) and permitting it to have different linear effects on the several administrations of the SAT, then we obtain the model in Fig. 8-25.

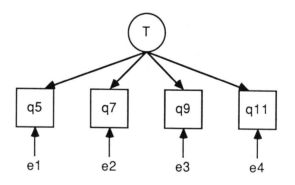

Figure 8-25: Factor model.

This model implies all three tetrad equations for the four measured variables and, judged from the sample, two of these implications are incorrect.

The simplest way to form a model that implies the single tetrad equation is to introduce latent variables implying that the correlations in the tetrad vanish when partialed on some latent variable. There should be a latent variable such that every trek between q5 and q9, between q7 and q11, between q5 and q11, and between q7 and q9 passes through that variable. But, in the simplest case, there must be treks between q5 and q7 and between q9 and q11 that do not pass through any latent variable common to all treks among the other pairs because tetrad equations involving these latter variable pairs do not hold in the data and should not be implied by the model.

An adequate model is obtained if we treat the latent variable as self-lagged (Fig. 8-26).

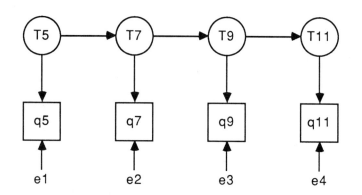

Figure 8-26: Single, self-lagged latent variable model.

This model implies the tetrad equation found to hold in the sample, and only that tetrad equation. It does not imply any vanishing partial correlations among the measured variables.

8.6. Roll Call Voting

In the mid 1960s a series of articles appeared in the *American Political Science Review* [79, 17, 26], all concerning data about constituent attitudes and congressional voting behavior. The sequence of articles is especially interesting both because of substantive issues and because of the very different methodological vews of the several authors. Miller and Stokes, who originally framed the substantive question discussed in all three articles, attempt to distinguish between two possible causal paths by which constituents influence their representatives in Congress. The principle methodological problem addressed by all the papers is that of finding the best causal explanation for the correlational data, and more specifically, the problem is to distinguish a number of possible causal models that might explain the same data.

Miller and Stokes argue for a particular causal model on the basis of plausibility and regression results, and then estimate the coefficients in submodels to determine the relative strengths of the different causal pathways. Cnudde and McCrone self-consciously employ a technique due to Simon and to Blalock, although they do not clearly characterize the technique.[32] The technique amounts to testing models by means of the overidentifying constraints they imply and eliminating those that imply constraints found not to hold in the data. Most of the constraints considered are vanishing partial correlations, but the authors apply no statistical tests. Using a body of substantive assumptions about the existence and direction of causal relationships among a subset of the variables they model, Cnudde and McCrone distinguish among possible causal structures for the remaining variables by showing that some structures imply constraints that fail to hold in the data. Forbes and Tufte rightly demand a justification of the assumptions that limit the number of overall causal structures examined. They show that, when Cnudde and McCrone's assumptions are violated, there are alternative models that imply no false constraints but which lead to quite different substantive conclusions. Forbes and Tufte fail to realize the role of explanation in theory assessment, however, and they wrongly consider all models that imply no false constraint to be equivalent.

Using the TETRAD program, we show how the Simon-Blalock procedure can be quickly, conveniently, and more exactly applied. We show that latent variable models can be eliminated. And, we show that models considered equivalent by Forbes and Tufte provide dramatically different levels of explanatory power.

Miller and Stokes' Article

In 1963, W. Miller and D. Stokes noted a high correlation between constituent attitudes and congressional roll call voting behavior in at least two broad

---

[32]For Simon's work, see [93, 94]. For Blalock's, see [7].

dimensions of policy, domestic intervention and civil rights. In later articles only data on civil rights is discussed, so we focus on that dimension. Miller and Stokes framed two possible mechanisms by which a correlation between constituents' attitudes and congressional voting could be explained. Voters might recruit candidates who share their attitudes, and those candidates who are elected then vote according to their own attitudes. Alternatively, incumbent politicians who wish to stay in office vote in accord with what they perceive to be their constituents' attitudes. Their discussion, and those that followed, included four variables. We list them and include our scheme of abbreviation, which we take from Cnudde and McCrone, in Fig. 8-27.

Attitudes of the Constituents
in a Representative's District   =   d

Representative's Attitudes   =   a

Representative's Perception
of Constituent's Attitudes   =   p

Roll Call Vote   =   r

Figure 8-27:   Variables for the roll call studies.

Miller and Stokes use regression studies to argue that p is a cause of r and a is a cause of r, as shown below.

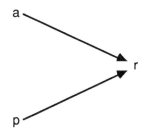

They then specify the causal model we show in Fig. 8-28. Their strategy is to determine the relative strengths of the causal paths from d to r. Following Sewall Wright, they attempt to analyze what proportion of the variance of r can be explained by the alternative causal pathways that correspond to the rival hypotheses they entertain.

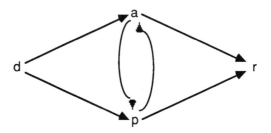

Figure 8-28: Miller and Stokes, 1963.

They cannot estimate coefficients because the model they specify is underidentified. Their strategy is, therefore, to consider two submodels that are identified, namely, the two we show in Fig. 8-29, and establish bounds on the values of certain coefficients.

They argue that, in the least favorable of these models, the sum of all the causal paths traveling from d to r that go through p explains more of the variance in r than does the sum of all the paths from d to r that go through a.

Cnudde and McCrone

The next article in the series, by Cnudde and McCrone, takes the analysis several steps further. They summarize their strategy

> ...the Simon-Blalock causal model analysis is used to resolve the two questions: are all the possible causal paths (in the Miller and Stokes model) operative? What is the direction of causation between the representative's perception and his attitude?

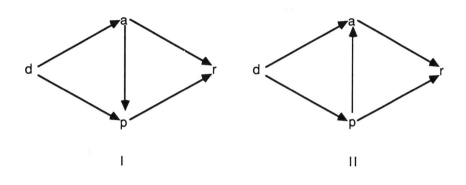

Figure 8-29: Two submodels.

They quote Blalock to summarize what they take to be the essence of the Simon-Blalock technique:

> ...to make causal *inferences* concerning the adequacy of causal models, at least in the sense that we can proceed by eliminating inadequate models that make predictions that are not consistent with the data.

Cnudde and McCrone make a host of assumptions that limit the number of models they consider.

1. There are no cycles in the directed graph.

2. Like Miller and Stokes, they assume that a causes r and that p causes r, and that r is a cause of no variable.

3. The variable d does not directly cause the variable r.

4. The variable d is not caused by any variable.

5. The variables d, a, and p are all trek connected.[33]

6. There are no latent variables (save error terms).

---

[33]This simply means that there is a trek between any two.

Given these assumptions, they consider models that vary only with regard to the causal ordering of d, a, and p. We show three of these models, those Cnudde and McCrone explicitly consider, in Fig. 8-30.

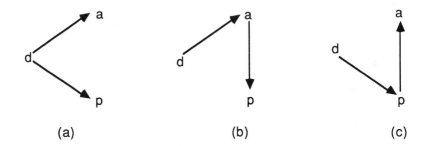

(a)　　　　　　　　　(b)　　　　　　　　　(c)

Figure 8-30: Three possible orderings among d, a, and p.

The first, model (a), postulates no direct causal link between a and p. They note that this implies

$$\rho_{da}\,\rho_{dp} = \rho_{ap}$$

which in turn implies (provided that neither ρ_{da} or $\rho_{dp} = 1$)

$$\rho_{ap.d} = 0$$

This prediction is false, and Cnudde and McCrone conclude that p and a have some direct causal connection. They then seek to establish which way the causal direction propagates. To do this they consider models (b) and (c). Model (b) implies that

$$\rho_{da}\,\rho_{ap} = \rho_{dp}$$

This prediction is also false, so this model can be ruled out. Model (c) implies that

$$\rho_{dp}\,\rho_{pa} = \rho_{da}$$

This equality holds closely in the data, although no statistical test is given, and the authors conclude that this half of the model is confirmed.

They then argue that a direct connection between p and r and between a and r cannot be removed, because in either case the extension of model (c) would imply an equation that does not hold in the data. Finding that the extension of model (c), shown in Fig. 8-31, predicts no false equations, they conclude that it fits the data as well as does the Miller/Stokes Model, but they consider model (c) superior because it is more parsimonious. We would put the issue differently.

Neither of these models imply any *very false* vanishing partial correlations, but the two models nonetheless have very different implications. Miller and Stokes' model implies no false constraints because it implies no constraints at all. The Cnudde model implies a constraint that happens to hold. To imply a constraint that holds closely is to explain it. The models are not equivalent on explanatory grounds, and model (c) is preferable.

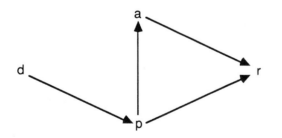

Figure 8-31: Cnudde and McCrone's suggested model.

Forbes and Tufte

Hugh Forbes and Edward Tufte use the roll call voting data to illustrate the need for caution when making conclusions based on causal models. The principal problem they emphasize is the same problem we belabor. *One must consider alternative causal models.* They attempt to show that Cnudde and McCrone have neglected to consider alternative causal models that are indistinguishable by "the Simon-Blalock technique" and yet lead to very different substantive conclusions. Forbes and Tufte are entirely right that alternative explanations must be considered, but they think there is no reason to have any preference between models that imply *no* constraints (and, therefore, no false ones), and models that imply no false constaints but that do imply *empirically correct* constraints on the data. We have argued at length in earlier chapters that this distinction is fundamental to the comparison of alternative explanations and is one of the keys to the success of the natural sciences.

Forbes and Tufte [26] consider the causal models shown in Fig. 8-32, all of which they suggest are empirically indistinguishable. They say the following about these models.

> Cnudde and McCrone have shown that model (1) fits the data; model (2) also fits: the addition of the link between district opinion and Congressmen's attitudes generates no new prediction equations that distinguish model (2) from (1). And model (3) also fits.... (p. 1260.)

They go on to insist that these models are distinguishable only by reliance on vague hunches and the like.

> How do we choose between these three different models, each of which suggests a different conclusion about the relationship between attitudes and perceptions? It should be apparent that the choice between them must rest (in the absence of additional data) on the investigator's hunch about what causal mechanisms are likely to exist in the real world. The only other imaginable basis for choice is the criterion of parsimony.... (p. 1260)

Some models fit the data because they imply constraints that hold in the data, and explain why those constraints hold. Other models fit the data because they could fit *any possible* data: they have a lot of parameters to gerrymander. We imagine that this difference is a very good basis for choice.

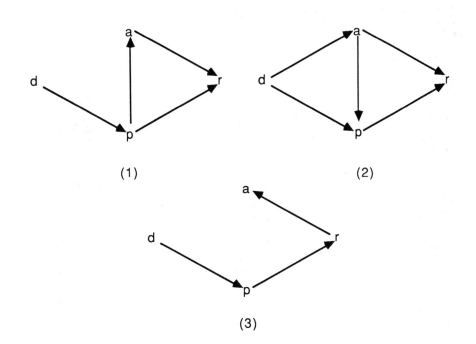

Figure 8-32: Three models from Forbes and Tufte.

The TETRAD Analysis

We ran TETRAD on all three of the models in Fig. 8-32, asking for statistical information about partial correlation equations and tetrad equations. We show the output for each in Fig. 8-33, Fig. 8-34, and Fig. 8-35.

One can see at a glance that none of the three models implies a false equation, but all three models are easily distinguished by what they do imply. Model (1) explains two of the four vanishing partial correlations that hold at a significance level of .177 or higher and it explains the tetrad equation that holds at a significance level above .83. Model (2), which Forbes and Tufte cannot imagine a way to distinguish from model (1), implies *no* equations. Model (3) does even better than model (1), for it implies all and only those equations that hold at .17 or higher.

If the only property of a model that matters is that it not imply a false equation, then these models are indeed indistinguishable, but then we must include a host of

The graph analyzed in this example is:
d->p p->a p->r a->r

The sample size is: 116

Partial	Residual	Impld.	Held	P(diff.)
d p . a	0.6291			0.0000
d p . r	0.4718			0.0000
d a . p	0.0454	y	y	0.6253
d a . r	0.0570		y	0.5470
d r . p	0.1086	y	y	0.2485
d r . a	0.4825			0.0000
p a . d	0.4708			0.0000
p a . r	0.1261		y	0.1776
p r . d	0.6701			0.0000
p r . a	0.6772			0.0000
a r . d	0.6030			0.0000
a r . p	0.4409			0.0000

Tetrad Equation	Residual	Impld.	Held	P(diff.)
d p ,a r = d a ,p r	0.1222			0.0136
d p ,r a = d r ,p a	0.1148			0.0040
d a ,r p = d r ,a p	0.0075	y	y	0.8388

Figure 8-33:   TETRAD output for model (1).

other models in this class (e.g., the complete graph among four variables). A causal model should explain the correlations (Thurstone's principle), but it should also explain the constraints those correlations satisfy (Spearman's principle). Only two of the three models Forbes and Tufte consider, and only a handful of the possible models, have this property. By paying attention to a model's explanatory power, we give ourselves an immense advantage in distinguishing among otherwise equivalent models.

The graph analyzed in this example is:
d->p d->a p->r a->p a->r

The sample size is: 116

Partial	Residual	Impld.	Held	P(diff.)
d p . a	0.6291			0.0000
d p . r	0.4718			0.0000
d a . p	0.0454		y	0.6253
d a . r	0.0570		y	0.5470
d r . p	0.1086		y	0.2485
d r . a	0.4825			0.0000
p a . d	0.4708			0.0000
p a . r	0.1261		y	0.1776
p r . d	0.6701			0.0000
p r . a	0.6772			0.0000
a r . d	0.6030			0.0000
a r . p	0.4409			0.0000

Tetrad Equation	Residual	Impld.	Held	P(diff.)
d p ,a r = d a ,p r	0.1222			0.0136
d p ,r a = d r ,p a	0.1148			0.0040
d a ,r p = d r ,a p	0.0075		y	0.8388

Figure 8-34: TETRAD output for model (2).

Latent Variable Models

None of the models considered in this series of articles entertains the possibility that the correlations are produced by unmeasured variables. With variables as deeply imbedded in social context as are those in this data set, the action of unmeasured factors cannot be dismissed without consideration. Forbes and Tufte's emphasis on considering alternatives is appropriate but too narrowly applied. Besides the alternatives they consider, there are any number of latent variable models that might account for the data. But for this data, latent variable models can

The graph analyzed in this example is:
d->p p->r r->a

The sample size is: 116

Partial	Residual	Impld.	Held	P(diff.)
d p . a	0.6291			0.0000
d p . r	0.4718			0.0000
d a . p	0.0454	y	y	0.6253
d a . r	0.0570	y	y	0.5470
d r . p	0.1086	y	y	0.2485
d r . a	0.4825			0.0000
p a . d	0.4708			0.0000
p a . r	0.1261	y	y	0.1776
p r . d	0.6701			0.0000
p r . a	0.6772			0.0000
a r . d	0.6030			0.0000
a r . p	0.4409			0.0000

Tetrad Equation	Residual	Impld.	Held	P(diff.)
d p ,a r = d a ,p r	0.1222			0.0136
d p ,r a = d r ,p a	0.1148			0.0040
d a ,r p = d r ,a p	0.0075	y	y	0.8388

Figure 8-35: TETRAD output for model (3).

be dismissed for the same reasons that some of Forbes and Tufte's alternatives can be dismissed: they do not explain the constraints the data satisfy.

Recall our principles for introducing latent variables, and their justification. When vanishing partial correlations hold that imply the tetrad equations that hold, do not introduce latent variables without good substantive reasons to do so. The latent variable models will not explain the vanishing partial correlations, and models without latent variables that imply the vanishing partial correlations will also imply the vanishing tetrad difference.

TETRAD shows us that in the roll call voting data, one tetrad equation holds, namely:

$$d\,a\,,r\,p = d\,r\,,a\,p$$

Its p value is .8388. Two partials, e.g.,

$$d\,a\,.\,p \text{ and } d\,r\,.\,p$$

hold with p values of .62 and .24, respectively, and are also explained by models (1) and (3). These vanishing partials imply the single tetrad equation that holds, and any models that explain these vanishing partial correlations will also explain the vanishing tetrad difference. The introduction of a latent variable that still allows the graph to imply the above tetrad equation would not allow the graph to explain these two partials. If we were to introduce a latent variable as a common cause of either d-a, d-r, or p-a, then we would prevent the explanation of the vanishing partial correlation equations involving these pairs.

Goodness of Fit Results

Before exhibiting the results of a chi square test on all the models we have considered so far, we would like to consider one more alternative.

Model (3) in Fig. 8-32 is difficult to believe. It asserts that a representative's roll call vote is a causal factor in the formation of his or her attitudes, but that a representative's attitudes have no influence at all on his or her roll call vote, as though a representative discovers what he or she thinks only by observing his or her own voting behavior. It seems rather more plausible to simply add a cause from a to r, allowing the relationship between a and r to be cyclic. TETRAD shows that the resulting model, shown in Fig. 8-36, explains the same vanishing partial correlations as does model (1) in Fig. 8-32, although it is less simple.

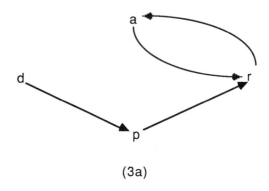

(3a)

Figure 8-36: Final candidate.

We ran the model above and those shown in Fig. 8-32 through EQS. The results are given in Table 8-7.

Model	DF	X^2	$p(X^2)$
(1)	2	1.365	0.505
(2)	1	1.128	0.288
(3)	3	3.207	0.361
(3a)	2	1.365	0.505

Table 8-7: Goodness of fit results.

Conclusion

All of these models perform acceptably under the chi square test, although model (2), which explains no equations, does markedly worse that the others.

Cnudde and McCrone's procedure, like Blalock's, shares the methodological sensibilities behind the TETRAD program. The program makes it possible to do this kind of analysis much more systematically, however, and to distinguish among a much broader class of alternative models. It also supplies statistical tests in place of informal judgments about vanishing partial correlations and vanishing tetrad differences.

8.7. The Effects of Summer Head Start

Data from the summer Head Start program present a case of considerable practical importance. At stake is a question about a causal effect: whether or not Head Start participation improves test scores and subsequent school performance. Head Start was evaluated in 1969 by Cicirelli *et al.* [16], who argued that the summer Head Start program had no effect on achievement or ability test scores. The data considered included (1) socioeconomic status variables for Head Start participants and nonparticipants matched by race and neighborhood, and (2) scores on two tests, the Illinois Test of Psycholinguistic Abilities and Metropolitan Readiness Test. Unfortunately, the tests were administered to participants only after participation in summer Head Start. Magidson [71], employing a causal model to make his case, took issue with a portion of the Cicirelli findings and argued that summer Head Start participation did have a positive effect on test scores. Magidson's conclusion was criticized by Bentler and Woodward [4] principally on the grounds that the effect was not statistically significant. They also suggested, but did not analyze, a different causal structure for the data. Pursuing the suggestion, Magidson and Sorbom argued that a second model also led to the conclusion that the program had the desired effect, but again the positive effect was not statistically significant. The Magidson-Sorbom model has been described again by Sorbom [100] and yet again by Joreskog and Sorbom in the LISREL VI manual.

The variables in Magidson and Sorbom's [72] model for data from white, 6-year-old participants and nonparticipants in summer Head Start, with their abbreviations, are

1. Mother's education (me),

2. Father's education (fe),

3. Father's occupation (fo),

4. Family income (i),

5. The child's score on the first of two tests given to Head Start participants at the end of the summer program (t1), and

6. The child's score on the second test (t2).

The sample correlations among these variables are given in Fig. 8-8.

Participants (n = 148)					
me 1.00					
fe	.466	1.00			
fo	.253	.203	1.00		
i	.361	.182	.377	1.00	
t1	.275	.265	.208	.084	1.00
t2	.256	.122	.251	.198	.664	1.00

Nonparticipants (n = 155)					
me 1.00					
fe	.561	1.00			
fo	.224	.342	1.00		
i	.306	.215	.387	1.00	
t1	.239	.215	.196	.115	1.00
t2	.281	.297	.234	.162	.635	1.00

Table 8-8: Head start correlation data.

The strategy Magidson and Sorbom pursue is to treat the participants and nonparticipants as separate groups to which the same causal model applies and to assume that all linear coefficients, save one associated with the effect of Head Start participation on cognitive ability, have the same values in the two groups. They assume that cognitive ability is a linear function of SES and of Head Start participation:

$$CA = aP + bSES + E$$

where P is a dummy variable equal to zero for nonparticipants and equal to 1 for participants. The object is to estimate the coefficient a. They use LISREL V, while our statistical analyses are done with EQS and LISREL IV.

Magidson and Sorbom's initial model for the SES indicators is pictured in Fig. 8-37.

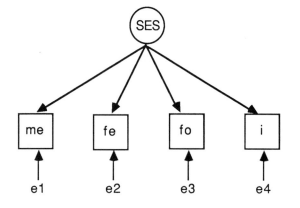

Figure 8-37: Magidson and Sorbom's initial SES model.

The fit for this model is unacceptable (chi square with 10 degrees of freedom is 43.6). The LISREL recommendation for revision of the model is to free a parameter for correlated error between me and fe, giving the model shown in Fig. 8-38. Here chi square is 31.04 with 22 degrees of freedom (p = .10). On the pooled data, however, this model gives a chi square with p = 0. This is not a happy result, since the fundamental assumption is that the submodel applies to the subgroups individually and jointly.

Magidson and Sorbom postulate that posttest scores depend on latent cognitive ability, which in turn depends on socioeconomic status and, perhaps, on Head Start participation. Their full model for each group is shown in Fig. 8-39.

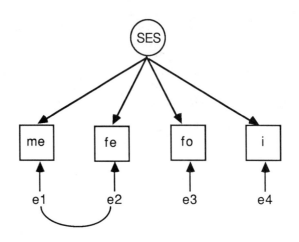

Figure 8-38: LISREL suggestion.

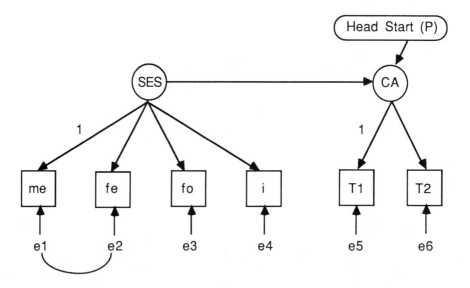

Figure 8-39: Magidson and Sorbom's full model.

Ignoring for the moment the Head Start dummy variable, and with all parameters except for the SES->CA structural coefficient specified to be the same in the two groups, chi square is 31.08 with 23 degrees of freedom, a statistic whose probability is about .10. But if correct, Magidson and Sorbom's revised model should apply to the participant and non-participant groups separately. Using EQS we find, for the participant group alone, that the chi square value (15.38 with 7 degrees of freedom) has a probability of .03. In view of the small sample size, this is not reassuring.

Difficulties with the Magidson-Sorbom Model

There are several difficulties with the Magidson-Sorbom model. First, the fit is unacceptable, both for the socioeconomic status model and for the model as a whole on the participant data. Poor fit is not a sufficient reason to reject a model if there are compelling reasons to think that the general assumptions are correct and if no plausible alternatives provide better fit. But in this case we have no powerful reasons to support the model's general assumptions, the sample size is not large, and we have no reason to believe that alternative models might not give much better fit. A second difficulty is the assumption that the structural parameters are constant across the two groups. That hypothesis is not tested in Magidson and Sorbom's analysis, but it could be given a rough test by estimating the coefficients separately on the two groups and comparing them. But there is little point in carrying out such a comparison until one has a common model that fits each group separately.

There are two further substantive difficulties. Magidson and Sorbom's model claims that occupation has no direct effect on income and that the correlation of the two is only obtained through a common socioeconomic status variable. This hypothesis does not seem likely to be a reasonable approximation to the truth. Finally, the Magidson-Sorbom model assumes that family socioeconomic status causes mothers education, father's education, father's occupation and family income. It is not clear that this assumption makes sense. For reasons described in an earlier chapter, family socioeconomic status ought, if anything, to be an effect of the these measured variables, not a common cause of them. The model assumes that parental education, occupation, and income have no effect on children's cognitive ability; the common socioeconomic status variable alone affects cognitive ability. This seems substantially less likely than that parental education, occupation, and income, no doubt through their effects on unmeasured intervening variables, have an effect on children's cognitive ability.

The TETRAD Analysis

In investigating alternative models for this case, we will consider three different initial hypotheses. We will first consider the initial model proposed by Magidson and Sorbom, which does not contain the correlated errors for fe and me. Second, we will consider an initial model obtained by adding an fo->i connection to Magidson and Sorbom's model. Third, we will investigate the hypothesis that the measured socioeconomic status variables affect some latent variable, which might be interpreted as cognitive ability or academic test taking ability, and the latent variable in turn affects test performances. We find a number of models that have conventionally acceptable fit for both participant and non-participant groups. Since we do not carry out a full search, there are quite possibly several other models that have equally good fit, explanatory power, and simplicity. We use the participant data with TETRAD to search for good models and test the models obtained both on the non-participant and on the participant data. Contrary to conventional wisdom that prohibits testing a model on the same data used to discover it (on the grounds that such tests are "tautological"), the participant data sometimes provides a more severe test of the models than does the non-participant data, producing much lower p values.

Magidson and Sorbom's Initial Model

When we pass the initial model through TETRAD and ask for the suggested sets, we obtain the results shown in Fig. 8-40. We note that the program does not suggest the fo-i trek which we consider to be required on substantive grounds.

We further note that the second unit of suggested treks could be simply realized by a common cause of fo, t1, and fe, if a trek between fe and fo were permissible. Equally, a common cause of t1, me, and fo could be implemented if a trek between me and t1 were permissible. The third unit of suggested sets does not contain a trek between fe and fo, but it does (in the second set) contain a trek between me and t1. Moreover, the second suggested set in the third unit contains the unique suggested set of the second unit. Both our heuristics and simplicity recommend implementing the second suggested set of trek additions in the third unit. We realize the recommended treks by correlating the errors of me and fe, and by introducing a new common cause of me, fo, and t1. The graph of the model is given in Fig. 8-41.

Sets of suggested treks at significance level = 0.5156

{ fo-t1 }

Sets of suggested treks at significance level = 0.6936

{ me-fo fe-t1 fo-t1 }

Sets of suggested treks at significance level = 0.7720

{ me-fe me-fo fe-t1 fo-t1 i-t1 }
{ me-fe me-fo me-t1 fe-t1 fo-t1 }
{ me-fe me-fo me-t1 fe-t1 i-t1 }
{ me-fe me-fo me-t1 fo-t1 i-t1 }

Figure 8-40: Suggested sets for Magidson and Sorbom's initial model.

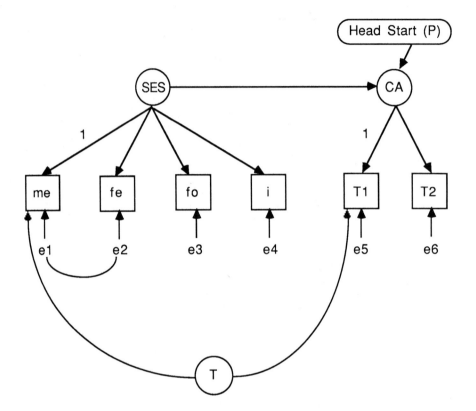

Figure 8-41: A revision suggested by TETRAD.

This model has a low TTR value, .1415. The initial model has a TTR of 1.34.

Occupation and Income

We now assume Magidson and Sorbom's initial model, but with the addition of fo->i. If we give this model to TETRAD and ask for suggested sets, TETRAD ignores the fo->i connection (because the model is not skeletal), and we get the same suggestions as before. We consider instead the Rttr chart. We choose a significance level of .7, roughly the level of the second unit of suggested sets of trek additions. The Rttr chart is given below:

The graph analyzed in this example is:
fo->i SS->me SS->fe SS->fo
SS->i SS->CA CA->t1 CA->t2

The significance level is: 0.7000

The sample size is: 148

Edge	Rttr	D(I-H)	I(H-I)
me->fe	0.383	7	1
fe->me	0.383	7	1
me C fe	0.383	7	1
me->fo	0.423	10	1
fo->me	0.423	10	1
me C fo	0.423	10	1
me->i	0.275	6	1
i->me	0.423	10	1
me C i	0.275	6	1
me->t1	0.192	6	1
t1->me	0.326	9	2
me C t1	0.192	6	1
me->t2	0.217	6	1
t2->me	0.326	9	2
me C t2	0.217	6	1
fe->fo	0.297	8	3
fo->fe	0.297	8	3
fe C fo	0.297	8	3
fe->i	0.158	4	3
i->fe	0.297	8	3
fe C i	0.158	4	3
fe->t1	0.261	7	0
t1->fe	0.419	10	1
fe C t1	0.261	7	0

```
fe->t2      0.276       6           1
t2->fe      0.419      10           1
fe C t2     0.276       6           1

fo->t1      0.365      10           1
t1->fo      0.656      15           2
fo C t1     0.365      10           1

fo->t2      0.443      10           1
t2->fo      0.656      15           2
fo C t2     0.443      10           1

i->t1       0.365      10           1
t1->i       0.377       9           2
i C t1      0.237       6           1

i->t2       0.443      10           1
t2->i       0.377       9           2
i C t2      0.235       6           1
```

The Total Tetrad Residual, or TTR, is: 0.79826

We eliminate all directed edges from test score variables to indicators of SES because they make no sense. The Rttr chart suggests several possible additions (Fig. 8-42).

Edge	Rttr	D(I-H)	I(H-I)
i->t2	0.443	10	1
fo->t2	0.443	10	1
fo C t	0.443	10	1
fe C t	0.261	7	0
fe->t1	0.261	7	0
me->fo	0.423	10	1
fo->me	0.423	10	1
me C f	0.423	10	1

Figure 8-42: The Rttr chart's best candidates.

A proper search would now treat each of these edges as second level nodes in a search tree and investigate third level nodes.[34] We will not pursue the search, however, but we will subsequently give chi square results for these models.

An Alternative Hypothesis

The Magidson-Sorbom model assumes that parental education, occupation and income are *not* causes of whatever abilities account for performance on the two tests. It seems to us more plausible that these measured variables do cause the capacities exhibited on the tests, and we will use TETRAD to explore that hypothesis. Since parental education, occupation, and income are highly correlated, we assume that they have a common unmeasured source of covariance, but we give no interpretation to this latent variable.

The initial model (neglecting error terms) we assume is shown in Fig. 8-43.

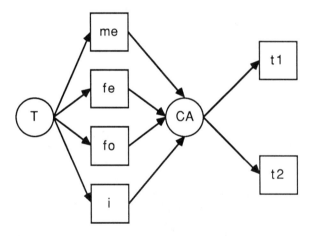

Figure 8-43: An alternative causal skeleton.

[34]We note in passing that the correlated error between me and fe, suggested by LISREL for addition to the Magidson and Sorbom initial model also has the highest Rttr value for that model. But when the causal connection between occupation and income is imposed, the Rttr chart shows that an me-fe connection is no longer distinguished either by Rttr value or by I(H-I).

This model is not a conventional multiple indicator model because it has directed edges from measured variables to latent variables. TETRAD will nonetheless suggest trek additions for it if we request them. The suggested treks are supposed to be those that will not prevent the implication of any tetrad equations that hold at the appropriate significance level. A rough but quick check of whether the TETRAD heuristic is working as it should can be obtained from the Rttr chart at the same significance level: every trek in any suggested set should have a I(H-I) value of 0. When we ask TETRAD to suggest trek additions to the initial model we obtain Fig. 8-44.

Sets of suggested treks at significance level = 0.0367

{ me-fe }
{ fo-i }

Sets of suggested treks at significance level = 0.0927

{ me-fe fe-t1 }
{ me-fe fe-t2 }
{ fe-t1 fo-i }
{ fe-t2 fo-i }

Sets of suggested treks at significance level = 0.2655

{ me-fe fe-t1 i-t1 }
{ me-fe fe-t1 i-t2 }
{ me-fe fe-t2 i-t1 }
{ me-fe fe-t2 i-t2 }
{ fe-t1 fo-i i-t1 }
{ fe-t1 fo-i i-t2 }
{ fe-t2 fo-i i-t1 }
{ fe-t2 fo-i i-t2 }

Figure 8-44: TETRAD's sets of suggested trek additions.

The Rttr chart with the significance level set at .1 shows that the first unit of suggested sets does have I(H-I) equal to zero but that the suggested trek additions in higher units are not reliable.

Of the suggested trek additions in the first unit, we prefer fo->i, for reasons already explained. If we add fo->i to the initial model and again ask for the Rttr chart at the same significance level we obtain

The graph analyzed in this example is:
me->CA fe->CA fo->i fo->CA i->CA
T->me T->fe T->fo T->i CA->t1 CA->t2

The significance level is: 0.1000

Edge	Rttr	D(I-H)	I(H-I)
me->fo	0.027	0	1
fo->me	0.027	0	1
fo C me	0.027	0	1
me->i	0.027	0	1
i->me	0.027	0	1
i C me	0.027	0	1
me->t1	0.186	3	3
t1->me	0.110	1	3
t1 C me	0.083	1	2
me->t2	0.186	3	3
t2->me	0.110	1	3
t2 C me	0.083	1	2
fe->fo	0.027	0	1
fo->fe	0.027	0	1
fo C fe	0.027	0	1
fe->i	0.027	0	1
i->fe	0.027	0	1
i C fe	0.027	0	1
fe->t1	0.186	3	3
t1->fe	0.145	3	1

t1 C fe	0.118	3	0
fe->t2	0.186	3	3
t2->fe	0.145	3	1
t2 C fe	0.118	3	0
CA->fe	0.027	0	1
CA->me	0.027	0	1
CA->fo	0.027	0	1
CA->i	0.027	0	1
CA->T	0.027	0	1
T->t1	0.186	3	3
T->t2	0.186	3	3
fo->t1	0.186	3	3
t1->fo	0.179	2	4
t1 C fo	0.152	2	3
fo->t2	0.186	3	3
t2->fo	0.179	2	4
t2 C fo	0.152	2	3
i->t1	0.186	3	3
t1->i	0.123	1	3
t1 C i	0.095	1	2
i->t2	0.186	3	3
t2->i	0.123	1	3
t2 C i	0.095	1	2

The Rttr chart shows that there are no outstanding elaborations at this stage in the search. A number of edges will reduce the TTR by .186 but cost three equations in explanatory power, and a number will reduce the Rttr by .145 and only cost 1 equation in explanatory power.

A thorough search would therefore generate a great many nodes at this level of the search tree. We will not conduct a thorough search, but we will consider the statistical properties of the model that adds the further edge fe->t1. For symmetry, we also consider the effects of adding fe->t1 and fe->t2 to our skeleton and fo->i.

Goodness of Fit Results

Figure 8-45 summarizes the chi square results for the models we have considered. We use the abbreviations "P" and "NP" to stand for the participant and nonparticipant data sets respectively.

Model	X^2 (P)	X^2 (NP)	$p(X^2)$ (P)	$p(X^2)$ (NP)
Magidson & Sorbom's Skeleton				
1) me C fe	15.38	11.79	.031	.107
2) me C fe, T->me, fo->t1	11.05	4.35	.026	.360
3) fo->i, i->t2	10.09	8.39	.121	.211
4) fo->i, fo->t2	11.66	8.12	.070	.230
5) fo->i, fo C t2	11.66	8.12	.070	.230
6) fo->i, fe C t1	9.12	8.12	.167	.236
7) fo->i, fe->t1	9.12	8.12	.167	.236
8) fo->i, me->fo	57.82	70.85	< .001	<.001
9) fo->i, fo->me	11.93	73.35	.064	<.001
10) me C fo, fo->i	11.93	3.11	.064	.795
Our Skeleton				
11) fo->i	10.22	6.83	.037	.145
12) fo->i, fe-t1	4.02	6.44	.260	.092
13) fo->i, fe->t1, fe->t2	4.02	6.44	.134	.040

Figure 8-45: Goodness of fit results.

These results were all obtained using the EQS program. The coefficient estimates are reasonably stable between groups for significant models, such as models 4 and

12.

Conclusion

Although we have not carried out a thorough search, the case does illustrate how TETRAD can be used in combination with substantive hypotheses about the domain. With the program, models are found that fit the data for both participant and nonparticipants in summer Head Start.

8.8. Achievement, Ability, and Approval

This section is concerned with two points. First, every case so far examined in this book can be processed using the version of TETRAD on the floppy disk, which is limited to 9 variables. On the personal computer, the program can, however, process models with as many as 23 variables. We do not know the size limits for models processed on the Microvax version of the program, but they are considerably larger. This section illustrates the use of the program on a series of models, each with 19 variables. All of the work was accomplished on a IBM compatible machine with 256K RAM and without an 8087 coprocessor. Processing models of this size can take as long as several hours, depending on the information requested. It is most conveniently done in batch mode while the user has something else to do that does not require the computer. The work described in this section took about an hour of user time and about half a day of computer time.

Second, we have emphasized throughout the importance of searching for alternative models. But for the most part the cases we have considered have shown how TETRAD can be used to search for elaborations of an initial model, not how the program can be used to search for alternative initial models. The case we consider here is chosen to illustrate *one way* in which TETRAD can be used to search for alternative skeletal, or nearly skeletal, models. The models we found were not subjected to a chi square test, but we are confident that all of them would yield p values that are essentially zero. The search we describe is partial, but a more thorough search could be executed using the same techniques. We stop with a skeletal model that might be given to TETRAD for further elaboration. We do not investigate these elaborations here, but consider only the problem of locating plausible initial models.

The Maruyama and McGarvey Study

The data we consider are contained in a study by Maruyama and McGarvey [74] of the causes of scholastic achievement. The data consist of correlations[35] of a number of measures of ability, socioeconomic status, peer popularity, evaluations of parents and teachers, and academic achievement. The measures, with our abbreviations, are as follows:

1. Duncan Socio-Economic Index (se),

2. Education of head of household (ed),

3. Number of rooms per person in house (rm),

4. Scores on standardized verbal tests (va),

5. Verbal grades (vg),

6. Peabody Picture Vocabulary Test (pv),

7. Raven's Progressive Matrices (pm),

8. Playground popularity (pp),

9. Seating popularity (sp),

10. Schoolwork popularity (wp),

11. Father's evaluation (fe),

12. Mother's evaluation (me), and

13. Teacher's evaluation (te).

Maruyama and McGarvey assume these variables form five clusters, with the members of each cluster sharing a common latent variable. The latent variables are named socio-economic status (SS), academic ability (AB), achievement (AC), acceptance by peers (AP), and acceptance by signficant adults (AS).

The model Maruyama and McGarvey consider is given in Fig. 8-46, in which we have omitted error terms. Maruyama and McGarvey are concerned with whether academic achievement (AC) causes "acceptance by peers," whether instead acceptance causes achievement, whether each has an effect on the other, or whether, finally, any covariation between acceptance and achievement is due to common causes. The model depicted in Fig. 8-46 is proposed "to test the competing alternatives." In effect, Maruyama and McGarvey simply use LISREL to estimate the standardized coefficients associated with AC->AP and AP->AC. They find that the first is .270 and the second is .232, and while they perform no

---

[35]The data are in fact partial correlations, with sex and grade level controlled for.

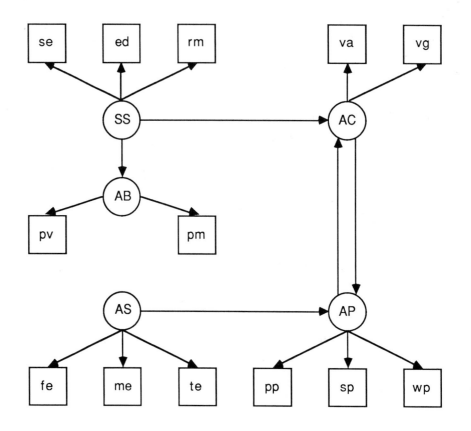

Figure 8-46: Maruyama and McGarvey's model.

formal test of significance of the difference, it seems likely that the difference is not significant. The overall model yields a chi square statistic with a p value of zero.

Their study is offered to illustrate a strategy for using LISREL to decide causal questions. There are any number of reasons for both rejecting the procedure and denying that the particular study is of any weight. The procedure does not really test the alternative causal relations between acceptance or approval and academic achievement. Maruyama and McGarvey note that there are a number of other alternative plausible conections among the latent variables and that their model excludes the very real possibility that acceptance and achievement have common causes. Their strategy is, in effect, to pick a particular causal model from among many alternative possibilities, and to have edges in the model that represent particular causal hypotheses of interest, and to use estimates of these coefficients to decide among the hypotheses. Without persuasive justification for the model assumed, this seems a risky strategy. The particular case is still more dubious. Maruyama and McGarvey obtain an insignificant difference from a model that fails a chi square test on a sample of middling size.[36]

Before we begin our search, we note that TETRAD makes it easy to apply another strategy. Citing Bentler and Woodward, Maruyama and McGarvey suggest that one might compare the two models obtained from theirs by deleting, respectively, the AP->AC edge and the AC->AP edge. An approximate comparison of these alternatives can be obtained in one step with TETRAD by omitting *both* edges from the model and asking for the Rttr chart (for latent-latent connections only) of the submodel that results. The output is obtained in about ten minutes.

Edge	Rttr	D(I-H)	I(H-I)
AC->AP	16.295	247	179
AP->AC	13.536	203	133

AC->AP does substantially more to reduce the TTR value than does AP->AC, and we would therefore expect the deletion of AC->AP from the Maruyama and McGarvey model to give poorer fit than the deletion of the AP->AC edge.

A TETRAD Search

Maruyama and McGarvey's study presents a case in which there are 13 variables clustered into 5 groups. There are an enormous number of ways of specifying causal connections among the 5 latent variables (in fact, 4^{10} different ways if no further variables are introduced), and we have few strong theoretical guides to exclude possibilities. We can be confident that peer and adult approval do not cause socioeconomic status, and neither does achievement. We can be less confident that achievement does not cause ability, and we have some evidence (see Brophy and Good [12]) that socioeconomic status has an effect on adult approval,

---

[36]Perhaps equally dubious, the data are partialed on a dichotomous variable (sex) and then the partial correlations are assumed to be generated by normally distributed random variables.

but we cannot be confident of much else *a priori*. When we have limited knowledge of this kind, the best we can do is to search for alternatives that give a reasonably good fit, explain patterns in the data, and are not excluded by what we think we know.

The actual problem is rather worse, since alternative clusterings are surely possible. We will, however, assume for purposes of illustration that the measured variables are clustered in the way Maruyama and McGarvey propose and consider how we might search through the possible causal connections among the latent variables.

Our procedure is to begin with a model in which there are *no* causal connections among the latent variables. Because there are no treks connecting variable pairs in most foursomes of variables, the disconnected cluster model will imply a great many tetrad equations and have an enormous TTR value. We give this model to TETRAD and ask for the Rttr chart for edges connecting latent variables. We add the connection that has the highest Rttr value, and run the modified model through TETRAD again. We continue in this way until there are edges from measured to measured variables, or from latent to measured variables, that have Rttr values greater than any addition connecting only latent variables. If at any stage we find that several alternative additions produce nearly the same Rttr value, the search branches, and every alternative is considered. Since the primary problem is to find latent variable models that dramatically reduce the TTR of the disconnected clusters, considerations about the explanation of tetrad equations plays a secondary role.

This search procedure is not very thorough, and it will undoubtedly overlook many excellent models. It is undoubtedly a far better search, however, than people are able to do without the aid of the program. We will not even carry out the full search procedure, but will rather follow only one line, noting where the search might reasonably branch.

We note at the outset that the Maruyama and McGarvey model has a TTR value of 12.9. Their model also implies some vanishing partial correlations, since it implies that the indicators of adult approval are uncorrelated with the indications of socioeconomic status and ability. At a significance level of .4, the model explains 52 vanishing partial correlations that are not rejected by the significance test and implies 38 vanishing partial correlations that do not hold. Another 165 vanishing partial correlations hold at that significance level but are not implied by the model. The tetrad residuals are, in this case, more powerful indicators of fit. There are 1031 tetrad equations that hold at the .4 significance level, and the model implies 240 that do not hold and 499 that do hold. We will consider only the TTR values in our search.

We begin our search with the model in which the five clusters are disconnected (Fig. 8-47). We give this model to TETRAD and ask for the Rttr chart. The connections among latent variables have the largest Rttr values, and of these, the connections between AC and AB most reduce the TTR value. In this case it makes

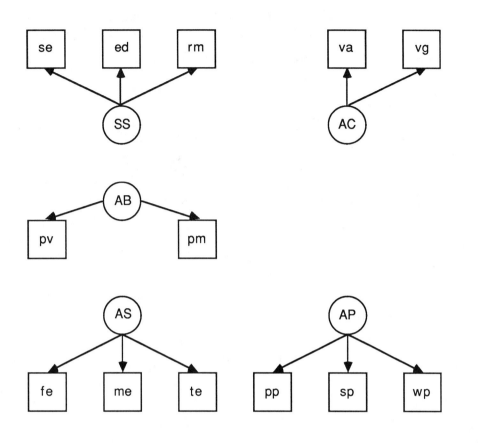

Figure 8-47: Disconnected model.

no difference for any connection which way the arrows go or whether there is a common cause. The relevant output is given below:

The graph analyzed in this example is:
AC->va AC->vg SS->rm SS->se SS->ed
AB->pm AB->pv AP->sp AP->pp
AP->wp AS->fe AS->me AS->te

The significance level is: 0.4000

Edge	Rttr	D(I-H)	I(H-I)
SS->AC	5.360	68	16
SS->AB	4.711	55	29
SS->AP	2.070	35	55
SS->AS	2.565	37	53
AC->AB	6.331	67	5
AB->AC	6.331	67	5
AC->AP	5.338	76	8
AP->AC	5.338	76	8
AC->AS	4.438	54	30
AS->AC	4.438	54	30
AB->AP	2.708	54	30
AP->AB	2.708	54	30
AB->AS	3.232	57	27
AS->AB	3.232	57	27
AP->AS	3.244	56	34
AS->AP	3.244	56	34

The Total Tetrad Residual, or TTR, is: 64.05317

Figure 8-48: Rttr output for the disconnected model.

Evidently a connection between ability and achievement is most important. We add AB->AC to the disconnected model, since it seems the most plausible connection between the two variables.

When we give the revised model to TETRAD and ask for the Rttr chart we find that connections between AB and SS have the highest Rttr value, 9.7. We can introduce a connection between AB and SS by means of a new latent variable, T, which serves as a common cause. One could as well introduce a direct effect of SS on AB. We obtain two alternative revised models (Figs. 8-49 and 8-50).

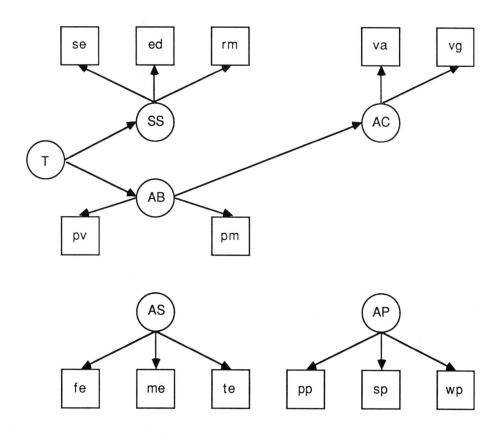

Figure 8-49: Disconnected model plus AB->AC, T->AB, T->SS.

We will pursue only the first branch of the search. When we again give the model of Fig. 8-49 to the program, we get an Rttr chart, which, after we have selected the best candidates, is shown in Fig. 8-51. T->AS has the highest Rttr value, 11.533. This is a plausible connection, supported by research cited by Brophy and Good [12]. The other edges shown are close, so again the search might branch, but

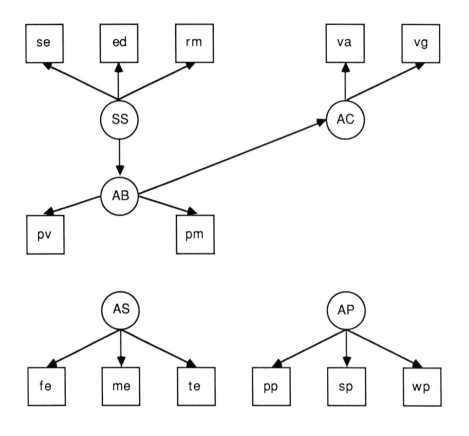

Figure 8-50: Disconnected model plus AB->AC, SS->AB.

we will follow only the line indicated by this alternative. We add T->AS to the model (Fig. 8-52). Continuing with the search, we give this model to TETRAD and request another Rttr chart. We show the relevant parts of it in Fig. 8-53.

The graph analyzed in this example is:
AC->va AC->vg SS->rm SS->se SS->ed AB->pm
AB->pv AB->AC AP->sp AP->pp AP->wp AS->fe
AS->me AS->te T->SS T->AB

The significance level is: 0.4000

The sample size is: 249

Edge	Rttr	D(I-H)	I(H-I)
AC->AP	10.771	171	111
AC->AS	10.610	163	119
T->AP	10.895	170	148
T->AS	11.533	176	142

Figure 8-51: The best candidates from the full Rttr chart.

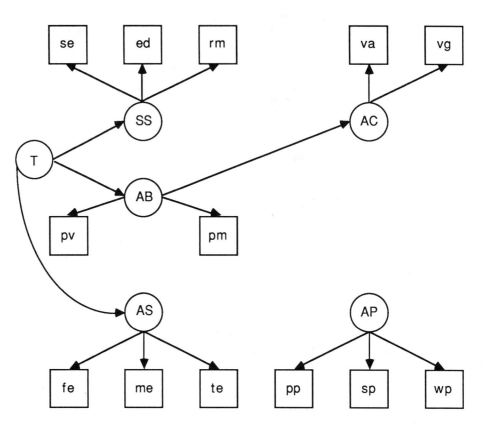

Figure 8-52: Disconnected model plus AB->AC, T->AB, T->SS, T->AS.

The graph analyzed in this example is:
AC->va AC->vg SS->rm SS->se SS->ed
AB->pm AB->pv AB->AC AP->sp AP->pp AP->wp
AS->fe AS->me AS->te T->SS T->AB T->AS

The significance level is: 0.4000

The sample size is: 249

Edge	Rttr	D(I-H)	I(H-I)
AC->AP	19.257	344	280
AP->AC	13.064	212	172
AB->AP	16.256	296	220
AP->AB	17.066	303	285
AP->AS	14.902	280	224
AS->AP	16.019	288	282
T->AP	16.072	260	220

Figure 8-53: Rttr output.

Here, there is a unique best edge, AC->AP. So far, we have the model in Fig. 8-54. Giving this model to TETRAD, we request an Rttr chart. The relevant output is shown in Fig. 8-55.

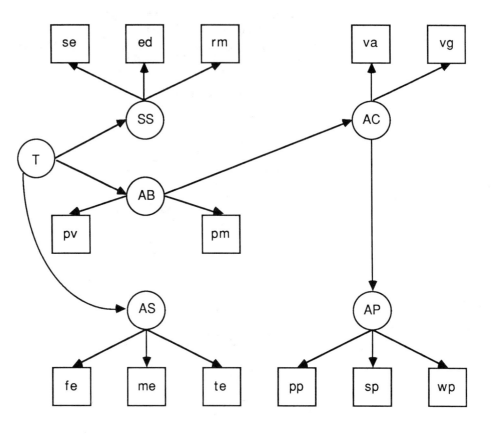

Figure 8-54: AB->AC, T->AB, T->SS, T->AS, and AC->AP.

The graph analyzed in this example is:
AC->va AC->vg AC->AP SS->rm SS->se SS->ed
AB->pm AB->pv AB->AC AP->sp AP->pp AP->wp
AS->fe AS->me AS->te T->SS T->AB T->AS

The significance level is: 0.4000

The sample size is: 249

Edge	Rttr	D(I-H)	I(H-I)
AC->SS	2.628	54	66
SS->AC	3.817	75	75
AC->AB	1.863	33	27
AP->AC	1.306	19	29
AC->AS	3.143	63	57
AS->AC	3.817	75	75
AC->T	1.863	33	27
T->AC	1.863	33	27
SS->AP	5.483	102	162
AP->SS	4.438	87	141
AB->AP	1.306	19	29
AP->AB	4.474	74	106
AP->AS	5.462	110	118
AS->AP	5.483	102	162
AP->T	4.474	74	106
T->AP	3.537	58	98

The Total Tetrad Residual, or TTR, is: 17.24747

Figure 8-55: Rttr output.

Notice that now the model implies no vanishing partial constraints. The model we have reached reduces the TTR to around 17.2, and it still explains 562 equations that hold at a significance level of .4. The Rttr chart contains three edges that look most promising, SS->AP, AP->AS, and AS->AP. That SS causes peer acceptance is certainly plausible, so we elaborate our model accordingly (Fig. 8-56).

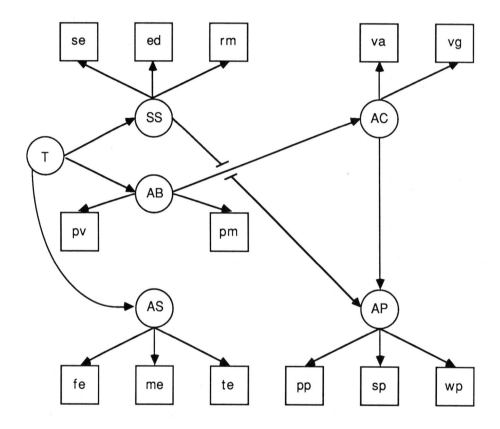

Figure 8-56: Final model.

Running this model through TETRAD shows that the Rttr chart now contains other edges that do more to reduce the TTR than any edge from a latent to another latent variable. The model's performance on TETRAD's standard measures is shown below.

The graph analyzed in this example is:
AC->va AC->vg AC->AP SS->rm SS->se SS->ed
SS->AP AB->pm AB->pv AB->AC AP->sp AP->pp
AP->wp AS->fe AS->me AS->te T->SS T->AB T->AS

The Total Tetrad Residual, or TTR, is: 11.76464

I-H, the total number of equations implied by the
model that do not hold in the data, is: 219

H-I, the total number of equations that hold in the
data but are not implied by the model, is: 631

The number of equations that hold in the data is 1031

The number of equations explained by the model is 400

Figure 8-57: TETRAD's standard output for the final model.

Compare this model with that of Maruyama and McGarvey. The new model is as plausible, and it has a TTR value of 11.7 compared to the Maruyama and McGarvey model TTR of 12.9. The new model implies no vanishing partial correlations that fail a significance test at a significance value of .4, whereas Maruyama and McGarvey's model implies 38 incorrect vanishing partial correlations. We expect, therefore, that the new model will provide a better fit, although we would still expect it to fail a chi square test at the .05 significance level.

We would not, on the basis of this data and this cursory search, put any weight on the substantive claims our model makes. We remind the reader that any number of equally good models might be found by making different choices at different stages in the search.

8.9. The Stability of Alienation

A study by Wheaton et al. [111] on the stability of alienation has become a standard example in manuals for computer programs that perform statistical analyses of structural equation models. Joreskog and Sorbom [52]discuss the example in the LISREL manuals, Bentler discusses the example in the EQS manual, and we introduce it here to illustrate the use of the TETRAD program. Covariance data for this case are on the floppy disk. The file name is "alien.dat."

The alienation study shows the use of both structural criteria and plausibility criteria in respecifying an initial causal model. The interpretation of variables in the initial model rules out a host of possible elaborations and, therefore, reduces the search space significantly.

The initial causal model is shown in Fig. 8-58. The probability of its chi square statistic (with 6 degrees of freedom) is less than .001.

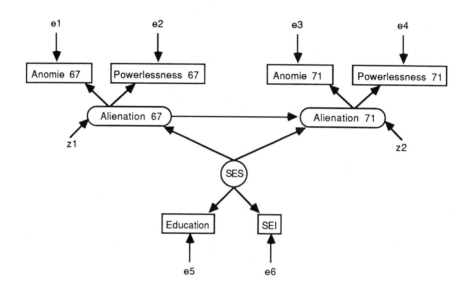

Figure 8-58: Alienation: Original model.

Alienation is a latent construct measured by anomie and powerlessness at two different times. SES is socioeconomic status, also latent, measured by Duncan's socioeconomic index and an index of educational achievement. Using the LISREL search procedure, the initial model is amended by freeing two parameters that correspond to correlations for error terms for the same indicator measured at different times. The revised model, shown in Fig. 8-59, has 4 degrees of freedom and p = .335, n = 932. It is proposed both by Joreskog and Sorbom, and by Bentler.

It is certainly plausible that indicators measured at different times have correlated errors, and the probability value of the chi square statistic is high. But a researcher who settled for this account of the data would have missed many possibilities. We can find alternative models with the TETRAD program, and then use LISREL or

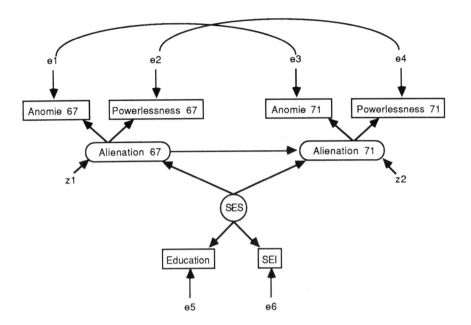

Figure 8-59: Alienation: Amended model.

EQS to compare the probabilities of their chi square statistics.

The TETRAD Analysis

We use the abbreviation scheme given in Fig. 8-60, and we give TETRAD the initial model shown in Fig. 8-61.

We will conduct two searches for modifications of this initial model. One of them, using the Suggested Sets of trek additions, is easy, almost instantaneous, and leads to an extremely good model. The other, using the Rttr chart, is much more tedious, but it recovers the same model found with the Suggested Sets and another that is nearly as good.

Alienation 67	=	A6
Alienation 71	=	A7
SES	=	SE
Anomie 67	=	a6
Anomie 71	=	a7
Powerlessness 67	=	p6
Powerlessness 71	=	p7
SEI	=	se
Education	=	ed

Figure 8-60: Abbreviation scheme.

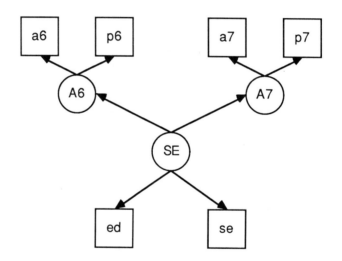

Figure 8-61: Alienation: Skeleton.

Using the Suggested Sets

Asking for three units of suggested sets, we get the results in Fig. 8-62. According to the suggested sets, it appears that a6-a7 is the best single trek to add to the skeleton. This trek can be realized as a direct cause from the value of a6 to the value of a7 or as a correlated error, but it cannot be interpreted as a cause from a7

```
Sets of suggested treks at significance level = 0.1307
-------------------------------------------------------

{ a6-a7 }


Sets of suggested treks at significance level = 0.4903
-------------------------------------------------------

{ a6-a7 p6-se p7-se }


Sets of suggested treks at significance level = 0.5296
-------------------------------------------------------

{ p6-a7 p6-se p7-ed p7-se }
{ p6-a7 p6-se A6->a7 p7-ed }
{ p6-a7 p6-se A6->a7 p7-se }
{ p6-a7 p6-se p7-ed A6->p7 }
{ p6-a7 p6-se p7-se A6->p7 }
{ p6-a7 p6-se SE->a7 p7-ed }
{ p6-a7 p6-se SE->a7 p7-se }
{ p6-a7 p6-se p7-ed SE->p7 }
{ p6-a7 p6-se p7-se SE->p7 }
{ a6-a7 p6-a7 p6-se p7-se }
{ a6-a7 p6-se A6->a7 p7-se }
{ a6-a7 p6-se p7-se A6->p7 }
{ a6-a7 p6-se SE->a7 p7-se }
{ a6-a7 p6-se p7-se SE->p7 }
{ a6-a7 p6-a7 p6-se p7-ed }
{ a6-a7 p6-se A6->a7 p7-ed }
{ a6-a7 p6-se p7-ed A6->p7 }
{ a6-a7 p6-se SE->a7 p7-ed }
{ a6-a7 p6-se p7-ed p7-se }
{ a6-a7 p6-se p7-ed SE->p7 }
```

The Total Tetrad Residual, or TTR, is: 0.37422

Figure 8-62: Suggested sets for skeleton.

to a6. We regard the correlated error as the most plausible realization of this suggested trek addition. The second suggested set contains a6-a7, and it also involves a pair of treks from se to the measures of powerlessness at two different times. It is certainly plausible that a measure of SES and a measure of powerlessness have correlated errors. It is natural to suppose that if SES is correlated with a measure of powerlessness at one time then it is correlated with the same measure at a later time, and the second set of suggested treks agrees with that judgment, which we can think of as a symmetry requirement imposed on our models. The socioeconomic index cannot, it would seem, be either a cause or an effect of the *responses* given to questionaire items, and so it seems less reasonable to implement the suggested treks by means of directed edges connecting p6, p7, and se.

An immediate realization of the second set of suggested treks is therefore a very plausible elaboration of the initial model, namely,

$$a6 \; C \; a7, \; p6 \; C \; se, \; p7 \; C \; se$$

This model has a chi square probability of .9103. In view of the goodness of fit and the fact that the models in the third unit of suggested sets of trek additions will all fail to explain one or more tetrad equations holding at a significance level of .49, we do not consider models from the third unit. In fact, it also turns out that all of the plausible models from the third unit of suggested trek additions have chi square probabilities lower than .9103.

We might, however, on grounds of symmetry with a6 and a7, reasonably add a fourth correlated error, between p6 and p7, to the model. If we do, the TTR is reduced to .008.

Searching with the Rttr Chart

The Rttr chart can be used with this case in a breadth first search. The techniques are just those described in our discussion of the Costner and Schoenberg case at the beginning of this chapter. We will not describe the search here, but only give its results. In addition to the model found with the suggested sets procedure, the Rttr search finds the model that adds the correlated errors

$$a6 \; C \; a7, \; a6 \; C \; se, \; a7 \; C \; se$$

to the initial model.

Additions To Skeleton	TTR	Equations Explained	$p(X^2)$
1) None	.3742	4	<0.0010
2) a6 C a7, se C p6, se C p7	.0158	3	0.9103
3) a6 C a7, a6 C se, a7 C se	.0226	3	0.8017
4) a6 C a7, se C p6, se C p7, p6 C p7	.0008	1	0.9936

Figure 8-63: Goodness of fit results.

The goodness of fit results for three models thus obtained are shown in Fig. 8-63.

Conclusion

With TETRAD's help we have found three models which perform substantially better on a chi square test than the one standardly exhibited in causal modeling texts. Two of these models lose a single degree of freedom in comparison with the model suggested in the LISREL and EQS manuals.

In fact, however, we have done something else at least equally important: *We have performed a search for alternative models.* In order not to make the discussion even more lengthy, we have not described all of the details of that search.

This case also exhibits something of the role that background knowledge can play in causal modeling with TETRAD. At several points in the analysis we appealed to the knowledge that a6 and a7, and similarly p6 and p7, were the same indicator measured at different times. We also appealed to our knowledge of the time order in eliminating possible causal connections.

9. A BRIEF HISTORY OF HEURISTIC SEARCH IN APPLIED STATISTICS

The methods used in the TETRAD program derive from work in statistics, biometrics and psychometrics that is now long forgotten but once captured the attention of some of the best workers in these subjects. That work forms a fascinating piece of the history of applied statistics. The story that follows is certainly not complete, especially in its recounting of more recent work.

We may forget how closely the development of statistics and probability was sometimes tied to the desire to be able to infer causes from frequencies. The earliest applications of social statistics were to causal questions, expecially in epidemiology and medicine. George Boole seems to have thought that the principal application of his algebra was to enable one to infer causes from probabilities, and to that end he embedded his algebra in a rather idiosyncratic theory of probability. Toward the close of the nineteenth century, Galton and Pearson developed the ideas of regression and correlation to attempt to describe the statistical manifestations of genetic inheritance.

Charles Spearman was an English psychologist who sought to combine the psychometric innovations of workers such as Binet with the new statistical methods that were emerging from mathematicians such as Pearson. Pearson did not like the result, and he and Spearman remained antagonists for a long while. In 1904 Spearman published "General Intelligence Objectively Determined and Measured" [102]. In it, from a variety of tests with a small sample of London school boys, Spearman argued that there is one common component to all manifestations or tests of "intelligence." Reading Spearman's paper today, one is struck by the bizzare choice of tests, many of which involved motor skills or sensory discrimination, and the absurd sample sizes, but that is not the point. The point is Spearman's *argument*, for it was the argument that caught the imagination of statisticians and psychometricians. Spearman's argument, given rather obscurely in this first paper but more clearly in subsequent papers, was as follows.

Suppose there are four measured variables x_1, x_2, x_3, and x_4, and their correlations (Pearson product-moment correlations, that is) have values that satisfy three equations:

$$\rho_{12}\rho_{34} - \rho_{13}\rho_{24} = 0$$
$$\rho_{12}\rho_{34} - \rho_{14}\rho_{23} = 0$$
$$\rho_{13}\rho_{24} - \rho_{14}\rho_{23} = 0$$

These constraints on the correlations can be explained in a powerful way by supposing that each of the measured variables is affected by a single common unmeasured variable, and that each of the measured variables is also affected by an unmeasured variable specific to it and having no effect on the other measured variables. The algebra is easy:

$$x_1 = a_1G + s_1$$
$$x_2 = a_2G + s_2$$
$$x_3 = a_3G + s_3$$
$$x_4 = a_4G + s_4$$

G, the s_i and the x_i are random variables, the a_i are undetermined constants. Multiplying each side of the first equation by the corresponding side of the second equation and averaging we get:

$$Exp(x_1x_2) = Exp(a_1a_2G^2 + a_1s_2G + a_2s_1G + s_1s_2)$$

For algebraic simplicity assume that all of the variables have mean 0. Since there is assumed to be no causal connection either between the several s_i variables or between these variables and G, their covariances should vanish, leaving

$$Cov(x_1x_2) = a_1a_2Var(G)$$

Analogous equations are obtained in the same way for the other covariances of the measured variables. Hence, for example

$$Cov(x_1x_2)Cov(x_3x_4) - Cov(x_1x_3)Cov(x_2x_4) =$$
$$a_1a_2a_3a_4Var(G)^2 - a_1a_3a_2a_4Var(G)^2 = 0$$

The correlation coefficient is just the covariance divided by the product of the standard deviations of the correlated variables, so the difference of the products of the correlations coefficients must also vanish.

Spearman's point was that the assumption of one common factor would explain why these constraints on the correlations, or *tetrad equations* as they came to be called, were satisfied in the population. The thing that must be emphasized, although it is simple enough, is this:

The one-factor model implies that the three tetrad equations will hold in the population no matter what the values of the coefficients a_i may be.

The converse is also true, Spearman thought. That is to say, if correlations among four variables satisfy the three associated tetrad equations, then the correlations can be generated from some one-factor model, with appropriate values for the linear coefficients. The three tetrad equations are the necessary and sufficient statistical conditions for the admissability of a one factor explanation of the correlations. This amounts to saying that a one-factor model implies no other independent constraints on the population covariance matrix besides the vanishing of all tetrad differences.

Analogous arguments apply for any larger number of measured variables. If there are n measured variables, then the number of possible tetrad equations among these variables is three times the number of ways of choosing four from n. If the correlations are due to the action of one common cause, then all of the tetrad equations must hold regardless of the values of the linear coefficients; conversely, if all of the tetrad equations hold, then the correlations can be generated by a one-factor model with appropriate values of the linear coefficients.

Spearman realized that the three tetrad equations could be derived from alternative models with multiple latent factors, provided the linear coefficients were chosen to have appropriate values, but only the one-factor model, he seems to have thought, would imply the tetrad equations no matter what the values of the coefficients might be. Spearman's dominant methodological idea, never fully articulated, seems to have been that the best explanation is one which generates constraints found in the population measures without having to assume special values for its parameters. In other words, he preferred those explanations which were robust or resilient over changes in the specification of the value of free parameters.

Whether Spearman realized it or not, he was appealing to a methodological idea that runs throughout the sciences. Kepler gave an analogous argument for the superiority of Copernican to Ptolemaic astronomy [35]. In the same years that Spearman was applying the argument to psychometrics, Harold Jeffreys, who was later to make distinguished contributions to statistics, and Arthur Eddington were making an analogous argument for Einstein's general theory of relativity.

In the years after 1904 Spearman and his students published a number of studies all of which supported his hypothesis of "General Intelligence," and critics such as Thorndike published contrary studies. Some critics, notably G. Thomson, argued that the tetrad equations need not be explained by a single common factor but could, instead, be satisfied if the test items were produced by a sufficiently large number of completely independent factors. The argument was rather muddled.

Neither Spearman nor his students nor his critics seem to have noted that there are a number of alternative models that have the same relationship to the tetrad equations as does the one-factor model. Pictorially, both of the models in Fig. 9-1 entail that three tetrad equations will hold in the population, no matter what the values of the linear coefficients.

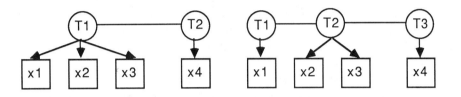

Figure 9-1: Alternatives to the one factor model.

It is hard to know what Spearman would have said about these alternatives. He might have dismissed them on the grounds that they are less simple than the one factor theory, which indeed they are. More likely, he would have held them to be "subtheories" of the one-factor model--that is, they amount to saying that the single factor consists of two or three causally connected components. Spearman had nothing against substructure.

In fact, however, the case is even worse, for three tetrad equations among four latent variables are robustly implied by models that have no latent factors but simply postulate directed effects of the measured variables on one another (Fig. 9-2). The example is but an instance of Sewall Wright's "path models." Wright's work was published in 1921 and drew immediate attention. As far as we know, however, none of the psychometricians of the day, Spearman included, entertained the thought that the responses their subjects gave to earlier items on batteries of mental tests might have an effect on the responses given to later items.

The increasing appreciation of the importance of sampling error made it urgent for Spearman to find a means to determine whether or not a tetrad difference is small enough to be plausibly regarded as due to sampling variation from a population in which the true value of the tetrad difference is zero. What was required was a knowledge of the sampling distribution of tetrad differences under the assumption that the underlying distribution of the variables is multinormal. In 1926 Spearman and Holzinger [49] produced an approximate formula for the variance of the sampling distribution of the tetrad residual, or tetrad difference, under the

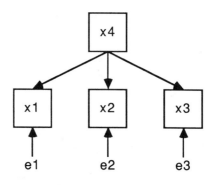

Figure 9-2: A path model that implies all three tetrad equations.

assumption that the difference is zero in the population. A year later they obtained an analogous formula for a collection of tetrad differences, again under the assumption that they are all zero.

Truman Kelley [57], a psychologist at Stanford and a capable statistician, had earlier derived an approximate formula for the sampling distribution of the ratio of the correlation products rather than the difference of the products. Spearman appears never to have used this statistic, and Kelley himself eventually gave up using it in favor of the tetrad difference. In retrospect, Kelley's strategy seems the better. Spearman was, in reality, making two inferences: (1) that the tetrad residual found in a sample was due to chance and the population tetrad difference was actually zero, and (2) that the zero tetrad difference in the population was due to the causal structure generating the data, not dependent on the particular values of the linear coefficients. But the tetrad difference is the difference of two small numbers, and the difference of two small numbers is small. Hence, whatever the model, if the linear coefficients were such as to produce small correlations, small tetrad differences would be expected in both the population and the sample. The ratio of two small numbers, by contrast, need not be small. Put in other terms, but still informally, Spearman's statistic has less power to discriminate between small tetrad differences due to causal structure and small tetrad differences due to small correlations.

In 1927 Spearman published, together with the statistical formulae, the most detailed defense of his theory. *The Abilities of Man* [103] drew a lot of attention, including some unwelcome attention from Pearson. Pearson wrote unflattering and anonymous assessments of the book in *Nature*, and then, with Moul, a critical but substantive contribution in *Biometrika* [84]. Pearson and Moul addressed the question of the sampling distribution for tetrad differences, assuming a vanishing difference in the population and multinormally distributed variables. They did not obtain an exact sampling distribution (and as far as we know the question is still open), and they did not improve on Spearman and Holzinger's formula for the sampling variance. They did, however, observe that the distribution of tetrad differences is certainly not normal. Pearson roundly criticized Spearman, principally on two counts: (1) that (using Spearman and Holzinger's formula for the sampling variance) the tetrad residuals in Spearman's data were sometimes quite large, and (2) that Spearman had used very small samples (e.g., 50 subjects) and, in his statistical analysis, had assumed that the sampling distribution of the tetrad differences was normal. Pearson's point was that the sampling distribution is only asymptotically normal, and the sampling variance formula could, therefore, only be used to decide the significance of a tetrad residual provided the sample sizes were reasonably large. Spearman's samples weren't.

Spearman didn't get the point, for he replied [104] that he made no assumption about the normality of the distribution of the tetrad differences. But if so, he could not have made the judgments he did about significance or converted from sampling variance to probable error in the way that was then customary, a transformation that assumes a normal distribution.

John Wishart [112] next took up the problem of the sampling distribution of tetrad differences. He did not attempt to find an exact sampling distribution, but he did find an exact formula for the variance of the distribution. The exact formula gave a larger standard deviation than does Spearman and Holzinger's approximate formula and had the effect of making Spearman's judgments in *The Abilities of Man* look a bit more reasonable.

Spearman was interested in tetrads because he saw in them an argument for his psychological theory. But others saw in his work something much more important, namely, a general procedure for finding the best linear causal models to account for statistical data. This ingenious work, pursued in different ways by Garnett [32], Kelley [57], and Holzinger [48], came to naught for reasons which we will describe subsequently, but it is the real key to our own heuristic search procedures. To explain their ideas, one statistical remark is necessary. Spearman's tetrad equations amount to a simple constraint on the population covariance matrix. Today, such constraints are given the slightly misleading name of "overidentifying constraints" because they usually determine more than one independent estimate of some parameter of the theory. Now there are other possible restrictions one could put on the covariance matrix, and in fact the *a priori* possibilities are endless. Garnett and Kelley , in effect, posed the following problem:

Find, for any linear causal model, the constraints on the population covariance matrix necessary and sufficient for the admissibiltiy of the model in the sense that the model will imply the constraints for all values of its linear coefficients and will not imply any further independent constraints.

This is an elegant problem, but one cannot hope to solve it for all possible cases. If, on the contrary, one could classify all of the possible linear models by the constraints necessary and sufficient for them, then by estimating from the sample covariance matrix which constraints are satisfied by the population covariance matrix, one could hope to find the best explanation for any body of data. Kelley fully realized there were far too many possible cases.

Garnett, and especially Kelley, worked out the constraints for a number of models, and the results are reported in Kelley's oddly titled *Crossroads in the Mind of Man*. Kelley's book contains analyses of the following cases:

1. Three variables, one specific factor (i.e., a latent error term), and one common factor (i.e., a latent common cause). (Two of the variables must be perfectly correlated).

2. Three variables, two specific factors, and one common factor. (The product of two of the correlations must equal the third.)

3. Three variables, three specific factors, and one common factor. (The absolute value of the product of every pair of correlations must be less than the third, and one or three of the correlations must be positive.)

4. Three variables, two common factors, no specific factors. (The multiple correlation coefficients of each variable with the other pair must all equal unity.)

5. Four variables, one common factor, four specific factors. (This is Spearman's case.)

6. Four variables, one common factor, three specific factors. (Kelley gives only a sufficient condition.)

7. Four variables, two common factors, four specific factors. (The condition is a slightly complicated inequality)

8. Five variables, two common factors, five specific factors. (The condition is the vanishing of a linear combination of 12 terms, each involving a product of five correlations. Kelley calls such a polynomial a "pentad."

9. Four variables, four specific factors, a common factor, and a factor common to x_1, x_2 or a factor common to x_3, x_4. (The tetrad differences, (12)(34) - (13)(24) and (12)(34) - (14)(23), are equal and, hence, of necessity the remaining tetrad difference vanishes.)

Kelley's work was very nice, in some ways the best done by the psychometricians of the time. As a strategy for locating the best linear causal model, however, it was clearly doomed. There are just far too many possible cases for a complete classification to be carried out. Each case that generates distinct algebraic constraints requires a distinct sampling statistic, and even the indefatigable Kelley did not obtain sampling variances for some of his cases. Kelley realized as much, and he wrote that "we do not have, and certainly cannot readily obtain, criteria for six, seven or more variables at a time." (p. 101)

On the other hand, the cases Kelley did cover offer a kind of *heuristic* guide in the search for models that will best explain the data. However large the model considered, it can be depicted as a directed graph, and the graph will have subgraphs consisting of only three, four, or five measured variables and their connections to each other and to latent variables. According to the structure of the subgraphs, constraints of the kinds that Kelley studied will be implied. Thus, one might hope to guide the selection of models by comparing the constraints (of the kind Kelley describes) that hold in the data with the constraints of the same kind implied by a hypothetical model and altering the model if necessary until what holds and what is implied fit together. This is exactly what Kelley himself did.

Kelley applied his analysis to a data set involving nine measured variables for a sample of 140 seventh graders. He settled for trying to fit the model to the vanishing tetrads found approximately in the data. The pentads were just too troublesome to calculate. Holzinger took over the same strategy for the same data in defense of a model that was closer to Spearman's views. A year later, in his *Statistical Resume of the Spearman Two Factor Theory*, Holzinger repeated the same strategy on various examples. He discussed, for example, the case in which there are four measured variables and only one tetrad equation holds and pointed out, as Kelley had, that the pattern can be accomodated by supposing there is an additional common factor (or as people would say today, a correlated error) between either of two pairs of the measured variables. Which pair had the additional common factor, he correctly noted, could be determined if there was an additional, fifth, measured variable.

Holzinger's *Statistical Resume* was nearly the last gasp of tetrad analyses. Spearman's argument that the best explanation is one that robustly implies the constraints found on the covariance matrix had briefly led to a strategy for scientific discovery. The strategy used one of the most commonly occurring constraints on a covariance matrix, the tetrad equation. It proposed to compute the tetrad equations implied by a model, compare them with the constraints satisfied by the data, and alter the model if there was a misfit. That strategy failed for computational reasons. The determination of the tetrad equations implied by an arbitrary model, even a model with as few as nine or ten variables, was excessively tedious.

The real death of these analyses of constraints on the covariance matrix came at the hands of Hotelling and Thurstone. In the early 1930s, Hotelling developed both principal components analysis and canonical correlation analysis. The two techniques enabled researchers to manipulate their data and define constructs which localized the variance of a set of variables or the correlation of two families of variables. But more important, perhaps, was Thurstone's contribution.

Thurstone's *The Vectors of Mind* [107] appeared in the middle of the 1930s, and it effectively ended the analysis of tetrad equations and overidentifying constraints among psychometricians and social scientists for another quarter century. Despite the denunciations of factor analysis one hears nowadays, Thurstone's book was elegant and revolutionary. Written in a lucid and courteous style, *Vectors of Mind* was, for its time, a mathematical *tour de force*, completely in command of the relevant matrix theory, geometry, and statistics. Equally important, however, it had a simple and appealing philosophical theme--*science is nothing more than simplification*--and it combined that theme with an easy algorithm for doing science as Thurstone conceived it, an algorithm that could be carried out by hand with pencil and paper. The procedure was not tied to any one theory of mental or social phenomena but to a general conception of science. In Thurstone's view science was nothing more than the erection of "constructs" which describe the data more simply, with fewer "degrees of freedom," and he provided an almost magical procedure by which science could be done, theory discovered, progress made.

Spearman's tetrads were discussed by Thurstone, but as an inferior and inadequate special case. The motivation behind them, and the conception of scientific explanation from which they sprang, was never mentioned. Spearman, a mediocre mathematician, a rude and aggressive controversialist, a man tied to one theory and without an automatic method for discovery, had little chance against Thurstone. Neither did Kelley and Holzinger, who quickly converted from the analysis of constraints on the covariance matrix to the methods of factor analysis.

In almost every way, save that it was an effective and easy procedure for producing theories, Thurstone's factor analysis was inferior to the efforts at constraint analysis pursued by Spearman, Wishart, Kelley, Holzinger, and others. Psychometricians had not entertained the possiblity that measured variables might have direct effects on one another or even on latent variables, nor had they analyzed models in which latent variables had *causal* effects on one another, but nothing in the earlier procedures prohibited such analyses. With factor analysis such relationships were impossible because they were beyond the algorithm, and the philosophical views that went with factor analysis discouraged researchers in psychometrics, and in the many other subjects to which factor analysis quickly spread, from even thinking of the possibility.[37] Thurstone's factor analysis did not, in any serious sense, conduct a search for alternative theories of the data. Instead it churned out a representative of a collection of statistically equivalent models. Perhaps worst of all, Thurstone's methods abandoned the insight into scientific explanation that had lain behind Spearman's procedures and had, for a brief while, threatened to bring statistical modeling into the spirit of the natural sciences. For Thurstone, constraints exhibited by the sample covariance matrix had to be satisfied, but they were to be satisfied by adjusting the linear coefficients--the factor loadings--in whatever way necessary. Thurstone was the Ptolemy of statistical modeling.

Thurstone's triumph, and the reasons for it, are evident in Guilford's *Psychometric Methods* [41], which appeared in 1936. Guilford gives a detailed and sympathetic treatment of Spearman's views and of tetrad methods, before recommending that they be abandoned in favor of Thurstone's factor analysis, which is described in even greater detail. Guilford's reasons for the preference were succinct:

> The use of the tetrad is a laborious procedure except when one is dealing with a small number of tests. The number of tetrads increases enormously as the number of tests increases. With 10 tests there are 630 tetrads and 20 tests there are 14,535. More effective and economical methods are now available; hence tetrads have little more than historical importance.

We have no pretense to surveying the history of statistical modeling from the mid-1930s to the present, and we have already ignored the important developments that had taken place in econometrics. But it is worth saying a few words about what happened to the fundamental idea of Spearman's school, namely, that linear causal models should be assessed by their ability to robustly entail constraints on the covariance matrix, no matter what the values of their linear coefficients.

---

[37]We think it is fairly clear why none of the psychometricians, from Spearman to Thurstone, considered models in which the latent variables have causal effects on one another. The psychometricians believed their latent factors were genetically determined traits or faculties or abilities. Since the traits were determined by genetics, they could have no causal effects on one another (and neither could they be causally influenced by the manifestations of these traits in observable behavior). Of course, since the traits might have common genetic causes, it was permissible for them to be correlated, as Thurstone's factor analysis allowed. Just why the psychometricians had this conviction is less clear, but two speculations are possible. The source of the study of correlation was Galton's and Pearson's genetic studies, and so it was natural enough for psychometricians to look to biological models. Second, the assumption that the traits manifested by test scores were genetic fit comfortably with their conviction of the superiority of the white race. Kelley, for example, ended his *Crossroads in the Mind of Man* [57] with a discussion of the implications of psychometrics for eugenics.

Constraints on the covariance matrix came to be known in the economics literature as "overidentifying constraints." For reasons we do not pretend to understand, many econometricians were much more interested in parameter estimation than in theory testing, and overidentifying constraints made consistent, unbiased estimation more difficult. For that reason some econometricians adopted the exact contrary of the views of the Spearman school and recommended avoiding models that imposed any constraints on the covariance matrix.

The connection between statistical models and causal notions was reinvigorated by Herbert Simon's work in the 1950s, which attempted to derive the causal claims of a statistical model from the identifiability relations of the variables of the model. The analysis seems to have given some applied statisticians encouragement to think explicitly about the connection between statistical models and the causal conclusions people habitually drew from them. In psychology, Campbell's work on inferring causal order from the correlations of time-lagged variables, and the work of Wold in economics had similar effects. The effect was perhaps most pronounced in sociology, a subject which came rather late to statistical methods and causal models. The leading practitioners, thinking the issues through afresh, in effect rediscovered many of the ideas of the Spearman school.

The clearest example is Blalock's *Causal Inferences in Nonexperimental Research* [7], which appeared in 1961. Blalock reinvented the procedure of examining the constraints on the covariance matrix robustly implied by a linear causal model. The models he considered were not, however, latent factor models of the kind considered by the psychometricians but were, instead, path models with no common unmeasured variables, models in fact of the very kind introduced by Wright. The constraints on the correlation matrix in these cases are not tetrad or pentad equations or the like, but constraints on partial correlations. Blalock makes no reference to any of work done by the Spearman school.

Spearman's ideas were noted by Herbert Costner and O. D. Duncan, however, who considered the patterns of tetrad equations implied by a number of simple latent variable models in which the latent variables have causal effects on one another and each latent variable affects two or more measured indicator variables. They do not refer to the work of Kelley or Holzinger, but their basic idea is much the same. Costner, in collaboration with Schoenberg, even proposed a more or less systematic procedure for revising linear models with latent variables by locating submodels having two causally connected latent variables each with two measured indicators. Such submodels imply a single tetrad equation, which is no longer implied if a measured indicator of one latent variable has a common factor or correlation with a measured indicator of the other latent variable. If the appropriate tetrad equation is not found to hold empirically, Costner and Shoenberg recommend modifying the model accordingly. Costner and Schoenberg's procedure is still occasionally cited but does not seem to have been much used, perhaps because it was confined to locating special sorts of erroneous model specifications and was not really algorithmic. Kelley and Holzinger would have liked the work. The development of computer programs such as LISREL that automatically carry out maximum likelihood estimates of parameters and perform significance tests led to a quite different strategy for revising models. The strategy is quite alien to the tradition of the Spearman school and to Costner and Schoenberg's procedure, for it pays no attention to robustly accounting for constraints satisfied by the sample covariance matrix. Instead, the revision procedure locates the fixed parameter for which a small variation will most increase the value of a fitting function, revises the model by adding the corresponding free parameter, reestimates, and tests to see if the difference in chi square values of the original and modified models is signficant. With this procedure an initial model may robustly explain constraints on the covariance matrix but the modified model may very well be unable to robustly explain those constraints. If the procedure is not quite as Ptolemaic as Thurstone's factor analysis, neither is it as Copernican as the constraint analyses of the Spearman school. Perhaps we should think of it as Tychonic.

The early psychometricians knew how to compute the covariances or correlations implied by an estimated model, given the variances of the exogenous variables and the values of the linear coefficients. With Kelley's results they knew how to determine the tetrad equations and certain other constraints for special cases. As far as we know, however, they had no general method for computing covariances and correlations when the models were, in contemporary jargon, nonrecursive, that is, when the directed graph of the causal model contained a cyclic path leading from one variable back to that same variable. No such models occurred in psychometrics, but they did occur elsewhere. The general solution to the problem was provided by an outsider, Samuel Mason. His doctoral thesis in the 1950s was devoted to the effects of loops in circuits, and it provided a general procedure for computing the correlations or covariances of a recursive or nonrecursive model, given the variances of the exogenous variables and the values of the linear coefficients. Mason's work was elaborated for social scientists by Heise in his *Causal Analysis*.

The moral to this story is that Spearman, Kelley, Holzinger and others had good ideas about scientific explanation and about how to search for good explanations of nonexperimental data. The idea was not entirely lost and persists here and there in recent work in statistical modeling. That it never came to fruition was due to computational problems, not to statistical difficulties. What was lacking was a general algorithm that would permit the rapid calculation of the tetrad equations (or other constraints) robustly implied by *any* linear causal model and would compare those constraints with the constraints approximately satisfied by the sample covariance matrix. That is a lot, of course, but it is more a problem in algorithm design than in statistical inference. With such a procedure embodied in a computer program, researchers would no longer have to bother with lengthy and tedious analyses of the implications of a very few causal models. The implications of any model would be immediately available. With such a procedure researchers would not have to resort to accepting or rejecting a model entirely, but could instead systematically examine the logical workings of parts of a complex model and modify the parts as need be. A program of this sort would, in fact, serve as a research tool for determining the kinds of results that Kelley, Holzinger, Costner, and Duncan wrung out by hand in a few simple cases. With it, one could locate *general rules* about what modifications of a model would or would not prevent the robust implication of particular tetrad equations or other constraints. If such general rules could be found and incorporated in a computer program, we would have the best result of all; with such a procedure, appropriately designed, researchers could implicitly search through millions of alternatives for those modifications of an initial hypothesis that best explain the constraints satisfied by the sample data. TETRAD is such a program.

10. MATHEMATICAL FOUNDATIONS

10.1. The Algorithm

The TETRAD program has four major components.

1. It determines the vanishing tetrad differences and vanishing partial correlations implied by any model given to it.

2. It determines the vanishing tetrad differences and vanishing partial correlations that pass a statistical test at a significance level set either by the user or automatically.

3. It determines which sets of treks can be added to the model to prevent the implication of "false" tetrad equations without preventing the implication of "true" tetrad equations implied by the initial causal model.

4. For each edge e not already present in a model, and for each correlated error e between vertices not connected by an edge, it calculates which vanishing tetrad differences and vanishing partial correlations would be implied if e were added to the model.

Computing the Implied Equations

The general rules the program uses to compute the tetrad equations implied by a directed graph are as follows.

If u, v, w, x, are four distinct measured variables in the graph, the graph implies the tetrad equation

$$\rho_{uv}\rho_{wx} = \rho_{ux}\rho_{vw}$$

if and only if

$$\left(\sum_{t \in T_{uv}} L(t) \right) \left(\sum_{t \in T_{wx}} L(t) \right) = \left(\sum_{t \in T_{ux}} L(t) \right) \left(\sum_{t \in T_{vw}} L(t) \right)$$

where $L(t)$ is the product of labels of the edges in a trek t, and T_{ij} is the set of treks between i and j.

TETRAD can be used on a particular class of theories called "statistical linear causal theories" (SLCTs) which will be defined precisely later. We will also prove

247

that the rule stated above correctly calculates the tetrad equations implied by any acyclic SLCT.

The TETRAD program uses a modification of a well known path finding algorithm[37] to compute the tetrad equations a model implies. It first calculates the open paths and the treks between each pair of variables in the graph. The program then calculates, for each pair u,v of measured variables, the trek sum for that pair. The products of the trek sums are then compared to determine whether or not they constitute an algebraic identity. If they do,[38] the model implies the corresponding tetrad equation. The program proceeds in this way through all foursomes of measured variables.

Suggesting Modifications

To determine the sets of suggested trek additions to an initial model, the program proceeds through all foursomes of measured variables. For each foursome, it locates an appropriate subgraph of the initial model and determines whether or not to recommend the addition of a trek between any pair of variables in the subgraph. The treks may be produced by edges directly connecting two measured variables, by a common error term connecting the measured variables, or by a directed edge from a latent variable already in the graph to one of the measured variables.

The program's recommendations do not distinguish between directed edges connecting two measured variables in either direction and the introduction of a new error variable connected to two measured variables. In the program's recommendations, all of these possibilities appear as a measured variable pair in a set of suggested treks. The program does distinguish, however, between these sorts of modifications and the addition of a directed edge between a latent variable and a measured variable. If the program recommends the addition of a directed edge between a latent and a measured variable, then a pair consisting of the latent and the measured variables occurs in the set of recommendations. For example, if TETRAD received the skeleton in Fig. 10-1 and it recommended the pair [T1 -> 4], then there is only one way to augment the skeleton, the one we show in Fig. 10-2. We suggest this distinction notationally by listing a suggested trek between two measured variables x, y as [x - y], but a suggested trek between a latent variable T1 and a measured variable w as [T1 -> w].

---

[37] [1], pp.195-201

[38] If there are no treks between a pair of variables on one side of an equation and no treks between a pair on the other side of the same equation, the graph implies the equation and TETRAD counts it as doing so.

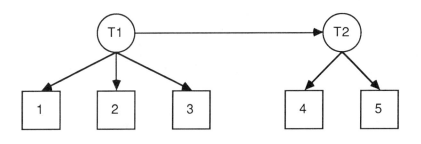

Figure 10-1: Skeleton.

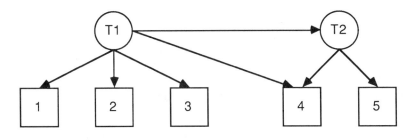

Figure 10-2: Augmented model.

How TETRAD Finds Its Recommendations

TETRAD makes suggestions about what sets of treks can be added to a model in order to better satisfy Thurstone's and Spearman's principles. TETRAD searches for sets of suggested treks that strictly satisfy Spearman's principle for a given significance level. However, the search is a *heuristic* search; that is, it is a fast search which probably, but not certainly, produces correct output. The sets of treks suggested by TETRAD may be incorrect in two ways; there may be sets of treks that strictly satisfy Spearman's principle that are not suggested, and some sets that are suggested may not strictly satisfy Spearman's principle.

TETRAD starts with the significance level set at 0.0 and increases it to a level at which at least one equation is considered false. For that significance level, the program does the following.

TETRAD first cycles through all sets of four measured variables and determines which equations hold empirically in the foursome at the current significance level. For each foursome, it puts any treks which, if added to the graph, would defeat the implication of equations that hold into a set called "don't pick" (DP).

TETRAD then cycles again through all foursomes of measured variables. For each foursome of variables, TETRAD considers whether or not the model implies a tetrad equation in those four variables that does not hold at the given significance level. If it does not, the program goes to the next foursome. If the model does imply an equation that does not hold in the data for those four variables, the basic strategy is to divide and conquer.

For each foursome of variables implying a tetrad equation that does not hold in the data, the program examines the **subgraph** consisting of

1. The four measured variables, say $x_1, \ldots, x_4$.

2. The latent variables adjacent to $x_1, \ldots, x_4$ (called parents).

3. The directed edges from parents to the measured variables they are adjacent to.

4. All treks, including theoretical variables which are not parents, between the parents.

For example, the graph in Fig. 10-3 is skeletal. The subgraphs for variables x_1-x_2-x_3-x_5 and variables x_1-x_2-x_5-x_6 are shown in Fig. 10-4.

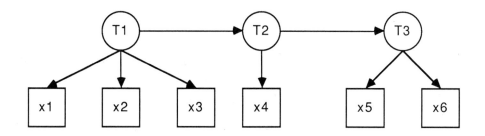

Figure 10-3: Skeleton

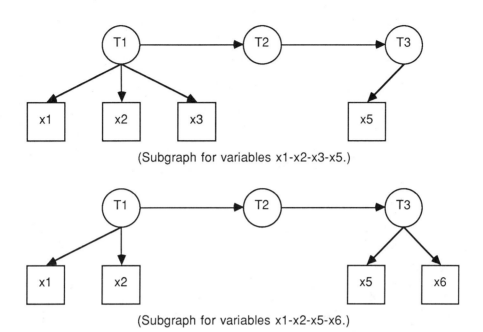

(Subgraph for variables x1-x2-x3-x5.)

(Subgraph for variables x1-x2-x5-x6.)

Figure 10-4: Subgraphs.

If this strategy is applied to skeletal graphs, there is a unique parent for each measured variable, and there are no treks between measured variables that do not go through a parent. If the graph is skeletal, the sets of suggested sets are probably, but not certainly, correct. However, if the graph is not skeletal, the sets of suggested sets are not even probably correct, and TETRAD issues a warning to that effect.

Based on the structure of the subgraph for each foursome, the program assigns the subgraph to one of nine types. The types are really equivalence classes of such subgraphs, where the equivalence relation is restricted to subgraphs that imply at least one tetrad equation.

Two skeletal subgraphs, A, B, with four measured variables are equivalent if and only if

1. There is a one-to-one map F:{measured and parent variables in A}-> {measured and parent variables in B}. We consider an edge to be an ordered pair of vertices, <v1,v2>. Thus F<v1,v2> = <F(v1),F(v2)>. Latent variables in the subgraph are parent variables in this definition

only if there is a direct edge from the parent to one of the four measured variables.

2. x_i is measured in A if and only if $F(x_i)$ is measured in B.

3. T_i is a parent in A if and only if $F(T_i)$ is a parent in B.

4. When variables in A are mapped into variables in B, or vice versa, A and B imply the same tetrad equations.

5. If any edge(s) from latent to measured variables or from measured to measured variables in A is added to A (forming $A_{augmented}$) and F(edge(s)) is added to B, then $A_{augmented}$ implies the same tetrad equations as $B_{augmented}$.

For example, all of the subgraphs having two parent variables connected by a trek and having each parent adjacent to two of the four measured variables, form a type.

We illustrate the nine types with a representative from each equivalence class (Figs. 10-6 and 10-5). In these illustrations, any number of latent variables may be inserted between the parent variables, so long as the path connections are retained, and no treks are introduced that violate the conditions stipulated in the diagrams.

Directed edge =   ⟶

Any trek =   ⎯⎯⎯

Latent variables =   T1, . . . ,T4

Measured variables =   x1, . . . ,x4

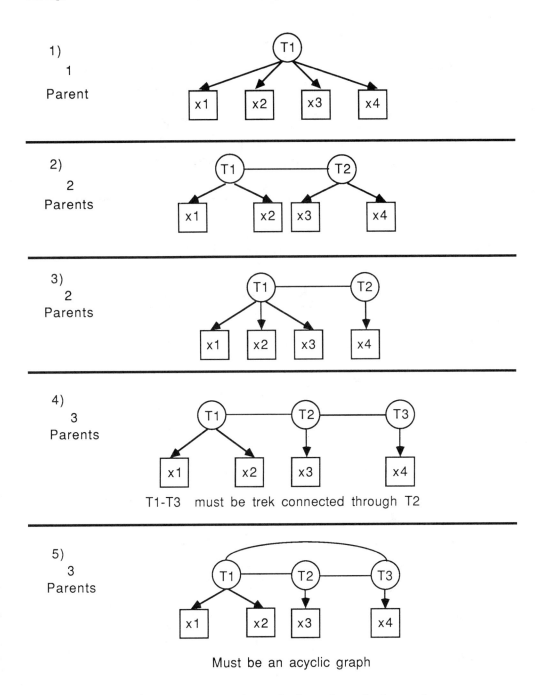

Figure 10-5: Representatives of subgraph equivalence classes.

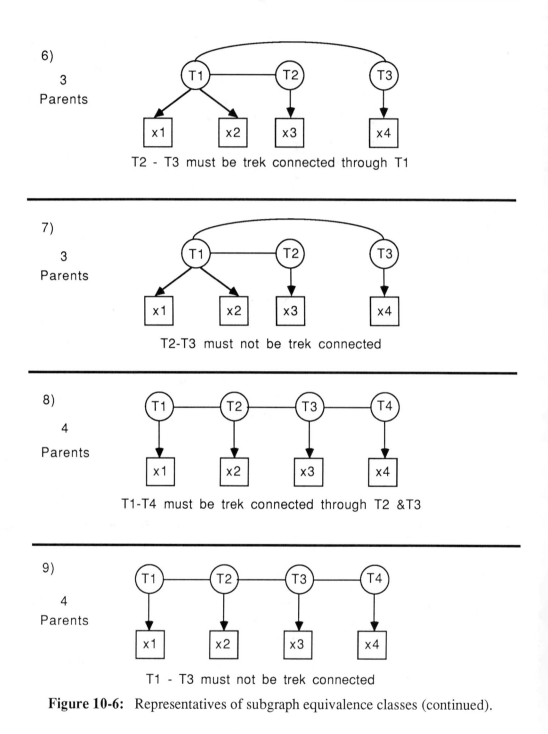

6)

3 Parents

T2 - T3 must be trek connected through T1

7)

3 Parents

T2-T3 must not be trek connected

8)

4 Parents

T1-T4 must be trek connected through T2 &T3

9)

4 Parents

T1 - T3 must not be trek connected

Figure 10-6: Representatives of subgraph equivalence classes (continued).

Based on the type of the subgraph, the program suggests all of the additional treks that will defeat the implication of the false equations involving the foursome of measured variables occurring in the subgraph. The algorithm is heuristic because it only considers, at this point, treks between variables *in* the subgraph. There might be an edge from a variable v *not in* the subgraph to a variable w *in* the subgraph that causes an equation involving only variables in the subgraph to be defeated and which is not considered in any other subgraph involving both v and w. In our experience this is rare. TETRAD removes any treks from this set of suggestions that are also in DP, thereby disallowing any candidates for addition that would violate Spearman's principle. After removing the treks that are also in DP, the program forms sets of treks LM_i that are locally minimal in the following sense

For the subgraph under consideration, each set LM_i, but no proper subset of LM_i, will, when added to the graph given to the program, defeat the implication of as many false tetrad equations involving the measured variables of the subgraph as is possible without defeating the implication of any true tetrad equations implied by the full graph.

As the program proceeds from foursome to foursome, it forms globally minimal sets GM_i that have a similar property. For each set GM_i, and no proper subset of GM_i, the set GM_i will defeat as many false equations involving all foursomes considered *so far* as is possible without defeating any true ones. After all foursomes are considered, the sets GM_i are the sets of suggested trek additions.

TETRAD outputs the sets and the first significance level at which the sets of the suggested trek additions are nonempty. It then increases the significance level until the sets of suggested trek additions are different.

Computing the Rttr Values

The Rttr value for an edge is the amount that the TTR will drop if that edge is added to the graph input. TETRAD adds that trek to the graph input and recalculates the TTR value. It recalculates the TTR value by determining what paths and treks would be added to a graph if a given edge were added. The difference between the original TTR and the recalculated TTR is the Rttr for the trek in question. The Rttr value is calculated for each edge that is not in the current model and for each correlated error between vertices that are not connected by an edge in either direction. Although guaranteed to be accurate, this procedure can be rather time consuming due to the large number of edges and correlated errors that must be considered.

10.2. Proofs of Correctness of the Algorithms Employed by TETRAD

Introduction

In this section three fundamental results about statistical linear causal theories will be proved. These theorems will be stated precisely later. Informally, they are

1. Any two theories with the same causal graph imply the same tetrad equations and the same vanishing partial equations.

2. For any acyclic theory, the algorithm employed by TETRAD correctly determines the tetrad equations implied by the theory.

3. For any theory, the algorithm employed by TETRAD correctly determines the partial equations implied by the theory.

The second and third points are not obvious for the following reason. When TETRAD determines whether or not a given tetrad or partial equation is implied by a theory, it does not correctly calculate the covariances in that equation. The covariances depend upon

1. the variances of independent variables

2. the open paths in the graph, and

3. the cycles in the graph.

TETRAD examines only certain open paths in determining which tetrad constraints and which vanishing partial correlations constraints are implied. The program nonetheless has been shown to correctly determine which partial correlation constraints are implied by models with cyclic or acyclic graphs. We have not proved that the program correctly determines which tetrad constraints are implied by a cyclic graph, although we have been unable to find any example in which the program has incorrectly determined which tetrad constraints were implied.

Before giving the formal definitions and lemmas needed to state and prove these theorems, we will give an example that illustrates them.

The covariance between x and y will be denoted by γ_{xy}, the variance of x will be denoted by σ^2_x, and the standard deviation of x will be denoted by σ_x.

Tetrad Equations

Assume that there is a set R of random variables {u,v,w,x,y,z} defined over a sample space Ω with a probability measure P, and a set of five homogeneous equations

$$w = a_{wu}u$$

$$x = a_{xu}u$$

$$y = a_{yv}v$$

$$z = a_{zv}v$$

$$v = a_{vu}u$$

where each a_{ij} is a real constant. The set of non-zero coefficients a_{ij} will be called the **equation coefficients**.

A causal graph <R,E> is associated with these equations (Fig. 10-3). The set of random variables R is the set of vertices of the graph. i is adjacent to j iff i causes j.

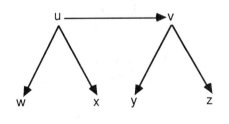

Figure 10-7: Example 1.

For each vertex x of positive indegree, x is specified as a function of all and only the vertices adjacent to x.

Note that the causal graph completely determines the form of the equations associated with it. However, different sets of equations can be associated with the same graph, since the graph does not fix the values of the coefficients.

According to the trek rules (which are described subsequently)

$$\gamma_{yz} = a_{yv}a_{zv}\sigma^2_v$$

Since v is not independent, its variance can be written in terms of the variances of variables which are independent. In this case,

$$\sigma^2_v = a^2_{vu}\sigma^2_u$$

Upon substitution, then,

$$\gamma_{yz} = a_{yv}a_{zv}a^2_{vu}\sigma^2_u$$

In the theory depicted in Fig. 10-7

$$\gamma_{yz} = a_{yv}a_{zv}a_{vu}^2\sigma^2_u$$

$$\gamma_{wx} = a_{wu}a_{xu}\sigma^2_u$$

$$\gamma_{wz} = a_{wu}a_{vu}a_{zv}\sigma^2_u$$

$$\gamma_{xy} = a_{xu}a_{vu}a_{yv}\sigma^2_u$$

Hence,

$$\gamma_{yz}\,\gamma_{wx} = \gamma_{wz}\,\gamma_{xy} = a_{wu}a_{zv}a_{xu}a_{yv}a_{vu}^2\sigma^2_u$$

These equalities obviously hold no matter what the values of the equation coefficients are. We shall say therefore that the theory described in Example 1 strongly implies the tetrad equation.

Some of the ideas illustrated in the example will now be defined more formally.

Definition 1: Given an ordered n-tuple $N = <c_1, \ldots, c_n>$, an object **o is in N** iff $o = c_i$ for some i between 1 and n inclusive. We shall also write that $o \, \varepsilon \, N$.

This notation is somewhat ambiguous since ε is also used to mean set membership, but the context will always make it clear which use of ε is intended.

Definition 2: A **digraph** is an ordered pair $<R,E>$, where R is a set of **vertices** and E is a set of **edges**. Each edge is an ordered pair of elements of R. The first element in an edge is called the **tail**, and the second element is called the **head**. An edge with a tail v_i and a head v_j is an edge **from** v_i to v_j; it is also said that the edge is **out of** v_i and **into** v_j. v_i is **adjacent** to v_j iff there is an edge from v_i to v_j. **Adj(i)** is the set of all variables adjacent to i. The **indegree** of a vertex v is equal to the number of distinct edges into v; the **outdegree** of a vertex v is equal to the number of distinct edges out of v.

Definition 3: A **path of length n** in a digraph $<R,E>$ is an ordered n+1-tuple of vertices $<v_1, \ldots, v_{n+1}>$ where for $1 \leq i \leq n$, $<v_i, v_{i+1}>$ is an edge in E. The path is said to **contain** edge $<v_i, v_{i+1}>$. The first vertex in the path is called the **source** of the path; the last vertex in the path is called the **sink** of the path. The path is said to **connect** the source to the sink. Two paths **intersect** iff they have a a vertex in common; any such common vertex is a **point of intersection**. A **cycle** is a path of at least length 1 in which the source equals the sink. A path **contains a cycle** iff it has a subpath which is a cycle. An **open path** is a path with no cyclic subpaths. A digraph is **acyclic** if and only if every path in the graph is open. A path with one vertex is an **empty path**. If path p is equal to $<v_1, \ldots, v_n>$ and path q is equal to $<v_n, \ldots, v_{n+m}>$, then **the concatentation of p and q** is equal to $<v_1, \ldots, v_n, \ldots, v_{n+m}>$ and is denoted by p&q.

Note that empty paths are the only paths that contains no edges. Also the concatenation of p with an empty path is p, and the concatenation of an empty path with p is p. The single vertex in an empty path is both its source and its sink.

Definition 4: A **trek t between two distinct vertices v_i and v_j** is a pair of open paths from some vertex u to v_j and v_i respectively that intersect only at u. The source of the paths in the trek is called the **source** of the trek. v_i and v_j are called the **termini of the trek**. Given a trek t between i and j, t_i will denote the path in t from the source of t to i and t_j will denote the path in t from the source of t to j.

One of the paths in a trek may be an empty path. However, since the termini of a trek are distinct, only one path in a trek can be empty. Fig. 10-8 illustrates some treks between v_i and v_j.

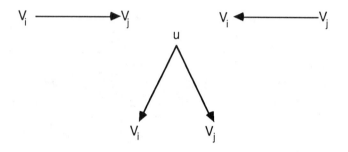

Figure 10-8: Examples of treks.

Definition 5: Let a **stochastic linear causal theory (SLCT)** be <<R,E>, (Ω,P), X, L> where

1. (Ω,P) is a probability space.

2. <R,E> is a labelled digraph. R is a set of random variables over (Ω,P). The variables in R have a joint distribution. Every variable in R has a non-zero variance. E is a set of directed edges between variables in R. There are no edges from a vertex to itself.

3. X is a consistent set of independent homogeneous linear equationals in random variables in R. For each i in R of positive indegree there is an equation in X of the form

$$i = \sum_{j \in Adj(i)} a_{ij} j$$

where each a_{ij} is a non-zero real number and each j is in R. This implies that each vertex i in R of positive indegree is a linear function of all and only the vertices adjacent to i. There are no other equations in X. A non-zero value of a_{ij} is the **equation coefficient** of j in the equation for i.

4. If vertices (random variables) u and v are not connected by a trek, then u and v are statistically independent.

5. L is a function with domain E such that $L(e) = a_{ij}$ iff head(e) = i and tail(e) = j. L(e) will be called the **label of e.** By extension, the product of labels of edges in any path or trek p will be denoted by L(p), and L(p) will be called the label of p. The label of an empty path is fixed at 1.

6. There is a subset of R called the **error variables.** Each error variable is of indegree 0 and outdegree 1. For every i in R of indegree $\neq$ 0 there is exactly one error variable with an edge into i.

If a SLCT contains loops it is possible that for some values of the equation coefficients some covariances between variables will be infinite. However, we will assume in all of the following proof that the covariances are well defined.

Definition 6: Variable i is **independent** iff i has zero indegree (no edges directed into i). Otherwise i is **dependent**.

Note that the *property* of independence is completely distinct from the *relation* of statistical independence. The context will make clear in which of these senses the term is used.

Each dependent variable has an "error variable" attached to it. In the actual operation of the TETRAD program these variables do not have to be explicitly given as input to the program; when a model is entered into TETRAD, it automatically adds an error variable to each dependent variable in the model.

Later, we will write various arithmetic expressions involving covariances and variances as sums, products, differences, and quotients of labels of treks and paths. In what follows we shall loosely interchange speaking of a monomial in an equation and the treks and paths whose labels it contains. For example, when a trek t is said to be equal to the product of two other treks p and q, this means that the product of labels of edges in t is equal to the result of multiplying the product of labels of edges in p by the product of labels of edges in q.

If t_1, t_2, t_3, and t_4 are distinct treks, it is possible for the product of labels of edges in t_1 and t_2 to be equal to the product of labels of edges in t_3 and t_4. This is because the same edges can occur in t_1 and t_2 as in t_3 and t_4, but be distributed between the treks differently. Similarly, it is possible for the monomial containing (the labels of) $t_1 t_2$ to be equal to the monomial containing (the labels of) $t_3 t_4$ even though they contain different treks.

Definition 7: In a SLCT, a **tetrad equation among four distinct variables x, y ,z, w** is any of

$$\gamma_{xy}\gamma_{zw} = \gamma_{xz}\gamma_{yw}$$

$$\gamma_{xy}\gamma_{zw} = \gamma_{xw}\gamma_{yz}$$

$$\gamma_{xz}\gamma_{yw} = \gamma_{xw}\gamma_{yz}$$

or an equivalent equation. A tetrad equation is also called a **vanishing tetrad difference**.

In a SLCT, a **partial equation among three distinct variables x, y, z** is any of

$$\rho_{xy.z} = 0$$

$$\rho_{yz.x} = 0$$

$$\rho_{xz.y} = 0$$

or an equivalent equation. A partial equation is also called a **vanishing partial correlation**.

A tetrad equation or partial equation is **strongly implied** by a SLCT $<<R,E>,(\Omega,P), X, L>$ iff it is implied by every theory $<<R,E>, (\Omega,P),X', L'>$ (that is, the theory implies the tetrad or partial equation for every value of the equation coefficients in X).

For the sake of brevity we will use "implied" synonomously with "strongly implied". In all of the following lemmas it will be assumed that tetrad and partial equations are among non-error variables only.

Mason's Rule

Mason has shown how to express the coefficient of a variable j in the equation of i in terms of the open paths connecting j to i and the loops in the graph. We will introduce a series of definitions needed to understand Mason's rule, stated in theorem 1.

Definition 8: Given a SLCT let P_{ij} be the set of paths from i to j.

Let $P_{ij}{}^o$ be the set of open paths from i to j.

Let T_{ij} be the set of treks between i and j.

We shall adopt the following conventions. Any lower case letter except t indexed by two variables i and j (such as p_{ij}) will represent a path in $P^o{}_{ij}$. t_{ij} will represent a trek in T_{ij}. $S(t_{ij})$ represents the source of the trek t_{ij}. "w.l.g." abbreviates "without loss of generality", "r.h.s." abbreviates "right hand side", and "l.h.s." abbreviates "left hand side".

Definition 9: An **independent equation for a dependent variable j in a SLCT <<R,E>,(Ω,P), X, L>** is an equation implied by X in which the variables which appear on the r.h.s. are independent and have a non-zero coefficient, and each variable occurs at most once on the r.h.s.

For example, in example 1 the equation $y = a_{yv}v$ is not an independent equation for y because v is not an independent variable. However, $y = a_{yv}a_{vu}u$ is an independent equation for y because all of the variables on the r.h.s. are independent variables, and each variable on the r.h.s. occurs at most once. In a given SLCT, the r.h.s. of every independent equation for a given dependent variable contains the same variables with the same coefficients.

We will adopt the following conventions. The set of independent variables in the theory is represented by "I". The sum over an empty set is equal to 0 and the product over an empty set is 1.

Definition 10: The **distributed form** of an expression or equation E is the result of carrying out every multiplication, but no additions, differences, or divisions in E.

If there are no divisions in an equation then its distributed form is a sum of monomials. For example, the distributed form of the equation $u = (a + b)(c + d)v$ is $u = acv + adv + bcv + bdv$.

Definition 11: Two expressions are **identically equal** iff they are equal for all values of the equation coefficients occurring in them.

If an expression is equal to ce, where c is a non-zero constant, and e is a product of equation coefficients raised to a positive integral power, then e is the **equation coefficient factor** of ce, and c is the **constant factor** of ce.

Henceforth, when we write "equal" or "=" in reference to products of labels of paths or treks we will mean identically equal unless we explicitly state otherwise. Similarly, "not equal" or "≠" in reference to products of labels of paths or treks will mean not identically equal unless we explicity state otherwise.

Definition 12: In a SLCT, a **loop** is a path of at least length 1 in which the source equals the sink, and no vertex (except the source) occurs in the path more than once; the source appears exactly twice.

A **loop touches an open path** iff the loop and the open path intersect in a vertex which is not the source of the open path. A **loop touches a loop** iff the two loops intersect.

A **loop is relevant to the variables i and j** iff it either touches some open path between i and j or it touches another loop relevant to the variables i and j.

U_x is the set of all independent variables that are the source of an open path to x. (Note that if x is independent then $x \in U_x$ since there is an empty path from every vertex to itself.)

U_{xy} is $U_x \cap U_y$.

RL_{ij} is the set of loops relevant to the variables i and j.

TL_{ij} is the set of loops touching any open path between i and j.

$*$ is a special operation on any expression e consisting of sums, products, and differences of labels of paths and loops in distributed form, in which all monomials in e that contain any two loops that touch or any loop touching a path are deleted.

E_{ij} is the **total effect of i on j**. By definition it is equal to

$$E_{ij} = \frac{\left[\sum_{p \in P_{ij}^{0}} L(p) \prod_{z \in RL_{ij}} \left(1 - L(z) \right) \right] *}{\prod_{z \in RL_{ij}} \left(1 - L(z) \right) *}$$

E^n_{ij} is the numerator of the total effect of i on j.

E^d_{ij} is the denominator of the total effect of i on j.

E^o_{ij} is the effect of the open paths from i to j. By definition, it is equal to

$$\sum_{p \varepsilon P_{ij}^0} L(p)$$

We will adopt the convention that E_{ii} is equal to 1.

The following theorem is Mason's rule. The proof of the theorem can be found in [3].

Theorem 1: If i is independent, then the coefficient of i in the independent equation for j is E_{ij}.

TETRAD's Algorithm for Determining the Tetrad Equations Implied by a SLCT

In this section, the algorithm TETRAD uses for determining the tetrad equations strongly implied by a graph are described, illustrated, and proved correct.

We will demonstrate below that in an acyclic SLCT a product of covariances $\gamma_{ij}\gamma_{kl}$ is equal to

$$\left[\sum_{t \varepsilon T_{ij}} L(t)\sigma^2_{S(t)}\right]\left[\sum_{t \varepsilon T_{kl}} L(t)\sigma^2_{S(t)}\right]$$

Tetrad represents a product of covariances occurring in tetrad equations by an expression which does not contain the variances of the sources of treks. The expression that TETRAD uses to represent a product of covariances P is *not* in general equal to P. However, the form that TETRAD represents P in does contain enough information (in conjunction with its representation of P') to determine whether or not a tetrad equation P = P' is implied by a given SLCT. For that reason the form that TETRAD represents products of covariances in will be called the Tetrad trek form of a product of covariances, even though the expression is not in general equal to a product of covariances. The **Tetrad trek form** of a product of covariances γ_{ij} and γ_{kl} is the distributed form of

$$\left[\sum_{t \varepsilon T_{ij}} L(t)\right]\left[\sum_{t \varepsilon T_{kl}} L(t)\right]$$

If the products of covariances in a tetrad equation are in Tetrad trek form then by extension we will say the tetrad equation is in Tetrad trek form. Note that each monomial in the product of covariances in Tetrad trek form is the product of two treks.

We will prove theorems about equations which are sums of monomials. Each monomial consists of a product of

1. equation coefficients raised to some positive integral power (products of open paths and loops)

2. a non-zero constant (a product of variances of independent variables)

3. one or negative one. (In the former case the monomial is said to be positive and have a positive constant factor, and in the latter case it is said to be negative and have a negative constant factor.)

In order to show that two such sums of monomials M and M' are identically equal it suffices to show that there is a one-to-one function mapping monomials in M onto identically equal monomials in M'.

Proving that two sums of monomials are not equal is a little harder. There are several reasons why there could fail to be a one-to-one function mapping monomials in M onto identically equal monomials in M' even though the sum of the monomials in M is identically equal to the sum of monomials in M'.

1. It could be that several monomials in M which are not identically equal to any monomial in M' sum to 0. For example if M is <a, -a, b> and M' = <b>, the sum of the monomials in M identically equals the sum of monomials in M' even though M' contains no monomial equal to a or -a. Note that a monomial m can be in a set of monomials in M that sum to 0 only if there is a monomial m' in M such that m and m' have identically equal equation coefficient factors but constant factors of opposite sign.

2. It could be that there is a sum of monomials in M equal to a sum of monomials in M'. For example, if M = <a, a, b> and M' = <2a, b> then the sum of the monomials in M identically equals the sum of monomials in M' even though M' contains no monomial equal to a. Note, however, that a sum m of monomials in M equals a sum of monomials m' in M' only if each monomial in m has an equation coefficient factor identically equal to the equation coefficient factor of some monomial in m', and vice-versa.

Taking into account these considerations, in order to show that the sum of monomials in M is not equal to the sum of monomials in M' it suffices to show that there exists a monomial m ε M such that

1. there is no monomial m' in M such that the constant factor of m is of

opposite sign of the constant factor of m', but the equation coefficient factor of m is equal to the equation coefficient factor of m', and

2. there is no monomial in M' whose equation coefficient factor equals the equation coefficient factor of m.

In the case of acyclic graphs each monomial in the equations we will consider is positive, so the first condition is satisfied. The only negative monomials in the equations that we will consider are monomials containing loops.

The Algorithm

Tetrad computes whether or not a given tetrad equation

$$\gamma_{uv} \, \gamma_{wx} = \gamma_{ux} \, \gamma_{vw}$$

is strongly implied by a given graph in the following way.

1. Tetrad attaches a unique error term to each dependent variable. Each error term is correlated only with the dependent variable it is associated with.

2. It computes

$$\sum_{t \in T_{uv}} L(t) \, , \, \sum_{t \in T_{wx}} L(t) \, , \, \sum_{t \in T_{ux}} L(t) \, , \text{ and } \sum_{t \in T_{vw}} L(t)$$

It forms the l.h.s. of the equation by the following multiplication, putting the product in distributed form.

$$\left[\sum_{t \in T_{uv}} L(t) \right] \left[\sum_{t \in T_{wx}} L(t) \right]$$

It forms the r.h.s. of the equation in an analogous way.

3. If there is any monomial on the l.h.s. of the equation that is not identically equal to any monomial on the r.h.s. of the equation, or vice-versa, it concludes that the tetrad equation is not strongly implied by the graph; otherwise it concludes that it is strongly implied by the graph.

An Example of the Algorithm

This procedure can be illustrated with the following example. Suppose that the graph in Fig. 10-7 is entered into Tetrad. Tetrad will perform the following actions.

1. First, it attaches a unique error term to each dependent variable. Each error term is uncorrelated with any variable except the dependent variable it is associated with. The graph depicted in Fig. 10-9 is formed.

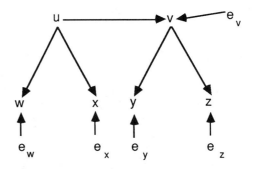

Figure 10-9: TETRAD adds error variables.

2. Next, it computes the sum of the products of labels of edges in every trek between every pair of variables in the tetrad equation.

Variable Pair	Trek Products
yz	$a_{yv}a_{zv}$
wx	$a_{wu}a_{xu}$
wz	$a_{wu}a_{vu}a_{zv}$
xy	$a_{xu}a_{vu}a_{yv}$

3. The l.h.s. and r.h.s. of the equation are formed as follows.

L.H.S. $a_{yv}a_{zv}a_{wu}a_{xu}$

R.H.S. $a_{wu}a_{vu}a_{zv}a_{xu}a_{vu}a_{yv}$

4. Finally, Tetrad compares the l.h.s. to the r.h.s. In this case the two sides are different, so it concludes that the tetrad equation is not strongly implied by the graph.

(Note that the graph depicted in example 1 does strongly imply this tetrad equation. But the graph with the inclusion of the error terms does not strongly imply the equation.) Tetrad does *not* directly calculate the covariances of any variable pairs when it determines which tetrad equations are strongly implied. The covariances depend upon

1. the variances of independent variables

2. the open paths in the graph, and

3. the cycles in the graph.

TETRAD examines only certain open paths in determining which tetrad equations and which vanishing partial correlations are implied. For these reasons, it is necessary to show that ignoring the variances of the sources of treks in calculations leads to the correct identification of tetrad equations strongly implied by a SLCT. This is done in the next two sections.

TETRAD's Algorithm Finds Only Tetrad Equations Strongly Implied by an Acyclic SLCT

In this section we will prove that every tetrad equation identified by TETRAD's algorithm as strongly implied by a SLCT S is strongly implied by S.

Lemma 1: In a SLCT, if i and j are two distinct independent variables, then no edge out of i occurs in any path containing j.

Proof: Let edge e out of i be in a path p. If j occurs in the same path p, then j either occurs before i or after i. If it occurs before i then i is not independent. If it occurs after i then j is not independent. Q.E.D.

Lemma 2: In a SLCT, no two treks in a monomial in a tetrad equation in Tetrad trek form have any terminus in common.

Proof: This follows directly from the definition of a tetrad equation and

Tetrad trek form.
Q.E.D.

Lemma 3: In a SLCT, if t is a trek with source i and t contains at most one edge out of i, then i is one of the termini of t.

Proof: If t contains only one edge out of its source, then one of the paths in t must be the empty path <i>. Since the sink of an empty path is equal to the source of an empty path, i is a sink of one path in t, and hence one of the termini of t.
Q.E.D.

Lemma 4: If t is a trek in SLCT S that contains an edge out of i, then either i is the source of the trek, or t contains a non-empty open path from the source of t to i.

Proof: Suppose that there is no non-empty open path from the source of t to i. Then one of the paths in t is <i>. It follows that i is the source of the trek.
Q.E.D.

Lemma 5: In a SLCT, if i is the source of a trek t, and i is not equal to k, then t contains at most one edge out of k.

Proof: Suppose, contrary to the lemma, that two edges out of k do occur in t. From the definition of an open path, it follows that the two edges of k do not both occur in a single open path. However, if the two edges out of k occur in distinct paths in the trek, then the two paths intersect at k. The two paths of a trek can intersect only at the source, and by hypothesis k is not the source of the trek. This is a contradiction.
Q.E.D.

Lemma 6: Given a tetrad equation among variables of an acyclic SLCT written in Tetrad trek form, for each monomial P on the l.h.s. that is identically equal to a monomial P' on the r.h.s., the set of sources of P is equal to the set of sources of P'.

Proof: P and P' each consist of the products of labels of edges in two treks. Let i and j be the sources of the treks of P, and k and z be the sources of the treks of P'. (We do not rule out the possibility that any of the four sources are equal.) In what follows T(x) will represent the trek with source x.

Suppose, contrary to the lemma, that P = P' but {i,j} is *not* equal to {k,z}. Since {i,j} is not equal to {k,z} it follows that there is a vertex on one side which is not equal to either vertex on the other side. Suppose, w.l.g. that i is not equal to k or z. By lemma 4, in order for the label of an edge out of i to appear in P', there are four possibilities.

1. There is a non-empty open path in T(k) from k to i.

2. There is a non-empty open path in T(z) from z to i.

3. i = k.

4. i = z.

The last two possibilities are false by hypothesis. We will assume w.l.g. that there is a non-empty open path in T(k) from k to i.

Similarly, the label of an edge out of k must appear in P. By lemma 4 there are four possibilites.

1. There is a non-empty open path in T(j) from j to k.

2. j = k.

3. i = k.

4. There is a non-empty open path in T(i) from i to k.

The third possibility is false by hypothesis. The fourth possibility is ruled out since it implies that there is a non-empty path from k to i and a non-empty path from i to k whose concatenation would form a cycle. This leaves the first two possibilities, each of which will be considered in turn. See Figs. 10-10 and 10-11.

Figure 10-10: Path from j to k.

Figure 10-11: j equals k.

The label of an edge out of z appears in P. By lemma 4 there are four possiblities.

1. There is a non-empty open path in T(i) from i to z.

2. There is a non-empty open path in T(j) from j to z.

3. j = z.

4. i = z.

The last possibility has been eliminated by hypothesis. This leaves three possibilities. Starting from the two cases of Figs. 10-10 and 10-11 this makes a total of six possible cases. It will now be shown that each of these cases is impossible.

Cases 1 and 2. See Figs. 10-12 and 10-13. The label of an edge out of j occurs in P'. By lemma 4, there are four possibilites.

1. There is a non-empty open path in T(k) from k to j.

2. There is a non-empty open path in T(z) from z to j.

3. k = j.

4. z = j.

If there are non-empty paths from either k or z to j then the graph has a cycle, which is a contradiction. If k = j, there is a cycle in the graph since by assumption there is a non-empty path from j to k. The fourth possiblity is covered in the cases below.

Figure 10-12: Case 1.

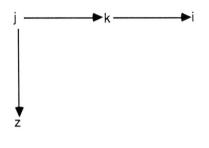

Figure 10-13: Case 2.

Case 3. See Fig. 10-14.

1. Let b be a non-empty path in T(k) from k to i, and a be a non-empty path in T(j) from j to k. T(j) contains every edge in b, since b appears on the r.h.s., and so must appear on the l.h.s. If it appears on the l.h.s., each of the edges in b appear in T(i) or T(j). However, T(i) cannot contain any edge in b, since this would imply that there was a cycle in the graph; hence, T(j) must contain every edge in b.

2. T(z) contains every edge in a. T(j) contains a and hence every edge in a appears on the r.h.s. Each edge in a occurs in T(k) or T(z). No edge in a occurs in T(k), since this would imply that there was a cycle in the graph. Therefore, every edge in a occurs in T(z).

3. The r.h.s. contains only one edge out of k. This can be shown by a reductio ad absurdum argument. Suppose that there are two edges out of k. Now neither of these edges occurs in T(i), since that would imply that there is a cycle. Therefore, both edges occur in T(j). But by lemma 5, T(j) contains only one edge out of k. It follows that there is only one edge on the r.h.s. out of k.

4. k is a terminus of T(k), by lemma 3.

5. k is a terminus of T(z). It has already been shown that T(z) contains a path from z to k. Since there is only one edge on the r.h.s. out of k, and that edge is in T(k), the sink of one of the paths in T(z) is k. This implies that k is a terminus of T(z). By lemma 2 this is a contradiction.

Figure 10-14: Case 3.

Case 4. See Fig. 10-15.

1. If the r.h.s. has two edges out of z, then there is a non-empty path from i to z in T(i). If there were no non-empty path from i to z in T(i) then both edges out of z would be in T(j). But since j is not equal to z, by lemma 5 T(j) does not contain two edges out of z. Hence, one of the edges out of z occurs in T(i). Since i is not equal to z, by lemma 4 there is a non-empty path from i to z in T(i).

2. Similarly, if the l.h.s. has two edges out of i, there is a non-empty path from z to i in T(z).

3. Either the r.h.s. contains at most one edge out of z or the l.h.s. contains at most one edge out of i. Otherwise there would be a non-empty path from i to z and a non-empty path from z to i. This would imply that there is a cycle in the graph, which is a contradiction.

4. Assume w.l.g. that the l.h.s. contains at most one edge out of i. It follows from lemma 3 that i is the terminus of a trek on the l.h.s.

5. T(j) contains a non-empty path to i since T(k) contains a non-empty path to i. All of the edges in this path appear on the l.h.s. and hence appear either in T(j) or T(i). No such edge appears in T(i), since this would imply that the graph had a cycle. Hence they all appear in T(j).

6. T(j) does not contain an edge out of i, since the l.h.s. contains at most one edge out of i, and T(i) contains at least one edge out of i.

7. i is one of the termini of T(j), since T(j) contains a non-empty path from j to i that terminates at i.

8. i is a terminus for two treks on the l.h.s. This contradicts lemma 2.

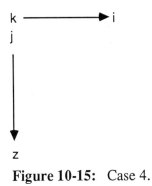

Figure 10-15: Case 4.

Case 5. See Fig. 10-16. The proof for this is the same as for Case 3, with z, k, i, and j substituted for i, j, k, and z respectively.

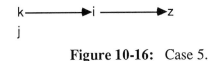

Figure 10-16: Case 5.

Case 6. See Fig. 10-17.

1. The l.h.s. contains at most one edge out of i. For suppose that there were two edges out of i on the l.h.s. By lemma 5, if there were two edges out of i, then both T(k) and T(z) would contain non-empty paths to i. None of the edges in these non-empty paths appear in T(i), since the graph is acyclic. Hence both non-empty paths appear in T(j). But this contradicts the definition of

a trek, since the paths in the trek intersect at a vertex that is not the source.

2. i is a terminus of T(i), by lemma 3.

3. T(j) contains a non-empty path to i, since T(k) contains a non-empty path from k to i. The edges in this path all appear on the l.h.s., so each of them appears in either T(i) or T(j). No such edge appears in T(i), since that would imply that the graph had a cycle. Therefore, each such edge appears in T(j).

4. T(j) does not contain any edge out of i, since the l.h.s. contains only one edge out of i, and T(i) contains that edge.

5. i is a terminus of T(j), since T(j) contains a path that terminates at i.

6. We have shown that i is the terminus of two treks on the l.h.s. But that contradicts lemma 2.

Figure 10-17: Case 6.

By Cases 1-6, it follows that the set of sources of the treks appearing on the l.h.s. equals the set of sources of the treks appearing on the r.h.s. Q.E.D.

Lemma 7: If

1. S is an acyclic SLCT

2. u, i, and j are variables in S

3. i ≠ j

4. p_{ui} is a path from u to i and v_{uj} is a path from u to j

then there exists at least one trek $t \varepsilon T_{ij}$ such that $p_{ui} = p_{uS(t)}\&t_i$ and $v_{uj} = v_{uS(t)}\&t_j$.

Proof: Since p_{ui} and v_{uj} have a common source they intersect. Let q be the last vertex in p_{ui} that intersects v_{uj}, r be the subpath of p_{ui} with source q, and s be the subpath of v_{uj} with source q. See Fig. 10-18. By the way that r and s are defined it follows that $p_{ui} = p_{uq}\&r$ and $v_{uj} = v_{uq}\&s$.

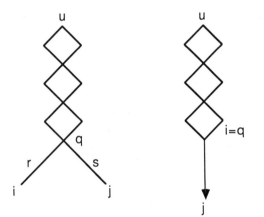

Figure 10-18: Trek T_{ij}.

The lemma is proved if we now show that q is the source of a trek t_{ij}. Note that r and s are not both empty, since that would imply that p_{ui} and v_{uj} intersect at their respective sinks, i and j. By hypothesis, however, i and j are distinct, so p_{ui} and v_{uj} do not intersect at their respective sinks. Furthermore r and s intersect only at q since by hypothesis no point on p_{ui} after q intersects any point on p_{uj}. r is an open path from q to i, s is an open path from q to j, one of r and s is non-empty, and r and s intersect only at q. This implies that q is the source of a trek t_{ij} consisting of r and s.
Q.E.D.

Lemma 8: If

1. S is an acyclic SLCT

2. u, i, and j are variables in S

3. $i \neq j$

4. p_{ui} is a path from u to i and v_{uj} is a path from u to j

then there exists at most one trek $t \in T_{ij}$ such that $p_{ui} = p_{uS(t)}\&t_i$ and $v_{uj} = v_{uS(t)}\&t_j$.

Proof: Let t_{ij} and t'_{ij} be treks such that $p_{ui} = p_{uS(t)}\&t_i = p'_{uS(t')}\&t'_i$ and $v_{uj} = v_{uS(t)}\&t_j = v'_{uS(t')}\&t'_j$.

We will show that $S(t) = S(t')$. Suppose $S(t) \neq S(t')$. $S(t)$ and $S(t')$ occur on both p_{ui} and v_{uj}. W.l.g. suppose that $S(t)$ occurs later in p_{ui} than $S(t')$ does. Then $S(t)$ also occurs later in v_{uj} that $S(t')$ does. For otherwise there is a cycle $v_{S(t)S(t')}\&p_{S(t')S(t)}$. Since $S(t)$ occurs later than $S(t')$ in both p_{ui} and v_{uj} it follows that t'_{ij} is not a trek, since $S(t)$ is not the source of t' but is a point of intersection of the paths in t'. This is a contradiction.

Since $S(t) = S(t')$ and the graph is acyclic, $p_{S(t)i} = t_i = t'_i$ and $v_{S(t)j} = t_j = t'_j$.
Q.E.D.

The following two lemmas show how to calculate the variance of random variables and covariances between random variables in terms of the covariances between other random variables. The proofs of these lemmas can be found in [2].

Lemma 9: If Q is a set of random variables with a joint probability distribution and

$$y = \sum_{j \in Q} a_j j$$

and

$$z = \sum_{j \in Q} b_j j$$

then

$$\gamma_{yz} = \sum_{i \in Q} \sum_{j \in Q} a_i b_j \gamma_{ij}$$

Lemma 10: If Q is a set of random variables with a joint probability distribution and

$$y = \sum_{j \in Q} a_j j$$

then

$$\sigma^2_y = \sum_{i \in Q} \sum_{j \in Q} a_i a_j \gamma_{ij}$$

Lemma 11: If

$$y = \sum_{j \in I} a_j j$$

and

$$z = \sum_{j \in I} b_j j$$

then

$$\gamma_{yz} = \sum_{i \in U_{yz}} a_i b_i \sigma^2_i$$

Proof: I is a set of independent variables. It follows that γ_{ij} is equal to 0 if $i \neq j$, and γ_{ij} is equal to σ^2_i if $i = j$. Substituting these values for γ_{ij} into the r.h.s. of the equation for γ_{yz} in lemma 9 shows that

$$\gamma_{yz} = \sum_{i \in I} a_i b_i \sigma^2_i$$

If i is in I, but i is not in U_{yz} then there are not open paths from i to y and z and it follows by Mason's rule that either a_i or b_i is zero. So the only non-zero terms in the sum are for $i \in U_{yz}$.
Q.E.D.

Lemma 12: If

$$y = \sum_{j \varepsilon I} a_j j$$

then

$$\sigma^2_y = \sum_{i \varepsilon U_y} a_i^2 \sigma^2_i$$

Proof: I is a set of independent random variables. It follows that γ_{ij} is equal to 0 if $i \neq j$, and γ_{ij} is equal to σ^2_i if $i = j$. Substituting these values for γ_{ij} into the r.h.s. of the equation for σ_y^2 in lemma 10 proves that

$$\sigma^2_y = \sum_{i \varepsilon I} a_i^2 \sigma^2_i$$

If i is in I, but i is not in U_y, then there is no path from i to y. It would follow by Mason's rule then that a_i is zero. Hence the only non-zero terms in the sum come from i in U_y.
Q.E.D.

Lemma 13:

$$\gamma_{xy} = \sum_{u \varepsilon U_{xy}} E_{ux} E_{uy} \sigma^2_u \qquad (1)$$

Proof: By Mason's rule, the coefficient of u in an independent equation for x is E_{ux}, and the coefficient of u in an independent equation for y is E_{uy}. The equation follows when these values for the coefficients are substituted into the r.h.s. of lemma 11.
Q.E.D.

Lemma 14:

$$\sigma^2_y = \sum_{u \varepsilon U_y} E_{uy} E_{uy} \sigma^2_u \qquad (2)$$

Proof: This is an immediate consequence of lemma 13.
Q.E.D.

The Fully Expanded Form of Tetrad and Partial Equations

We wish to put tetrad equations and partial equations in a form which consists of a sum of monomials, each of which is the product of

1. equation coefficients raised to some positive integral power (products of open paths and loops)

2. a non-zero constant (a product of variances of independent variables)

3. one or negative one.

In order to get the desired form, we will first prove some lemmas about partial equations.

Lemma 15: In a SLCT, if x, y, and z are distinct variables, then $\rho_{xz.y} = 0$ iff $\rho_{xz} = \rho_{xy}\rho_{yz}$.
Proof: By definition,

$$(3)$$

$$\rho_{xz.y} = \frac{\rho_{xz} - \rho_{xy}\rho_{yz}}{\sqrt{1 - \rho_{xy}^2}\sqrt{1 - \rho_{yz}^2}}$$

$\rho_{xz.y}$ is not well-defined unless ρ_{xy} and ρ_{yz} are not equal to one. We will now show that neither ρ_{xy} nor ρ_{yz} is equal to one. The only way that the correlation between x and y could be one is if x were a linear function of y alone. In that case either x or y is a dependent variable. Every dependent variable is a function of an error variable, and by hypothesis, none of x, y, and z is an error variable. It follows that x cannot be a linear function of y alone. Hence ρ_{xy} is not equal to one. Similarly it can be shown that ρ_{yz} is not equal to one. It follows that $\rho_{xz.y}$ is well-defined.

The l.h.s. of equation 3 equals 0 iff the numerator of the r.h.s. equals 0. Q.E.D.

Lemma 16: In a SLCT, if x, y, and z are distinct variables, then $\rho_{xz.y} = 0$ iff $\gamma_{xz}\sigma^2_y = \gamma_{xy}\gamma_{yz}$.
Proof: By lemma 15 $\rho_{xz.y} = 0$ iff $\rho_{xz} = \rho_{xy}\rho_{yz}$. By definition of correlation, $\rho_{xz} = \rho_{xy}\rho_{yz}$ implies that

$$\frac{\gamma_{xz}}{\sigma_x \sigma_z} = \frac{\gamma_{xy} \gamma_{yz}}{\sigma_z \sigma_x \sigma^2_y}$$

Multiplying each side by $\sigma^2_y \sigma_x \sigma_z$ we obtain

$$\gamma_{xz} \sigma^2_y = \gamma_{xy} \gamma_{yz}.$$

Q.E.D.

A partial equation $\rho_{xz.y} = 0$ is equivalent to the equation

(4)

$$\gamma_{xz} \sigma^2_y = \gamma_{xy} \gamma_{yz}.$$

By lemmas 13 and 14 the l.h.s. of equation 4 equals

$$\left[\sum_{u \varepsilon U_{xz}} \left(E_{ux} E_{uz} \sigma^2_u \right) \right] \left[\sum_{v \varepsilon U_y} \left(E_{vy} E_{vy} \sigma^2_v \right) \right]$$

which by definition is

$$\left[\sum_{u \varepsilon U_{xz}} \left(\frac{E^n_{ux} E^n_{uz} \sigma^2_u}{E^d_{ux} E^d_{uz}} \right) \right] \left[\sum_{v \varepsilon U_y} \left(\frac{E^n_{vy} E^n_{vy} \sigma^2_v}{E^d_{vy} E^d_{vy}} \right) \right]$$

We place each term on the l.h.s. of equation 4 over a common denominator D. In order to do this each $E^n_{ux} E^n_{uz} E^n_{vy} E^n_{vy}$ in the numerator is multiplied by a factor which for a particular u and v we will call d_{uv}. So the l.h.s. of equation 4 becomes

(5)

$$\sum_{u \varepsilon U_{xz}} \sum_{v \varepsilon U_y} \frac{E^n_{ux} E^n_{uz} E^n_{vy} E^n_{vy} d_{uv} \sigma^2_u \sigma^2_v}{D}$$

Similarly, each term on the r.h.s. of equation 4 can be placed over a common denominator D'. Then this expression becomes

(6)

$$\sum_{u \varepsilon U_{xy}} \sum_{v \varepsilon U_{yz}} \frac{E^n_{ux} E^n_{uy} E^n_{vy} E^n_{vz} d'_{uv} \sigma^2_u \sigma^2_v}{D'}$$

Multiply formulas 5 and 6 by DD'. Equation 4 is equivalent to

$$(7)$$

$$\sum_{u \in U_{xz}} \sum_{v \in U_y} E^n_{ux} E^n_{uz} E^n_{vy} E^n_{vy} d_{uv} D' \sigma^2_u \sigma^2_v$$

$$= \sum_{u \in U_{xy}} \sum_{v \in U_{yz}} E^n_{ux} E^n_{uy} E^n_{vy} E^n_{vz} d'_{uv} D \sigma^2_u \sigma^2_v$$

Similarly, a covariance equation $\gamma_{xy}\gamma_{zw} = \gamma_{xz}\gamma_{yw}$ can be written as

$$(8)$$

$$\sum_{u \in U_{xy}} \sum_{v \in U_{zw}} E^n_{ux} E^n_{uy} E^n_{vz} E^n_{vw} d_{uv} D' \sigma^2_u \sigma^2_v$$

$$= \sum_{u \in U_{xz}} \sum_{v \in U_{yw}} E^n_{ux} E^n_{uz} E^n_{vy} E^n_{vw} d'_{uv} D \sigma^2_u \sigma^2_v$$

D, D', d_{uv}, and d'_{uv} are all products of E^d terms. Hence each term in equations 7 and 8 consists of products of E^n and E^d terms times a product of variances.

Forming the **fully expanded form of a partial equation** is a two step process.

1. In the distributed form of equation 7 replace each E^n and E^d factor by its definition in terms of products of loops and paths.

2. Take the distributed form of the resulting equation.

The **fully expanded form of a tetrad equation** is formed in the analogous way from equation 8. [fully expanded tetrad equation]

By extension, we will say that either side of a tetrad equation (a product of covariances) or a partial equation is in fully expanded form if it is the distributed form of one side of equations 8 or 7 respectively.

In the case of an acyclic SLCT, d_{uv}, d'_{uv}, D, and D' are all equal to one. In the case of a cyclic SLCT, each d_{uv}, d'_{uv}, D, and D' factor in a monomial in the fully expanded form of a tetrad or partial equation is either one or a product of loops. The following example illustrates the differences between Tetrad trek form and fully expanded form of a product of covariances (one side of a tetrad equation) in an acyclic SLCT. Since in the case of an acyclic SLCT all of the d_{uv}, d'_{uv}, D, and D' are equal to one, we won't have to examine the other side of the tetrad equation. In this example we have set the labels of all edges from error variables to one. The SLCT in the example is the one depicted in Fig. 10-19.

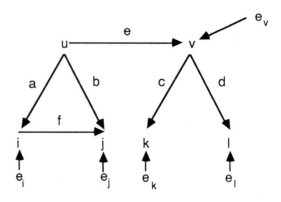

Figure 10-19: Example used to illustrate equation forms.

$$\gamma_{ij} = (ab + fa^2)\sigma^2_u + f\sigma^2_{e_i}$$

$$\gamma_{kl} = cde^2\sigma^2_u + cd\sigma^2_{e_v}$$

Tetrad trek form

$$\gamma_{ij}\gamma_{kl} = abcd + cdf$$

Fully expanded form

$$\gamma_{ij}\gamma_{kl} = abcde^2\sigma^4_u + fa^2cde^2\sigma^4_u + abcd\sigma^2_u\sigma^2_{e_v} + fa^2cd\sigma^2_u\sigma^2_{e_v}$$
$$+ cde^2f\sigma^2_u\sigma^2_{e_i} + cdf\sigma^2_{e_v}\sigma^2_{e_i}$$

Given the SLCT in Fig. 10-19 one term in equation 8 is $E^n_{ui}E^n_{uj}E^n_{uk}E^n_{ul}\sigma^4_u$. Using the definition of E^n, $E^n_{ui} = a$, $E^n_{uj} = (b + af)$, $E^n_{uk} = ce$, and $E^n_{ul} = de$. Placing these values into $E^n_{ui}E^n_{uj}E^n_{uk}E^n_{ul}\sigma^4_u$ the result is $a(b + af)cede\sigma^4_u$. Taking the distributed form of $a(b + af)cede\sigma^4_u$ the result is $abcde^2\sigma^4_u + a^2cde^2f\sigma^4_u$, which are two of the monomials appearing in the fully expanded form.

Note that a monomial in the Tetrad trek form of the product of two covariances is the product of two treks. A monomial in the fully expanded form of the product of two covariances in a SLCT is a product of open paths and loops. The open paths from a given independent variable u can be formed into treks and paths from u to the sources of the treks.

Lemma 17: In an acyclic SLCT, if i is independent, then the coefficient of i in an independent equation for j is equal to

$$\sum_{p \in P_{ij}^0} L(p)$$

Proof: In an acyclic SLCT,

$$\prod_{z \in RL_{ij}} \left(1 - L(z) \right)$$

is equal to one. The lemma follows from this fact, the definition of E_{ij}, and Mason's rule.
Q.E.D.

Lemma 18: Given an acyclic SLCT and two distinct variables i and j

$$(9)$$

$$\gamma_{ij} = \sum_{t \in T_{ij}} \left(L(t) \, \sigma^2_{S(t)} \right)$$

Proof: By lemmas 17 and 13

$$(10)$$

$$\gamma_{ij} = \sum_{u \in U_{ij}} \left[\left(\sum_{p \in P^O_{ui}} L(p) \right) \left(\sum_{q \in P^O_{uj}} L(q) \right) \left(\sigma^2_u \right) \right]$$

By lemmas 17 and 14

$$(11)$$

$$\sum_{t \in T_{ij}} \left(L(t) \, \sigma^2_{S(t)} \right)$$

$$= \sum_{t \in T_{ij}} \left[L(t) \sum_{u \in U_{S(t)}} \left(\left(\sum_{a \in P^O_{uS(t)}} L(a) \right) \left(\sum_{b \in P^O_{uS(t)}} L(b) \right) \sigma^2_u \right) \right]$$

We will call the r.h.s. of equation 10 expression 10 and the r.h.s. of equation 11 expression 11. We will show that expressions 10 and 11 are equal by showing that there is a one-to-one function f mapping monomials in expression 10 to equal monomials in expression 11.

U_{ij} is empty iff T_{ij} is empty. Hence, expression 10 is equal to 0 iff expression 11 is equal to 0.

Suppose then that U_{ij} is not empty. One monomial in expression 10 is equal to $L(p)L(q)\sigma^2_u$ where $p \ \varepsilon \ P^o_{ui}$ and $q \ \varepsilon \ P^o_{uj}$. One monomial in expression 11 is $L(t)L(a)L(b)\sigma^2_u$, where $a \ \varepsilon \ P^o_{uS(t)}$ and $b \ \varepsilon \ P^o_{uS(t)}$.

By lemmas 7 and 8, for each pair of paths $p \ \varepsilon \ P^o_{ui}$ and $q \ \varepsilon \ P^o_{uj}$ there is a unique t, $a \ \varepsilon \ P^o_{uS(t)}$, and $b \ \varepsilon \ P^o_{uS(t)}$ such that $p = a\&t_i$ and $q = b\&t_j$. Let f map $L(p)L(q)\sigma^2_u$ to $L(t)L(a)L(b)\sigma^2_u$. Clearly for each monomial m, $f(m) = m$.

For every monomial m in expression 11 there is a monomial m' in expression 10 such that $m = f(m')$, since $a\&t_i \ \varepsilon \ P^o_{ui}$ and $b\&t_j \ \varepsilon \ P^o_{uj}$, and $f(L(a\&t_i)L(b\&t_j)) = m$.

Finally, we will show that if m and m' contain different paths, then f(m) and f(m') contain different paths or treks. If m and m' contain different paths, then since the SLCT is acyclic, they contain different vertices and $m \neq m'$. Since $m = f(m)$ and $m' = f(m')$ it follows that $f(m) \neq f(m')$, which implies that f(m) and f(m') contain different paths or treks.

It follows that f is a one-to-one function from monomials in expression 10 to equal monomials in expression 11. Hence, expression 10 equals expression 11.
Q.E.D.

According to lemma 18 a tetrad equation $\gamma_{ij}\gamma_{kl} = \gamma_{jk}\gamma_{il}$ can be written in the form

$$\tag{12}$$

$$\left[\sum_{t \ \varepsilon \ T_{ij}} L(t)\sigma^2_{S(t)}\right]\left[\sum_{t \ \varepsilon \ T_{kl}} L(t)\sigma^2_{S(t)}\right]$$

$$= \left[\sum_{t \ \varepsilon \ T_{jk}} L(t)\sigma^2_{S(t)}\right]\left[\sum_{t \ \varepsilon \ T_{il}} L(t)\sigma^2_{S(t)}\right]$$

Call the distributed form of this equation the **full trek form** of the tetrad equation.

Lemma 19: Given a tetrad equation F among variables of an acyclic SLCT written in Tetrad trek form, if there is a one-to-one function f mapping each monomial P on the l.h.s. of F to an identically equal monomial P' on the r.h.s., then F is strongly implied by the SLCT.

Proof: The Tetrad trek form of F is the same as the full trek form except that in the Tetrad trek form the variances are left out of each monomial. It follows from lemma 6 that if P = P' then the set of sources of P equals the set of sources of P'. Hence, if P = P' then P times the variances of the sources of the treks in P equals P' times the variances of the sources of the treks in P'. It follows that P = P' iff the monomials corresponding to P and P' in the full trek form are equal. Hence, if there is a one-to-one function mapping monomials on the l.h.s. of the Tetrad trek form of F onto equal monomials on the r.h.s., then there is a one-to-one function mapping monomials on the l.h.s. of the full trek form of F onto equal monomials on the r.h.s. This implies the SLCT strongly implies F. Q.E.D.

TETRAD's Algorithm Finds All Tetrad Equations Strongly Implied by an Acyclic SLCT

In this section it will be proved TETRAD's algorithm finds all strongly implied tetrad equations in an acylic graph. This amounts to showing that if a tetrad equation is strongly implied by a SLCT then when products of covariances of the variables are written in Tetrad trek form, there is a one-to-one function f mapping each monomial P on the l.h.s. of the equation to an identically equal monomial P' on the r.h.s.

Lemma 20: If a tetrad equation is strongly implied by an acyclic SLCT, then when the tetrad equation is written in Tetrad trek form, there is a one-to-one function mapping each monomial on the l.h.s. onto an identically equal monomial on the r.h.s.

Proof: Suppose that $\gamma_{ij}\gamma_{kl} = \gamma_{jk}\gamma_{il}$ is strongly implied by a SLCT. In each monomial in the full trek form of this equation we will call the products of labels of the treks the equation coefficient factors, and the products of the variances of the sources the constant factors.

Since the tetrad equation is strongly implied, there is a one-to-one function mapping monomials on the l.h.s. of the full trek form onto identically equal monomials on the r.h.s., for the following reasons. Suppose not. There are two cases

1. there is a monomial on one side that is not on the other side, but is part of a sum of monomials equal to zero, or

2. there is a sum of monomials on the l.h.s., each with equation coefficent factor e, that is equal to a sum of monomials on the r.h.s., each with equation coefficient factor e, but no one-to-one function mapping monomials with equation coefficient factors e on the l.h.s. onto equal monomials on the r.h.s.

The first case is impossible. Since there are no loops in an acylic SLCT, there are no negative monomials in the full trek form, and hence no sum of monomials on the r.h.s. or on the l.h.s. equals zero.

The second case is also impossible. By lemma 6, each pair of monomials with equation coefficient factor e also has equal constant factors. The only way that there could be no one-to-one function mapping the monomials with equation coefficient factors e on the l.h.s. onto monomials with equation coefficient factors e on the r.h.s. is if there were more monomials on one side with equation coefficient factor e than on the other side. If that were the case, then the sum of the monomials containing e on each side would not be equal. This is a contradiction.

The Tetrad trek form of the tetrad equation is the same as the full trek form except that the constant factors (the products of variances) are left out of each monomial. It follows that if there is a one-to-one function mapping monomials on the l.h.s. of the full trek form of the tetrad equation onto equal monomials on the r.h.s., then there is a one-to-one function mapping monomials on the l.h.s. of the Tetrad trek form of the tetrad equation onto equal monomials on the r.h.s.
Q.E.D.

TETRAD's Algorithm for Identifying Implied Tetrad Equations is Correct

Theorem 2: A tetrad equation is strongly implied by an acyclic SLCT iff when the equation is written in Tetrad trek form, there is a one-to-one function f mapping each monomial P on the l.h.s. of the equation to an identically equal monomial P' on the r.h.s.

Proof: This follows immediately from lemmas 20 and 19.
Q.E.D.

A Tetrad Equation Among Covariances is Strongly Implied Iff A Tetrad Equation Among Correlations is Strongly Implied

Theorem 3: In a SLCT, if u, v, w, and x are distinct variables then $\gamma_{uv}\gamma_{wx} = \gamma_{ux}\gamma_{vw}$ iff $\rho_{uv}\rho_{wx} = \rho_{ux}\rho_{vw}$.

Proof: Suppose that $\gamma_{uv}\gamma_{wx} = \gamma_{ux}\gamma_{vw}$. By definition, no variable in a SLCT has a standard deviation equal to 0. Divide each side of the equation by $(\sigma_u\sigma_v\sigma_w\sigma_x)$. But

$$\rho_{uv}\rho_{wx} = \frac{\gamma_{uv}\,\gamma_{wx}}{\sigma_u\sigma_v\sigma_w\sigma_x}$$

and

$$\rho_{ux}\rho_{wv} = \frac{\gamma_{ux}\gamma_{wv}}{\sigma_u\sigma_x\sigma_w\sigma_v}$$

Hence,

$$\rho_{uv}\rho_{wx} = \rho_{ux}\rho_{wv}$$

The only if clause can be proved similarly.
Q.E.D.

Adding Edges Cannot Add New Implied Tetrad Equations

The theorem to be proved in this section states that adding edges to a model M can only defeat equations that are implied by M; equations that are not implied by M cannot be implied by the augmented model.

Lemma 21: Given a tetrad equation among variables of a SLCT in fully expanded form, if there is a monomial t that has an equation coefficient factor equal to the equation coefficient factor of a monomial u, then the constant factor of t is equal to the constant factor of u.

Proof: Let the equation coefficient factor of t be e_t and the constant factor of t be c_t. Define e_u and c_u analogously.

The equation coefficient factor of each monomial is a product of open paths from independent variables times some loop products. Let {i,j} be the set of sources of the open paths in e_t and $\{k,z\}$ be the set of sources of the open paths in e_u. c_t is equal to $\sigma^2_i \sigma^2_j$ and c_u is equal to $\sigma^2_k \sigma^2_z$. We will now show that if e_t equals e_u then $\{i,j\} = \{k,z\}$, which in turn implies that c_t equals c_u.

Suppose, contrary to the lemma that $e_t = e_u$ but $\{i,j\} \neq \{k,z\}$. Suppose w.l.g. that i is not equal to k or z. It follows from lemma 1 that i does not occur on any path containing k or z, nor can it appear in any loop. But according to lemma 1 and the definition of total effects, the equation coefficient factor of e_t is an open path with source i times some loops. Hence, the label of an edge out of i appears as a factor in e_t. e_u is a product of labels of edges on open paths with source k or z times some loops. It follows then that the label of an edge from i does not appear as a factor in e_u since no edge from i occurs in any path from k or z or any loop. Hence e_t does not consist of the same equation coefficients raised to the same powers as e_u. This contradicts our assumption.
Q.E.D.

Definition 13: An equation is in **reduced form** iff there is no sum of monomials on the l.h.s. that is identically equal to zero, and no sum of monomials on the r.h.s. that is identically equal to 0.

Lemma 22: A SLCT strongly implies a tetrad equation F iff when F is written in fully expanded and reduced form, there is a one-to-one function mapping each monomial m on the l.h.s. to a monomial m' on the r.h.s., such that the equation coefficient factor of m equals the equation coefficient factor of m'.

Proof: The if clause follows from lemma 21.

The only if clause will be proved by a reductio ad absurdum. Suppose that F is not strongly implied. Since the equation is in reduced form we know that there is no sum of monomials on the l.h.s. that is equal to zero, and no sum of monomials on the r.h.s. that is equal to zero. It follows that there is a sum of monomials on the l.h.s., each with equation coefficent factor e, that is equal to a sum of monomials on the r.h.s., each with equation coefficient factor e, but no one-to-one function mapping monomials with equation coefficient factors e on the l.h.s. onto equal monomials on the r.h.s. By lemma 21, each pair of monomials with equation coefficient factor e also has equal constant factors (but may be opposite in sign). The only ways that there could be no one-to-one function mapping the monomials with equation coefficient factors e on

the l.h.s. onto monomials with equation coefficient factors e on the r.h.s. is if either there were more monomials on one side with equation coefficient factor e than on the other side, or the monomials with equation coefficient factor e on one side had opposite signs from the monomials with equation coefficient factor e on the other side. In either case, the sum of the monomials containing e on each side would not be equal. This is a contradiction.
Q.E.D.

Definition 14: A SLCT M = <<R,E>, (Ω,P), X, L> is a subtheory of M' = <<R',E'>, (Ω,P), X', L'> iff E is included in E', L' is an extension of L, and R is included in R'.

Theorem 4: If M is a subtheory of M', then every tetrad equation among variables of M that is strongly implied by M' is also strongly implied by M.

Proof: We will show that if a tetrad equation among variables of M is not strongly implied by M, then it is not strongly implied by M'.

Note first that it follows from the definition of subgraph that the set of paths of M is a subset of the set of paths of M'.

Take any tetrad equation A among variables of M

$$\gamma_{ij}\gamma_{kl} = \gamma_{il}\gamma_{jk}$$

that is not strongly implied by M. Write A in fully expanded and reduced form, assuming the existence of the paths of model M. The equation when written in this form will be called A_M. Since A_M is not strongly implied by M, by lemma 22 it follows that after as many equal monomials as possible are subtracted from each side, there are monomials that remain that have equation coefficient factors that are not equal. Let t be the equation coefficient factor of a monomial such that no monomial on the other side of the equation has an equation coefficient factor equal to t. Suppose w.l.g. that t appears on the r.h.s. of A_M.

Now consider equation A when written in fully expanded form assuming the existence of the paths of model M'. The equation when written in this form will be called $A_{M'}$. Since the set of paths of M is a subset of the treks of M', it follows that the set of monomials appearing in A_M is a subset of the set of monomials appearing in $A_{M'}$. In particular, the monomial with equation coefficient factor t appears on the r.h.s. of $A_{M'}$.

Note that every monomial in A_M' but not in A_M contains an edge in E' - E, and hence has an equation coefficient factor different from that of t, which does not contain an edge in E' - E. t is not identically equal to the equation coefficient factor of any monomial on the l.h.s. of A_M by supposition, and is not equal to the equation coefficient factor of any monomial in A_M' but not in A_M. Hence t does not equal the equation coefficient factor of any monomial on the l.h.s.

The monomial containing t is not part of a sum of monomials on the r.h.s. of A_M' that equals zero, since it was not part of a sum of monomials on the r.h.s. of A_M that equals zero, and each monomial in A_M' that is not in A_M has an equation coefficient factor not equal to t. Hence if A_M' is put into reduced form the monomial containing t is still present.

By lemma 22, A_M' is not strongly implied.

The Causal Graph Determines the Tetrad Equations

The main result to be proved in this section is that any two theories with the same causal graph (cyclic *or* acyclic) imply the same tetrad equations. The importance of this theorem is that it indicates that it is possible to determine which tetrad equations are implied by a SLCT solely by examining the graph of the theory.

Definition 15: Two digraphs <R,E> and <R',E'> are **isomorphic** iff there exists a one-to-one function Z with domain R and range R' such that for each v_i and v_j in R, $<v_i,v_j> \varepsilon$ E iff $<Z(v_i), Z(v_j)> \varepsilon$ E'.

The following definition defines isomorphism between either sets of tetrad equations or sets of vanishing partial correlations.

Definition 16: Suppose that there are two SLCTs T = <<R,E>,(Ω,P), X, L> and T' = <<R',E'>, (Ω',P'), X', L'>, and there is a one-to-one function Q: R->R'. For any tetrad (partial) equation F among variables of T let Q'(F) be the result of substituting Q(r) for each variable r in F. **The set of tetrad (partial) equations among variables of T is isomorphic to the set of tetrad (partial) equations among variables of T'** iff for each tetrad (partial) equation F among variables of T, F is strongly implied by T iff Q'(F) is strongly implied by T'.

Theorem 5: Any two SLCTs $T = <<R,E>, (\Omega,P), X, L>$ and $T' = <<R',E'>, (\Omega',P), X', L'>$ with isomorphic graphs strongly imply isomorphic sets of tetrad equations.

Proof: Suppose $<R,E>$ is isomorphic to $<R',E'>$. By definition there is a one-to-one function $Q: R->R'$ such that $<x,y> \varepsilon E$ iff $<Q(x),Q(y)> \varepsilon E'$. We will show that Q is the function mapping $R:->R'$ establishing the isomorphism between the sets of tetrad equations.

Let F be an arbitrary tetrad equation of T written in fully expanded and reduced form, and F' the equation in T' obtained by substituting $Q(r)$ for each variable r in F.

The equation coefficient factor of each monomial in F is an arithmetical function of labels of paths in T. Similarly, the equation coefficient factor of each monomial in F' is an arithmetical function of labels of paths in T'. By the isomorphism of the graphs of T and T', it follows that there is a one-to-one function mapping monomials on the l.h.s. of F onto monomials on the r.h.s. of F that have equal equation coefficient factors iff there there is a one-to-one function mapping monomials on the l.h.s. of F' onto monomials on the r.h.s. of F' that have equal equation coefficient factors. By lemma 22, F is strongly implied by T iff F' is strongly implied by T'.
Q.E.D.

Proof of Correctness of the Algorithm for Identifying Vanishing Partial Correlations

According to TETRAD $\rho_{xz.y} = 0$ iff

1. for all $t \varepsilon T_{xz}$, $y \varepsilon t$, and

2. either for all $t \varepsilon T_{yz}$, $t_z \varepsilon P^o_{yz}$, or for all $t \varepsilon T_{yx}$, $t_x \varepsilon P^o_{yx}$

In this section we will prove that TETRAD's algorithm for identifying the vanishing partial correlations implied by a SLCT is correct.

TETRAD's Algorithm Finds Only Vanishing Partial Correlations Strongly Implied by a SLCT

Lemma 23: In a SLCT, for all variables u, y, z, if

1. $y \neq z$

2. there is a path from u to y

3. there is a path from u to z

then there is a trek between y and z whose source is the last point on p_{uy} that intersects p_{uz}.

Proof: Suppose p_{uy} is a path from u to y and p_{uz} is a path from u to z. p_{uy} and p_{uz} intersect in at least one point, since they intersect at u. Let x be the last point on p_{uy} that intersects p_{uz}. Let p_{xy} be the subpath of p_{uy} from x to y, and p_{xz} be the subpath of p_{uz} from x to z. p_{xy} and p_{xz} do not intersect anywhere except at x. Let p'_{xy} and p'_{xz} be paths from x to y and z respectively, formed by removing all cycles from p_{xy} and p_{xz} respectively. Since y is not equal to z at least one of p_{xy} and p_{xz} is not an empty path. It follows that p'_{xy} and p'_{xz} form a trek between y and z whose source is x.

Lemma 24: In a SLCT, for all vertices u, y, z, if

1. $y \neq z$

2. u is the source of an open path p to y, and

3. for all $t \; \varepsilon \; T_{yz}$, $t_z \; \varepsilon \; P^o_{yz}$

then every open path from u to z is the concatenation of two open subpaths, one from u to y and one from y to z.

Proof: Suppose not. It follows that there is an open path q from u to z that does not contain an open subpath from u to y and and an open subpath from y to z. It follows that q is an open path from u to z that does not contain y. By lemma 23 there is a trek t in T_{yz} whose source is the last point on p that intersects q. Since q does not contain y, the source of t is not y. It follows that t_z is not in P^o_{yz}.
Q.E.D.

Lemma 25: In a SLCT, for all vertices u, y, z, if

1. $y \neq z$, and

2. for all $t \in T_{yz}$, $t_z \in P^o_{yz}$

then any open path from u to y concatenated with any open path from y to z forms an open path from u to z.

Proof: Suppose contrary to the lemma that for all $t \in T_{yz}$, $t_z \in P^o_{yz}$ and there is an open path p from u to y and an open path q from y to z such that the concatenation of p and q is not an open path from u to z.

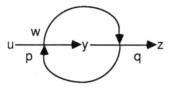

Figure 10-20: Open path from u to z.

(See Fig. 10-20.) If p&q is not an open path from u to z, it is a path with a cycle; hence, p intersects q at some point that is not equal to y. Let w be the last point on p that intersects q. There is an open path from w to y and an open path from w to z that intersect only at w. Since y does not equal z, least one of these paths is non-empty. Therefore w is the source of a trek t in T_{yz} such that t_z is not in P^o_{yz}, which is a contradiction. Q.E.D.

Lemma 26: In a SLCT, for all distinct vertices y, z, if

1. u is the source of an open path p to y and

2. for all $t \in T_{yz}$, $t_z \in P^o_{yz}$

then $TL_{uy} \cup TL_{yz} = TL_{uz}$.

Proof: See Fig. 10-21. By lemma 25 the concatenation of any open path from u to y concatenated with any open path from y to z forms an open

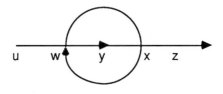

Figure 10-21: $TL_{uy} \cup TL_{yz} = TL_{uz}$.

path from u to z. If a loop m intersects an open path from u to y or an open path from y to z (not at u), then it intersects an open path from u to z (not at u). Hence $TL_{uy} \cup TL_{yz}$ is included in TL_{uz}.

By lemma 24 every open path from u to z consists of two open subpaths, one from u to y and one from y to z. Hence any loop m that intersects an open path from u to z (not at u), intersects either an open path from u to y or an open path from y to z (not at u). (If m intersects a path from y to z at y, it does not touch y, but it does touch a path from u to y.) It follows that TL_{uz} is included in $TL_{uy} \cup TL_{yz}$.
Q.E.D.

Lemma 27: In a SLCT, for all distinct vertices u, y, z, if for all $t \varepsilon T_{yz}$, $t_z \varepsilon P^o_{yz}$ then $RL_{uy} \cap RL_{yz} = \{\}$.

Proof: Suppose contrary to the theorem that for all $t \varepsilon T_{yz}$, $t_z \varepsilon P^o_{yz}$ but $RL_{uy} \cap RL_{yz} \neq \{\}$. See figure 10-22. If $RL_{uy} \cap RL_{yz} \neq \{\}$ it follows that there is a sequence of loops $m_1, \ldots, m_n$ such that m_1 touches an open path p in P^o_{uy}, m_n touches an open path q in P^o_{yz}, and for all $1 \leq i < n$, m_i touches m_{i+1}. There is a path r from some point $x' \neq y$ in q to some point x in p which runs through the sequence of touching loops. (Since m_n touches q, it must intersect q at some point $\neq y$.) There is a subpath $q_{x'z}$ of q from x' to z that does not intersect y. There is a subpath p_{xy} of p from x to y. It follows that $r \& p_{xy}$ is a path from x' to y. Let x'' be the last point on $q_{x'z}$ that intersects $r \& p_{xy}$. $x'' \neq y$ since $q_{x'z}$ does not contain y. By lemma 23, there is a trek t between y and z whose source is x''. Since the source of t is not equal to y, t_z is not in P^o_{yz}. This is a contradiction.

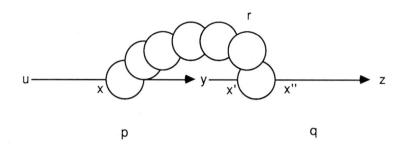

Figure 10-22: If $RL_{uy} \cap RL_{yz} \neq \{\}$.

Q.E.D.

Lemma 28: In a SLCT, for all distinct vertices u, y, z, if for all t ε T_{yz}, t_z ε $P^o{}_{yz}$ then $RL_{uy} \cup RL_{yz} = RL_{uz}$.

Proof: Suppose m is in RL_{uz}. It follows that either m is in TL_{uz} or there is a chain of touching loops from m to a loop in TL_{uz}. By lemma 26 TL_{uz} is included in $TL_{uy} \cup TL_{yz}$. It follows that m is either in $TL_{uy} \cup TL_{yz}$ or there is a chain of touching loops from m to a loop in $TL_{uy} \cup TL_{yz}$. In either case m is in $RL_{uy} \cup RL_{yz}$. Hence RL_{uz} is included in $RL_{uy} \cup RL_{yz}$.

Suppose m is in $RL_{uy} \cup RL_{yz}$. It follows that either m is in $TL_{uy} \cup TL_{yz}$ or there is a chain of touching loops from m to a loop in $TL_{uy} \cup TL_{yz}$. By lemma 26 $TL_{uy} \cup TL_{yz}$ is included in TL_{uz}. By definition then m is either in TL_{uz} or there is a chain of touching loops from m to a loop in TL_{uz}. In either case m is in RL_{uz}. Hence $RL_{uy} \cup RL_{yz}$ is included in RL_{uz}.
Q.E.D.

The following facts should be noted about the distributed form of the quantity

$$\prod_{z \,\varepsilon\, RL_{ij}} \left(1 - L(z) \right) \quad *$$

1. the first monomial is equal to 1

2. every subsequent monomial is a product of subsets of pairwise non-touching loops in RL_{ij}

3. each product of subsets of loops in RL_{ij} occurs in at most one monomial

4. the sign of a monomial is positive if the number of loops it contains is even and negative if the number of loops it contains is odd.

Lemma 29: In a SLCT, for all distinct vertices u, y, z, if

1. u is the source of an open path to y

2. for all $t \in T_{yz}, t_z \in P^o_{yz}$

then $E^d_{uy} E^d_{yz} = E^d_{uz}$.

Proof: We will show that there is a one-to-one function mapping monomials on the l.h.s. to identically equal monomials that have the same sign on the r.h.s.

First we will show that each monomial m in E^d_{uz} can be mapped onto an equal monomial m' in $E^d_{uy} E^d_{yz}$. Take an arbitrary monomial m in E^d_{uz}. It is either equal to 1 or it consists of a product of some subset of loops of RL_{uz} that do not touch each other. If it is equal to 1 it is equal to some monomial m' in the distributed form of $E^d_{uy} E^d_{yz}$, since both E^d_{uy} and E^d_{yz} contain a monomial equal to 1. If m is not equal to 1 then by lemmas 27 and 28 the loops in m can be uniquely partitioned into m_1, a subset of loops in RL_{uy}, and m_2, a subset of loops in RL_{yz}. Since no pair of loops in m touch each other, no pair of loops in m_1 touch each other and no pair of loops in m_2 touch each other. Hence m_1 is a monomial in E^d_{uy} and m_2 is a monomial in E^d_{yz}. Map m on the l.h.s. onto the product m' of m_1 and m_2 on the l.h.s. The monomial m' is equal to m.

Now we will show that m and m' have the same signs. If the sign of m is positive then m contains an even number of loops. In that case, the number of loops in m_1 and m_2 are either both even or both odd. In either case the sign of m' is positive. If the sign of m is negative, then the number of loops in m_1 is even and the number of loops in m_2 is odd, or vice-versa. In either case, the sign of m' is negative.

Next, we will show that every monomial m' in $E^d_{uy} E^d_{yz}$ has some monomial m in E^d_{uz} mapped onto it. Suppose that some product of loops m_1 and m_2 appears in $E^d_{uy} E^d_{yz}$ where m_1 is a subset of non-touching loops in RL_{uy} and m_2 is a subset of touching loops in RL_{yz}. By lemma 28 each loop in m_1 or m_2 is also in RL_{uz} and by lemma 27 no loop appears in both m_1 and m_2. Hence $m_1 m_2$ is a subset of loops in RL_{uz}. Furthermore, by lemma 27 no loop in m_1 touches any loop in m_2; otherwise RL_{yz} and RL_{uy} would not be disjoint. It follows that $m_1 m_2$ is a monomial in E^d_{uz}.

Finally, we will show that monomials m and n in E^d_{uz} which contain different subsets of loops are mapped onto distinct monomials m' and n' in $E^d_{uy} E^d_{yz}$. (We will consider the monomial equal to 1 to contain the empty set of loops.) We have already shown that m and n will be mapped onto some monomials m' and n' respectively in $E^d_{uy} E^d_{yz}$. Let $m' = m'_1 m'_2$, where m'_1 is a subset of loops in RL_{uy} and m'_2 is a subset of loops in RL_{yz}. Similarly, let $n' = n'_1 n'_2$. Since m'_1 and m'_2 partition m, and n'_1 and n'_2 partition n, and m and n contain different subsets of loops, $m'_1 m'_2$ is distinct from $n'_1 n'_2$.
Q.E.D.

Lemma 30: In a SLCT, for all distinct vertices u, y, z, if

    1. u is the source of an open path to y, and

    2. for all $t \in T_{yz}$, $t_z \in P^o_{yz}$

then $E^o_{uz} = E^o_{uy} E^o_{yz}$.

Proof: We will show that there is a 1-1 function from each monomial m' in $E^o_{uy} E^o_{yz}$ to an equal monomial m in E^o_{uz}.

First we will show that an arbitrary monomial m' in the distributed form of $E^o_{uy} E^o_{yz}$ can be mapped onto an equal monomial m in E^o_{uz}. m' is a product of open paths p in P^o_{uy} and q in P^o_{yz}. By lemma 25 p&q is an open path in P^o_{uz}. Map m' onto the monomial m in P^o_{uz} that corresponds to p&q. Clearly m and m' are equal.

Next we will show that every monomial m in E^o_{uz} has some monomial m' in $E^o_{uy} E^o_{yz}$ mapped onto it. By lemma 24 every path in P^o_{uz} is the concatenation of two paths, one in P^o_{uy} and one in P^o_{yz}. Hence every monomial m in E^o_{uz} has some monomial m' in $E^o_{uy} E^o_{yz}$ mapped onto it.

Finally, we will show that distinct monomials m' and n' in $E^o_{uy} E^o_{yz}$ are mapped onto distinct monomials m and n in E^o_{uz}. Let m' = $m'_1 m'_2$, where m'_1 is in E^o_{uy} and m'_2 is in E^o_{yz}; similarly let n' = $n'_1 n'_2$. The only way that different pairs of paths could be concatenated into the same path is if m'_1 were a subpath of n'_1 and n'_2 were a subpath of m'_2, or vice-versa. Since m'_1 and n'_1 are both open paths from u to y, neither can be a subpath of the other. Hence m' and n' are mapped onto distinct monomials m and n.
Q.E.D.

Lemma 31: In a SLCT, for all distinct vertices u, y, z, if

1. u is the source of an open path to y, and

2. for all t ε T_{yz}, t_z ε P^o_{yz}

then $E^n_{uz} = E^n_{uy} E^n_{yz}$.

Proof: On the l.h.s., each monomial in the distributed form of E^n_{uz} is a monomial m in E^d_{uz} times a monomial p in E^o_{uz}, where p does not touch any loops in m.

On the r.h.s., each monomial in E^n_{yz} is a monomial m' in E^d_{yz} times a monomial p' in E^o_{yz}, where p' does not touch any loops in m'. Similarly, each monomial in E^n_{uy} is a monomial m'' in E^d_{uy} times a monomial p'' in E^o_{uy}, where p'' does not touch any loops in m''.

By lemma 29, E^d_{uz} is equal to $E^d_{uy} E^d_{yz}$. By lemma 30, E^o_{uz} is equal to $E^o_{uy} E^o_{yz}$. In order to show that $E^n_{uz} = E^n_{uy} E^n_{yz}$ all that must be shown is that the monomials in $E^o_{uz} E^d_{uz}$ but not in E^n_{uz} equal the monomials in $E^o_{uy} E^d_{uy} E^o_{yz} E^d_{yz}$ but not in $E^n_{uy} E^n_{yz}$.

By lemma 24 every open path p from u to z is made up of an open path q from u to y concatenated with an open path r from y to z. By lemmas 27 and 28 m can be partitioned into m_1, a subset of loops in RL_{uy}, and m_2, a subset of loops in RL_{yz}. Take an arbitrary monomial x on the l.h.s. that consists of the product of p with some subset m of loops. Associate x with the monomial x' on the r.h.s. that consists of q times m_1 times r times m_2. We will show that x is deleted from the l.h.s. by the * operation iff x' is deleted from the r.h.s. by the * operation.

A monomial is deleted from either side iff it either contains two loops that touch, or it contains a loop that touches a path. It has already been shown in the proof of lemma 29 that x is removed from the l.h.s. because two loops touch iff the corresponding monomial on the r.h.s. is also removed because it contains two touching loops. Hence, we will consider only the case in which a monomial is removed because it contains a path touching a loop.

Suppose x is deleted from the l.h.s. If x is removed because p touches one of the loops in m, then one of the loops in m touches p on an open path q from u to y or an open path r from y to z. Suppose some loop in m touches an open path q from u to y. The loop in m that touches q must be in m_1, since any loop that touches q is in RL_{uy}. It follows that q times m_1 is deleted from the r.h.s. Similarly, if one of the loops in m touches r, then r times m_2 is deleted from the r.h.s. In either case x' does not appear on the r.h.s.

Suppose now that x' is deleted from the r.h.s. because one of the loops in m touches either q or r. But if a loop touches q or r, it touches p also. Hence x is removed from the l.h.s.
Q.E.D.

Lemma 32: In a SLCT, for all distinct vertices y, z, if

    1. u is the source of an open path to y, and

    2. for all $t \in T_{yz}$, $t_z \in P^o_{yz}$

then $E_{uz} = E_{uy} E_{yz}$.

Proof: $u \neq z$ since there is an open path from u to y and the source of every trek between y and z is y.

If u = y, then $E_{uz} = E_{yz} = E_{uy} E_{yz} = E_{yy} E_{yz} = E_{yz}$.

If $u \neq y$ then the lemma follows from lemmas 29 and 31.
Q.E.D.

Lemma 33: In a SLCT, for all distinct vertices y, z, if

1. for all $t \, \varepsilon \, T_{yz}$, $t_z \, \varepsilon \, P^o_{yz}$

2. $T_{yz} \neq \{\}$

then $U_y = U_{yz}$.

Proof: Since $U_{yz} = U_y \cap U_z$, U_{yz} is included in U_y. It remains to show that U_y is included in U_{yz}. If u is in U_y then there is an open path p from u to y. p can be extended to an open path from u to z, since there is a path in P^o_{yz}. Hence u is in U_z. By definition, u is in U_{yz}.
Q.E.D.

Lemma 34: In a SLCT, for all distinct vertices x, y, z, if

1. for all $t \, \varepsilon \, T_{xz}$, $y \, \varepsilon \, t$

2. for all $t \, \varepsilon \, T_{yz}$, $t_z \, \varepsilon \, P^o_{yz}$, and

3. $T_{yz} \neq \{\}$

then $U_{xy} = U_{xz}$.

Proof: Suppose the antecedent is true but $U_{xz} \neq U_{xy}$. If $U_{xz} \neq U_{xy}$ there are two possibilities, each considered below.

Suppose that there is an independent variable u that is the source of open paths p and q to x and z respectively, but u is not the source of an open path to y. By lemma 23 there is a trek between x and z that consists of subpaths of p and q. But since every t in T_{xz} contains y, u is the source of an open path to y.

Suppose that there exists an independent variable u that is the source of open paths to x and y but not z. By lemma 25 the concatenation of any open path from u to y with any open path from y to z is an open path from u to z. By hypothesis there is an open path from y to z. Hence there is an open path from u to z, which is a contradiction.
Q.E.D.

Lemma 35: In a SLCT, for all distinct vertices x, y, z, if

1. for all $t \in T_{xz}$, $y \in t$
2. $T_{yz} \neq \{\}$ and for all $t \in T_{yz}$, $t_z \in P^o{}_{yz}$, or,
3. $T_{yx} \neq \{\}$ and for all $t \in T_{yx}$, $t_x \in P^o{}_{yx}$

then

$$\gamma_{xz} = \frac{\gamma_{xy}\, \gamma_{yz}}{\sigma^2{}_y}$$

Proof: Suppose w.l.g. that for all $t \in T_{yz}$, $t_z \in P^o{}_{yz}$ and $T_{yz} \neq \{\}$.

By lemmas 13 and 14

(13)

$$\frac{\gamma_{xy}\, \gamma_{yz}}{\sigma^2{}_y}$$

$$= \frac{\left[\sum_{u \in U_{yz}} \left(E_{uy} E_{uz}\, \sigma^2{}_u \right)\right]\left[\sum_{u \in U_{xy}} \left(E_{ux} E_{uy}\, \sigma^2{}_u \right)\right]}{\sum_{u \in U_y} \left(E_{uy} E_{uy}\, \sigma^2{}_u \right)}$$

By lemma 33 $U_y = U_{yz}$. By lemma 32 $E_{uz} = E_{uy} E_{yz}$. Hence, the r.h.s. of equation 13 equals

(14)

$$\frac{\left[\sum_{u \in U_y} \left(E_{uy} E_{uy} E_{yz}\, \sigma^2{}_u \right)\right]\left[\sum_{u \in U_{xy}} \left(E_{ux} E_{uy}\, \sigma^2{}_u \right)\right]}{\sum_{u \in U_y} \left(E_{uy} E_{uy}\, \sigma^2{}_u \right)}$$

Since E_{yz} occurs in every monomial in the sum we can move it out of the sum. It follows that expression 14 equals

$$(15)$$

$$\frac{E_{yz}\left[\sum_{u\,\varepsilon\,U_y}\left(E_{uy}E_{uy}\sigma^2_u\right)\right]\left[\sum_{u\,\varepsilon\,U_{xy}}\left(E_{ux}E_{uy}\sigma^2_u\right)\right]}{\sum_{u\,\varepsilon\,U_y}\left(E_{uy}E_{uy}\sigma^2_u\right)}$$

Cancellation of the common monomials in the numerator and denominator shows that expression 15 is equal to

$$(16)$$

$$E_{yz}\left[\sum_{u\,\varepsilon\,U_{xy}}\left(E_{ux}E_{uy}\sigma^2_u\right)\right]$$

Now E_{yz} can be moved into the sum, so expression 16 is equal to

$$(17)$$

$$\sum_{u\,\varepsilon\,U_{xy}}\left(E_{yz}E_{ux}E_{uy}\sigma^2_u\right)$$

By lemma 32 it follows that expression 17 is equal to

$$(18)$$

$$\sum_{u\,\varepsilon\,U_{xy}}\left(E_{uz}E_{ux}\sigma^2_u\right)$$

By lemma 34 $U_{xz} = U_{xy}$. Hence, 18 equals

$$(19)$$

$$\sum_{u\,\varepsilon\,U_{xz}}\left(E_{uz}E_{ux}\sigma^2_u\right)$$

By lemma 13, expression 19 equals γ_{xz}.
Q.E.D.

Lemma 36: In a SLCT, for all distinct vertices x, y, z, if

    1. for all $t\,\varepsilon\,T_{xz}$, $y\,\varepsilon\,t$, and

    2. either for all $t\,\varepsilon\,T_{yz}$, $t_z\,\varepsilon\,P^o{}_{yz}$ or for all $t\,\varepsilon\,T_{yx}$, $t_x\,\varepsilon\,P^o{}_{yx}$

then if $T_{yz} = \{\}$ or $T_{yx} = \{\}$ then $T_{xz} = \{\}$.

Proof: Suppose $T_{xz} \neq \{\}$. It follows that there are paths from some variable u to x and z, and that one of these paths contains y. Hence there are paths from u to x, u to y, and u to z. By lemma 23, T_{yx} and T_{zy} are not empty.

Q.E.D.

Lemma 37: In a SLCT, for all distinct vertices x, y, z, if

1. for all $t \, \varepsilon \, T_{xz}$, $y \, \varepsilon \, t$, and

2. either for all $t \, \varepsilon \, T_{yz}$, $t_z \, \varepsilon \, P^o{}_{yz}$ or for all $t \, \varepsilon \, T_{yx}$, $t_x \, \varepsilon \, P^o{}_{yx}$

then $\rho_{xz.y} = 0$.

Proof: There are two cases to consider: either T_{yz} or T_{yx} is empty, or not.

Suppose first that either either T_{yz} or T_{yx} is empty. For all distinct a, b if T_{ab} is empty, it follows from lemma 23 that there is no independent variable that is the source of open paths to a and b. This implies by lemma 13 that $\rho_{ab} = 0$. Hence, if T_{yz} or T_{yx} is empty, then $\rho_{yz}\rho_{yx} = 0$. If T_{yz} or T_{yx} is empty, then by lemma 36 T_{xz} is also empty and $\rho_{xz} = 0$. So, if T_{yx} or T_{yz} is empty, $\rho_{yz}\rho_{yx} = \rho_{xz} = 0$. This implies by definition that $\rho_{xz.y} = 0$.

The second case is if neither T_{yz} nor T_{yx} is empty. In that case, by lemma 35

$$\gamma_{xz} = \frac{\gamma_{xy}\, \gamma_{yz}}{\sigma^2{}_y}$$

By lemma 16, $\rho_{xz.y} = 0$.

Q.E.D.

TETRAD Finds All Vanishing Partial Correlations Strongly Implied by a SLCT

Lemma 38: If $\rho_{xz.y} = 0$ then

1. for all $t \in T_{xz}$, $y \in t$, and

2. for all $t \in T_{yz}$, $t_z \in P^o_{yz}$ or for all $t \in T_{yx}$, $t_x \in P^o_{yx}$.

Proof: Again, we assume that x, y, and z are not error variables.

We will prove the contrapositive of the theorem, that is if

1. there exists a $t \in T_{xz}$ that does not contain y, or

2. there is a $t \in T_{yz}$ such that t_z not in P^o_{yz} and there is a $t \in T_{yx}$ such that t_x not in P^o_{yx}

then $\rho_{xz.y} \neq 0$. We will show that in either case

$$\gamma_{xz}\, \sigma^2_y \neq \gamma_{xy}\, \gamma_{yz}$$

Once this is proved, the lemma follows from lemma 16.

We will now consider the case where there exists a $t \in T_{xz}$ that does not contain y and we will show that in fully distributed form

(20)

$$\gamma_{xz}\, \sigma^2_y \neq \gamma_{xy}\, \gamma_{yz}$$

(See Fig. 10-23.)

By definition, the fully expanded form of inequality 20 is the distributed form of

(21)

$$\sum_{u \in U_{xz}} \sum_{v \in U_y} E^n_{ux} E^n_{uz} E^n_{vy} E^n_{vy} d_{uv} D' \sigma^2_u \sigma^2_v$$

$$\neq \sum_{u \in U_{xy}} \sum_{v \in U_{yz}} E^n_{ux} E^n_{uy} E^n_{vy} E^n_{vz} d'_{uv} D \sigma^2_u \sigma^2_v$$

Note the following facts about the monomials in inequality 21.

1. If E_{ab} is not equal to 0, then it's distributed form is a sum of monomials, at least one of which is equal to an open path from a to b. Hence, if x and z are dependent upon u, and y is dependent upon v, then $E^n_{ux} E^n_{uz} E^n_{vy} E^n_{vy}$ contains one monomial that is the product of open paths from u to x, u to z, v to y, and v to y. Since it contains open paths from u to x and u to z, it also

contains a trek between x and z.

2. For all a and b, every monomial in the distributed form of E^n_{ab} contains an open path from a to b as one factor.

3. For all a and b, E^d_{ab} is a product of terms of the form $(1 - L)$, where L is the label of a loop. Hence one monomial in the distributed form of any product of denominators is 1.

4. d_{uv}, d'_{uv}, D, and D' are all products of denominators in Mason's rule. Hence one monomial in the distributed form of each of them is 1.

It follows that the equation coefficient factor of one monomial in the distributed form of the l.h.s. of inequality 21 is the product of open paths from u to x and z respectively, and open paths from v to y.

We will now show that there is a monomial on the l.h.s. of inequality 21 whose equation coefficient factor is not equal to the equation coefficient factor of any monomial on the r.h.s. of inequality 21. See Fig. 10-23.

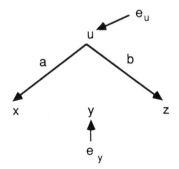

Figure 10-23: Trek product contains no edge from non-error variable into y.

First we will set all edges out of error variables to one. If the equation coefficient factor of monomial m is not equal to the equation coefficient factor of m' when the labels of the edges out of error variables have been set to one, the same is true when the labels of the edges out of error variables have not been set to one. For suppose there is some monomial m with equation coefficient factor x on the r.h.s. that is not equal to a monomial m' with equation coefficient factor x' on the l.h.s. when the edges out of error variables are all labelled by one. Now consider the monomials m and m' when the edges out of the error variables have not been set to one. Their equation coefficient factors are xy and x'y' respectively, where y is a product of labels not occuring in x, and y' is a product of labels not occurring in x' (since y and y' contain only edges from error variables). Clearly, if x ≠ x', then xy ≠ x'y'.

By hypothesis, there is a trek t from x to z that does not contain y. Suppose that the source of t is u, and the label of t is ab. The concatenation of the edge from e_u to u with t_x is an open path from an independent variable to x, and the concatenation of the edge from e_u to u with t_z is an open path from an independent variable to z. Since the label of the edge from e_u to u is 1, it follows that there is a product of open paths from an independent variable to x and z that is equal to ab. If y is independent then the only open path to y is from y, and that path is labelled 1. If y is not independent, there is an edge from the error variable e_y to y labelled 1. In either case, there is a monomial on the l.h.s. of inequality 21 whose equation coefficient factor is equal to ab.

We will now show that there is no monomial in on the r.h.s. of inequality 21 whose equation coefficient factor is equal to ab. Every monomial on the r.h.s. of inequality 21 contains a trek between x and y and a trek between y and z. These treks must contain an edge into or out of y that is not from e_y. But if there are any edges into or out of y in ab they are edges from e_y. It follows that no monomial on the r.h.s of inequality 21 has an equation coefficient factor equal to ab.

We will now show that no monomial whose equation coefficient factor is equal to ab but whose constant coefficient is negative occurs on the l.h.s. of inequality 21. The only monomials on the l.h.s. of inequality 21 whose constant coefficients are negative contain loops. But ab does not contain any loops.

It follows that the l.h.s. of inequality 21 does not equal the r.h.s. of inequality 21.

Now consider the case where there is a $t \in T_{yz}$ such that t_z is not in P^o_{yz} and there is a $t \in T_{yx}$ such that t_x is not in P^o_{yx}. We will show that this also implies

$$\gamma_{xz} \sigma^2_y \neq \gamma_{xy} \gamma_{yz}$$

By supposition, there are treks $t_{yz} \in T_{yz}$ and $t_{xy} \in T_{xy}$ such that neither trek contains an edge out of y. By the previous remarks there is some monomial on the r.h.s. of inequality 21 whose equation coefficient factor contains just the edges in two treks between x and y and y and z respectively.

We will now show that there is some monomial m on the r.h.s. of inequality 21 whose equation coefficient factor contains no edges out of y, and that there is no monomial whose equation coefficient factor equals that of m, but whose constant factor is of opposite sign. We shall say that a monomial s is strictly less than t iff, for all edges e, the number of occurrences of e in s is less than or equal to the number of occurrences of e in t, and there is some edge that occurs fewer times in s than in t. On the r.h.s. of inequality 21 there are monomials whose equation coefficient factors consist solely of the product of two treks, one between x and y, and one between y and z. It follows from the hypothesis that there is a product of treks between x and y, and y znd z respectively that contains no edge out of y. Find such a product of treks m that contains no edge out of y, and has the property that no other product of treks is strictly less than m. By the remarks made above, m appears on the r.h.s. of inequality 21. If there is a monomial m' whose constant coefficient is opposite in sign to that of m, then m' contains loops, since only monomials containing loops have negative constant coefficients. But then the product of treks contained in m' is strictly less than m, which is a contradiction.

We will now show that there is no monomial m' on the l.h.s. of inequality 21 with an equation coefficient factor equal to m. Each monomial on the l.h.s. of inequality 21 contains a trek t_{xz}. There are two cases to consider.

1. t_{xz} contains an edge into y.

2. t_{xz} does not contain an edge into y.

Suppose first that t_{xz} contains an edge into y. It also contains an edge out of y, since y is not one of the termini of the trek. However, if it contains an edge out of y then it contains an edge that is not in m. Hence no monomial containing a trek t_{xz} that contains an edge into y has an equation coefficient factor equal to that of m.

Suppose that t_{xz} does not contain an edge out of y. Since t_{xz} contains no edges out of y, and y is not a terminus of t_{xz}, it does not contain y at all. We have already show that if there is a trek between x and z that does not contain y then the r.h.s. of inequality 21 does not equal the l.h.s.

It follows then that if there exists a trek $t \varepsilon T_{yx}$ such that t_x is not in P^o_{yx} and a trek $t \varepsilon T_{yz}$ such that t_z is not in P^o_{yz}, or there exists a tε t_{xz} that does not contain y, then

$$\gamma_{xz} \sigma^2_y \neq \gamma_{xy} \gamma_{yz}$$

Q.E.D.

TETRAD's Algorithm for Identifying Vanishing Partial Constraints Is Correct

Theorem 6: $\rho_{xz.y} = 0$ iff

    1. for all $t \varepsilon T_{xz}$, $y \varepsilon t$, and

    2. either for all $t \varepsilon T_{yz}$, $t_z \varepsilon P^o_{yz}$, or for all $t \varepsilon T_{yx}$, $t_x \varepsilon P^o_{yx}$

Proof: This follows immediately from lemmas 37 and 38.
Q.E.D.

Adding Edges Cannot Add New Implied Partial Equations

Theorem 7: If M is a subtheory of M', then every partial equation among distinct variables of M that is strongly implied by M' is also strongly implied by M.

Proof: Let T^M_{xz} be the set of treks between x and z in M, and $T^{M'}_{xz}$ be the set of treks between x and z in M'. By theorem 6, for any three distinct variables x, y, and z, M strongly implies $\rho_{xz.y} = 0$ iff

    1. for all $t \varepsilon T^M_{xz}$, $y \varepsilon t$, and

    2. either for all $t \varepsilon T^M_{yz}$, $t_z \varepsilon P^o_{yz}$, or for all $t \varepsilon T^M_{yx}$, $t_x \varepsilon P^o_{yx}$.
Also by theorem 6, for any three distinct variables x, y, and z, M' strongly implies $\rho_{xz.y} = 0$ iff

    1. for all $t \varepsilon T^{M'}_{xz}$, $y \varepsilon t$, and

    2. either for all $t \varepsilon T^{M'}_{yz}$, $t_z \varepsilon P^o_{yz}$, or for all $t \varepsilon T^{M'}_{yx}$, $t_x \varepsilon P^o_{yx}$.
The set of treks in M is a subset of the subset of treks in M'. It follows

then that if

1. for all $t \in TM'_{xz}$, $y \in t$, and

2. either for all $t \in TM'_{yz}$, $t_z \in P^o_{yz}$, or for all $t \in TM'_{yx}$, $t_x \in P^o_{yx}$.

then

1. for all $t \in TM_{xz}$, $y \in t$, and

2. either for all $t \in TM_{yz}$, $t_z \in P^o_{yz}$, or for all $t \in TM_{yx}$, $t_x \in P^o_{yx}$.

Hence if M' strongly implies $\rho_{xz.y} = 0$ then M strongly implies $\rho_{xz.y} = 0$.

Q.E.D.

Part III

Using TETRAD, EQS and LISREL

11. USING TETRAD WITH EQS AND LISREL

TETRAD is a program for helping to discover *causal structure*. It will not estimate parameters in a statistical model, nor will it perform a *statistical* test of the model as a whole. Fortunately, there are programs that will. The LISREL and EQS programs are among the most widely used computer packages for estimating and testing structural equation models. EQS is always, and LISREL is usually, straightforward to use on models found with TETRAD.

The appearance of the LISREL programs made available full information maximum likelihood estimation and testing. Under the assumption of normality, the program made possible the estimation and testing of a great range of structural equation models. The LISREL programs impose certain classifications of variables, however, and these classifications and the restrictions that accompany them can sometimes cause difficulties in representing causal models. In the first part of this chapter we describe these restrictions and ways to circumvent them.

The EQS program is considerably easier to use than LISREL, but the PC version can often take 15 minutes or more for a single run. If one wants to estimate and test 20 models, say, 5 hours might be required. In the second section of the chapter we explain how to run EQS in batch mode so that large numbers of models can be run without the attention or time of the user.

11.1. LISREL and Its Restrictions

The LISREL programs are described in detail in a series of manuals. We have used the *LISREL IV User's Guide* [52] and the *LISREL VI User's Guide* [54]. LISREL requires the user to classify the variables of a model according to the following scheme:

$$
\begin{array}{lll}
\text{ksi} & = & \text{exogenous and latent} \\
\text{eta} & = & \text{endogenous and latent} \\
\text{x} & = & \text{measured and dependent on ksi variables} \\
\text{y} & = & \text{measured and dependent on eta variables}
\end{array}
$$

Each of these variable types has an associated covariance matrix:

phi	=	covariance matrix of error vars. for ksi vars.
psi	=	covariance matrix of error vars. for eta vars.
theta delta	=	covariance matrix of error vars. for x vars.
theta epsilon	=	covariance matrix of error vars. for y vars.

The program permits the user to specify covariances and variances among the phi variables, the psi variables, the theta delta variables, and the theta epsilon variables. In directed graph representations of a causal model, covariances of these sorts are represented as undirected (or bidirected) edges connecting error variables.

The LISREL classification of variables carries with it some restrictions on possible causal and structural representations, including the following.

1. x variables cannot depend on eta variables;

2. x variables cannot depend on other x variables;

3. y variables cannot depend on other y variables;

4. y variables cannot depend on ksi variables; and

5. No error variable from one error type can covary with an error variable from *any other type*.

In what follows we will use the following abbreviation scheme.

ksi	=	K
eta	=	N
x	=	x
y	=	y
psi	=	s
phi	=	p
theta delta	=	td
theta epsilon	=	te

To illustrate the effect of these restrictions, we show, in Fig. 11-1, a simple model that is easily expressed in LISREL's formalism. Fig. 11-2 shows all of the additions to this model that can be represented in that formalism. In Fig. 11-3 we show a few of the many elaborations of the original model that *cannot* be represented (as is) in the LISREL formalism.

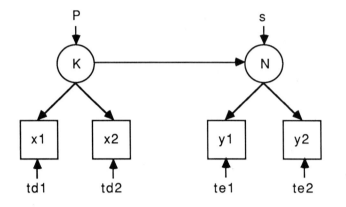

Figure 11-1: LISREL model.

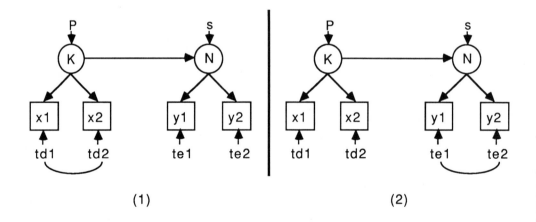

Figure 11-2: Simple variants representable in LISREL.

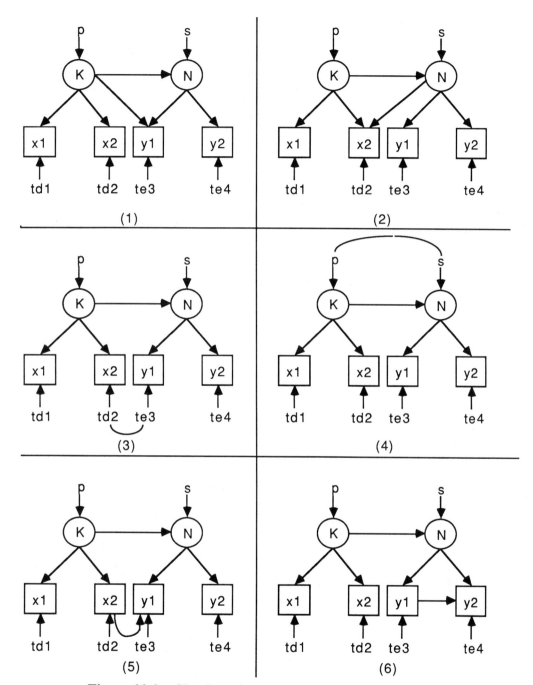

Figure 11-3: Simple variants not representable in LISREL.

11.2. Overcoming the Restrictions

To circumvent LISREL's restrictions, we need only find representations that LISREL will accept and that are appropriate substitutes for the models LISREL will not accept. We understand a substitution to be appropriate if a model and its substitute are intertranslatable.[40] We suggest two ways to do this.

1. Specifying ksi variables as eta variables.

Usually a ksi variable can be specified as an eta variable. You must also change all the x variables that were previously indicators of the ksi variables to y variables that are indicators of the new eta variables, and you must change the error variable types as well. This kind of move will solve the problem of representing variants 1, 2, 3, and 4 of Fig. 11-3. We show the solutions in Fig. 11-4. This kind of solution is straightforward enough. We are simply changing the LISREL type for certain variables in our model. We are not introducing any new variables, or eliminating any that our original model contained. This technique will work just in case an unacceptable model has an alphabetic variant that LISREL will accept.

2. Introducing surrogate eta variables.

In case a model contains a causal relation between measured variables, e.g., variants 5 and 6 in Fig. 11-3, the strategy just described is not sufficient. One y variables still cannot cause another y variable. Only LISREL variables of the eta type, and no other, can be represented as both causes and effects. For a LISREL representation of models such as variants 5 and 6, therefore, y variables must be converted into eta variables. This can be done by replacing a y variable and its error term in the original model with a system of new variables as shown in Fig. 11-5. Variables subscripted with an o stand for original, and variables subscripted with an n stand for new. Notice that s_n occupies the same "function" in the new model that te_o did in the old model. Notice also that the error term for y_n is always fixed at 0. To get the new model from the old model, simply replace every occurrence of y_o with n_n. This does nothing to change the substance of the old

---

[40]That is to say, models I and II are equivalent provided that for every variable of model I there is a definition of that variable in terms of the variables of model II, and for every variable of model II there is a definition in terms of the variables of model I, and the two models, respectively conjoined with their definitions of the terms in the other model, are mathematically equivalent. See Glymour [34, 35] and Glymour and Spirtes [105].

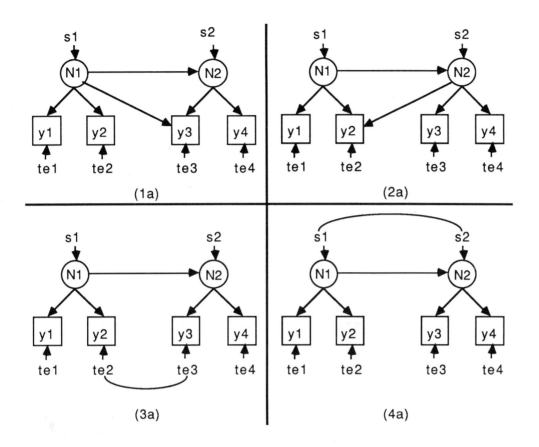

Figure numbers (1a), (2a), (3a), (4a)

Figure 11-4: Solutions to variants 1, 2, 3, and 4.

model, because in the new model

$$y_n = 1(n_n) + 0$$

which amounts to saying the two variables are identical. In effect we have created a surrogate variable for the old y which can now enter into causal relationships with other variables of its type. We show the solutions to variants 5 and 6 as solutions 5a and 6a in Fig. 11-6. Lest users feel uncomfortable with this technique, it should be noted that LISREL has an identical technique already built into its set of options. When a model in LISREL is specified with the option "FIXEDX" in

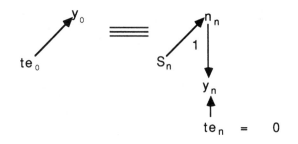

Figure 11-5: Converting a y variable into an eta variable and a y variable.

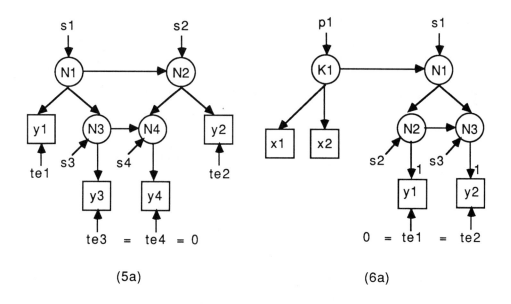

(5a)   (6a)

Figure 11-6: Solutions to variants 5 and 6.

the model line, this essentially identifies x variables with ksi variables in the same way that we identified y variables with eta variables above. To say "FIXEDX" in LISREL is to create the situation in Fig. 11-7 for each x variable input.

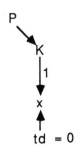

Figure 11-7: LISREL's FIXEDX.

By specifying "FIXEDX" a user can estimate and test a model in which measured variables are exogenous. One is actually creating a surrogate ksi variable for each measured variable; since ksi variables are allowed to be exogenous in the LISREL formalism, this accomplishes precisely the same thing.

An Example: Authoritarian-Conservatism Again

We can illustrate the preceding points by showing the construction of a LISREL input file for a measurement model (Fig. 11-8) of the psychological attitude called authoritarian-conservatism discussed in Chapter 8, Section 8.3. To make a LISREL model from this causal model we assume that all errors are uncorrelated. We treat q1-q5 as eta variables, so that we can represent the causal links from q2 to q5 and q5 to q3. It would not do to correlate error terms for q2-q5 and for q3-q5. The model in Fig. 11-8 includes a causal chain from q2 to q3 and, thus, a source of correlation between q2 and q3 that is not AC. A model that correlated the error terms for q2-q5 and q3-q5 would not include a source of correlation between q2 and q3 that did not stem from AC.

We treat AC as an eta variable that has no indicator. The full LISREL model is shown in Fig. 11-9. The variables in parentheses are just to help identify which LISREL variables correspond to which variables in the causal model. We assume the coefficient of the AC->q1 path is fixed at unity, and the error terms for all y variables are fixed at 0. One possible LISREL input file for this model is shown in Fig. 11-10.

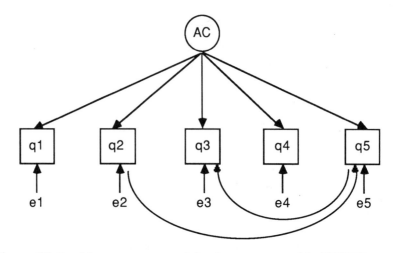

Figure 11-8: Measurement model to be represented in LISREL.

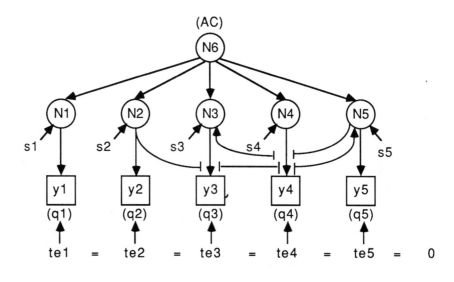

Figure 11-9: Full LISREL model.

```
ANCHORING: Q2->Q5, Q5->Q3
DA NI=5 NO=3001 MA=KM
LABELS
*
'Q1' 'Q2' 'Q3' 'Q4' 'Q5'
KM SY
*
2.0987
0.7161 2.0286
0.4505 0.3356 1.7258
0.7746 0.5012 0.3525 2.0759
0.4263 0.3421 0.3149 0.3014 1.0658
MO NK=0 NX=0 NE=6 NY=5 GA=ZE LX=ZE
TE=ZE TD=ZE PH=ZE PS=DI,FR
PA BE
*
0 0 0 0 0 0
0 0 0 0 0 1
0 0 0 0 1 1
0 0 0 0 0 1
0 1 0 0 0 1
0 0 0 0 0 0
MA BE
*
1 0 0 0 0 -1
0 1 0 0 0 -.5
0 0 1 0 -.3 -.5
0 0 0 1 0 -.5
0 -.3 0 0 1 -.5
0 0 0 0 0 1
MA LY
*
1 0 0 0 0 0
0 1 0 0 0 0
0 0 1 0 0 0
0 0 0 1 0 0
0 0 0 0 1 0
MA PS
*
.5 .5 .5 .5 .5 .5
OU PM TO SE
```

Figure 11-10: LISREL input file for Fig. 11-9.

11.3. EQS

EQS is a recent program authored by Peter Bentler. The input to EQS is much easier than the LISREL formalism, and it is much easier to detect input errors in the EQS program. An EQS input file for the same model just considered is shown in Fig. 11-11.

```
/TITLE
AC1.DAT: FACTOR MODEL + q2->q5, q5->q3;
/SPEC
VAR=5; CAS=3101; ME=ML;
/LABELS
V1=Q1; V2=Q2; V3=Q3; V4=Q4; V5=Q5; F1=AC;
/EQUATIONS
V1 =  F1 + E1;
V2 = .5*F1 + E2;
V3 = .5*F1 + .3*V5 + E3;
V4 = .5*F1 + E4;
V5 = .5*F1 + .3*V2 + E5;
/VARIANCES
E1 TO E5 = .5*;
/MATRIX
2.0987
0.7161 2.0286
0.4505 0.3356 1.7258
0.7746 0.5012 0.3525 2.0759
0.4263 0.3421 0.3149 0.3014 1.0658
/END
```

Figure 11-11: EQS input file.

Changing this input file to create variants of the measurement model pictured in Fig. 11-8 is trivial. The problem is in waiting for the output. Examining a serious number of alternative models interactively is prohibitive if one has a personal computer without an 8087 coprocessor. To overcome this, EQS can be run repeatedly in batch within a simple ."bat" file.[41]

---

[41]We are indebted to Eric Wu, one of the programmers of EQS, for promptly answering our query with the suggestion we describe here.

When EQS is called from DOS version 2.1 or higher, it loads and then prompts for three pieces of information:

1. the input filename,

2. the data filename, and

3. the output filename.

The data filename is optional. In the input file shown above, we have included the covariance matrix as a part of the input file. It is possible to leave the data in a separate file, but we have found it easier to include the data within the input file. If the data is included in the input file, the response to EQS's prompt for a data file is simply a carriage return.

To run EQS in batch you need

1. a command file that ends in ".bat",

2. a series of files, each containing answers to the three prompts EQS gives in a single run, and

3. a series of input files.

Suppose we have three variants of the measurement model pictured in Fig. 11-8, and suppose the input files for each, with covariance data, are called, respectively,

AC1.dat

AC2.dat

AC3.dat

We would then form three files, called "In1", "In2", and "In3", that contain the answers to EQS's prompts for three runs. We show the contents of file "In1" in Fig. 11-12.

```
AC1.dat

AC1.out
```

Figure 11-12: File "In1".

"AC1.dat" must occur on the *first* line of the file "In1." The second line is blank because in this case there is no data file, and a blank line here is the same as a carriage return. The third line tells EQS to send the output to file "AC1.out."

The ."bat" might be called "run.bat", and it would look as shown in Fig. 11-13.

```
Eqs <In1
Eqs <In2
Eqs <In3
```

Figure 11-13: The file "Run.bat"

To execute the "Run.bat" file, simply type "Run" at the DOS prompt. The first line of the file tells DOS to run EQS, and to get the answers for its prompts from the contents of file "In1." The left angle bracket is a DOS command to change the input stream from the console to a text file. EQS will use the file "AC1.dat" as an input file, it will know there is no separate data file, it will put the output in the file "AC1.out", and, when it is finished, DOS will call it again and tell it to now answer its prompts from the contents of file "In2." Any number of models can be run this way.

12. RUNNING TETRAD

TETRAD is an interactive command-driven program which is simple to use. This chapter includes a description of the format of input files, a description of each command, some transcripts of actual TETRAD sessions, and a description of the types of errors that can occur.

12.1. Installing TETRAD

Two versions of TETRAD have been provided on your distribution disk. One of these versions (TETRAD) is designed for computers that do not have an 8087 coprocessor chip; the other version (TET87) is designed for computers that do have this chip. The two programs act in an identical fashion, except that TET87 is considerably faster than TETRAD.

To run TETRAD you will need to install all of the following files on the same directory.

```
TETRAD.COM
TETRAD.000
TETRAD.001
HELP.TXT
ERROR.TXT
```

To run TET87 you will need to install all of the following files on the same directory.

```
TET87.COM
TET87.000
TET87.001
HELP.TXT
ERROR.TXT
```

The sample data and graph files may be installed in any directory.

12.2. Entering and Exiting TETRAD

In order to successfully run TETRAD (TET87) your current directory must be the directory in which the TETRAD (TET87) program resides. For example, if TETRAD.COM (TET87.COM) is in directory "\tetrad," then "\tetrad" must be your current directory.

In order to invoke TETRAD (TET87) simply type "TETRAD" ("TET87") at your monitor prompt.

In the rest of this chapter, we refer to the TETRAD program, but everything we say also applies to TET87. After entering a command, the user must hit the "return" key before the command will be executed.

Upon entering TETRAD, a number of messages are printed out. Finally, a ">" is printed. This symbol is a prompt that indicates that TETRAD is waiting for the user to enter a command.

The program is exited by typing "EXIT" at the prompt.

12.3. Getting Help

Online help summarizing the action of each command C is available by entering TETRAD and typing "help C". The list of commands that TETRAD recognizes can be obtained by simply typing "help". A list of each of the commands and the action that it invokes is also provided in this chapter.

12.4. Input Files

The TETRAD program requires both a directed graph and correlation or covariance data for the measured variables in that graph. The file from which TETRAD reads the correlation of covariance data will be called the **covariance file**. The file from which TETRAD reads the directed graph will be called the **graph file**. Using your favorite editor, these files may be created before the TETRAD program is run. Alternatively, they may be created within the TETRAD program using "EDIT," a simple line editor that is part of TETRAD. In this section we explain how to create covariance files and graph files.

Variable Labels

In both the covariance file and in the directed graph, variables must have names. The conventions for naming variables are very simple

1. Any alphanumeric character[42] can be used in a variable name.

2. Each variable name must be one or two characters long.

3. Names for *measured* variables must begin with a *lowercase* letter or a numeric character.

4. Names for *latent* or unmeasured variables must begin with an *uppercase* letter.

5. One and the same variable must have the same name in the covariance file and in the directed graph.

6. Uppercase letters are distinct symbols from lowercase letters.

Covariance Files

A TETRAD covariance file is a normal text file. With the IBM PC operating system, MS DOS, as many as eight letters can occur in the filename and three more in an extension. Other operating systems may have different conventions. The extension is not necessary although it can be useful. Examples of data filenames are

```
Data1
Data1.pas
1adata
Theory1.dat
```

The first non-blank line of a covariance file must be an integer which represents the sample size. It occurs on a line by itself.

---

[42]The set of alphanumeric characters include all letters, upper and lower case, and all numbers.

After the sample size, the only information in a covariance file is a correlation or covariance for each pair of measured variables. The user may enter either correlational data or covariance data in the covariance file; TETRAD converts all covariances into correlations. In what follows we mean "correlation or covariance" whenever we say just "covariance." By a "number" we always mean a real number or integer. There are two distinct ways of representing the covariance data in a file.

Covariances on Each Line

In the first way of representing covariances, a separate line in the covariance file must be created for each covariance. Each line contains, in order

1. one correlation, entered as a number;

2. the two variable names which correspond to the covariance, separated by at least one space from the covariance number and from each other; and

3. a carriage return.

No latent variables may occur in the covariance file. Every pair of measured variables appearing in the covariance file must have exactly one number associated with it in the covariance file. (Each variable must also be paired with itself; that is, for each variable x, there must be an entry for the pair x x.)

An example of a line in a covariance file is

```
.576   x1   x2
```

The order of the variable names in a line does *not* make a difference. The covariance in the example could just as well be entered as

```
.576   x2   x1
```

Note, however, that it would be illegal to enter both of the above lines in a single covariance file, since that would assign more than one (albeit equal) covariance to a single pair of variables.

The covariances do not have to be entered in any particular order. The sequences in Fig. 12-1 (which are all *fragments* of covariance files) are all the same as far as the TETRAD program is concerned.

```
.24  x1 x2        .45  x1 x3        .86 x3 x2
.45  x1 x3        .86  x2 x3        .24 x1 x2
.86  x2 x3        .24  x1 x2        .45 x3 x1

    (1)               (2)               (3)
```

Figure 12-1: Equivalent input sequences

The fragments of covariance files shown in Fig. 12-2 are *illegal* and will not be read correctly by the program.

```
.24x1 x2                          Correlations
.45 x1 x3                         .24 x1 x2
.86 x2 x3                         .45 x1 x3
                                  .86 x2 x3
( There is no space between
( the correlation and the         (Titles are not allowed.)
( first variable name.     )


x1 x2 .24                         .24 x1 x2  .45 x1 x3
x1 x3 .45                         .86 x2 x3
x2 x3 .86
                                  (Only one correlation is
(The correlation                  ( allowed per line. )
(must come first.)
```

Figure 12-2: Illegal covariance files

To illustrate these points, suppose we have constructed a simple measurement model for socioeconomic status, with four indicators: father's education, father's occupation, mother's education, and family income. Our abbreviation scheme is as follows.

socioeconomic status = SE
father's education = fe
father's occupation = fo
mother's education = me
family income = in

We show our hypothetical model in Fig. 12-3.

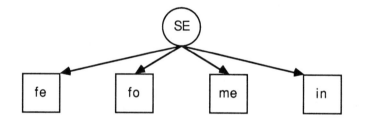

Figure 12-3:

Suppose that the covariance matrix is the one shown in Fig. 12-4. Using our favorite text editor (or the "EDIT" command in TETRAD), we convert this matrix into the covariance file pictured in Fig. 12-5.

	fe	fo	in	me
fe	1.0	.30	.24	.27
fo		1.0	.60	.40
in			1.0	.32
me				1.0

Figure 12-4: SES correlations

```
1024
.30   fe   fo
.24   fe   in
.27   fe   me
.60   fo   in
.40   fo   me
.32   in   me
1.0   fe   fe
1.0   fo   fo
1.0   me   me
1.0   in   in
```

Figure 12-5: Separate line SES covariance file

A Matrix Representation of Covariances

A covariance file may, instead, contain an upper triangular matrix representation of covariances. To represent the covariance matrix of Fig. 12-4, simply create the file in Fig. 12-6.

Once again, no latent variables may appear in the covariance file. The variable names must all be separated by at least one space and must all occur on the same line. The order of the numbers that follow obviously matters, but the spacing does

```
1024
fe      fo     in     me
1.0     0.30   0.24   0.27
        1.0    0.60   0.40
               1.0    0.32
                      1.0
```

Figure 12-6: Matrix representation of covariance file

not. It also does not matter what line a number occurs on. TETRAD will simply keep reading numbers until the (upper triangle) of the matrix has been completely filled. If fewer numbers than are needed to fill out the matrix have been entered into the covariance file, TETRAD will issue an error message and refuse to process the data; if more numbers than are needed to fill out the matrix have been entered into the covariance file, then TETRAD will issue a warning, but proceed normally.

Graph Files

TETRAD treats a directed graph as a set of ordered pairs. Each ordered pair represents a directed edge in the graph, and the directed edge in turn represents a hypothetical causal connection. The first element of the ordered pair represents the cause, and the second element represents the effect. The set

$$\{<Se,fe>,<SE,fo>,<SE,me>,<SE,in>\}$$

describes the directed graph shown in Fig. 12-3.

The user should form such a set of edges to represent the graph of the theory to be investigated. Each line of a graph file contains one edge represented by the name of the cause, at least one space, and the effect. It does not matter which edge is entered first, but of course it *does* matter, in each edge, which vertex or variable name is entered first. A graph file for the above example is shown in Fig. 12-7.

The set of variables that TETRAD considers to be in the graph is derived from the covariance file, *not* the graph file. If there are variables in the covariance file that are not in the graph file, these variables are considered to be part of the graph, even though there are no edges into or out of them. This has implications for the TTR,

```
SE fe
SE fo
SE me
SE in
```

Figure 12-7: Example of a graph file

the TPR, and the pi value of a model. It is possible for tetrad equations to be implied among variables which are in the covariance file but not in the graph file; the residuals of these equation will be counted as part of the TTR. The same is true of the TPR. Furthermore, the pi value of a model depends upon the number of edges in a base model. (See section 12-9. The default base model is one in which one latent variable is connected to each measured variable. The base model that is constructed by default has edges to each measured variable that appears in the covariance file, regardless of whether or not it also appears in the graph file.

12.5. Output Files

The user may specify the name of a file where output is to be sent by using the "OUTPUT" command. The "OUTPUT" command will prompt the user for the file name. If the output file has not been specified, then any command producing output will prompt the user for it. After the output file has been specified, all subsequent output will be sent to that file until the user issues another "OUTPUT" command that specifically changes the output file.

12.6. View and Edit

Two small subsystems with their own set of commands have been incorporated into TETRAD. "VIEW" is for viewing output files, and "EDIT" is for creating or modifying input files. Since each of these commands reads files into memory, using them on large files will use large amounts of memory. TETRAD will produce an error message if the file is too large to fit into memory. Each of these subsystems is intended for use on files which have maximum line lengths of 80 characters.

12.7. The Run Command and Menus

The easiest way to use TETRAD is through the "RUN" command. Each output command, except the "RUN" command, is used to produce output about one specific feature of a model. The purpose of the "RUN" command is to allow the user to use a single command to produce output about a variety of features of a model.

The "RUN" command is used in conjunction with the "SETOUTPUT" command. The "SETOUTPUT" command provides the user with a menu of possible outputs that can be produced by the "RUN" command. Any combination of desired outputs can be produced by choosing the desired outputs from the menu of the "SETOUTPUT" command, and then issuing the "RUN" command. It should be emphasized that the outputs selected from the "SETOUTPUT" command do not themselves produce any output, nor do they have any effects on any command except the "RUN" command. An example of the use of the run command is shown below. Note that "RUN" prompts for any information that it needs that has not already been specified; if the information had already been specified, then the information would not have been prompted for. Further details about "RUN" and "SETOUTPUT" are in Section 12-9.

The "SETPARAMETER" command prompts the user for all of the program parameters. Unlike the "SETOUTPUT" command, this command affects all of the output output commands.

While many of the other commands make the use of TETRAD more convenient, most of the features of TETRAD can be invoked using just these three commands together with the "EXIT" command.

The following is a transcript of an actual TETRAD run. Input typed in by the user is shown in boldface. User input is always followed by a carriage return which is generally not shown. However, on lines where the user enters only a carriage return, this has been symbolized by <CR>. Any italic text between a "{" and a "}" is a comment that has been added to the transcript to explain the commands. All of the examples in this chapter will assume that the covariance file used was d1.dat and the graph file used was d1graph (both shown below).

d1.dat has the following contents.

```
500
1.0  x1  x1
1.0  x2  x2
1.0  x3  x3
1.0  x4  x4
1.0  x5  x5
```

```
1.0   x6  x6
1.0   x7  x7
1.0   x8  x8
1.0   x9  x9
0.562 x1  x2
0.658 x1  x3
0.471 x2  x3
0.750 x1  x4
0.524 x2  x4
0.866 x3  x4
0.774 x1  x5
0.550 x2  x5
0.790 x3  x5
0.969 x4  x5
0.783 x1  x6
0.563 x2  x6
0.674 x3  x6
0.880 x4  x6
0.949 x5  x6
0.779 x1  x7
0.565 x2  x7
0.674 x3  x7
0.875 x4  x7
0.942 x5  x7
0.989 x6  x7
0.760 x1  x8
0.555 x2  x8
0.655 x3  x8
0.855 x4  x8
0.920 x5  x8
0.956 x6  x8
0.957 x7  x8
0.787 x1  x9
0.566 x2  x9
0.674 x3  x9
0.878 x4  x9
0.946 x5  x9
0.993 x6  x9
0.990 x7  x9
0.958 x8  x9
```

d1graph has the following contents.

```
T1  T2
T2  T3
T1  T3
T1  x1
T1  x2
T1  x3
T2  x4
T2  x5
T2  x6
T3  x7
T3  x8
T3  x9
```

In the following TETRAD session, the user sends output about the suggested sets and the tetrad equations to a file called "firstout". The transcript is as follows. (C:\ is the prompt produced by the operating system before the program is invoked.)

C:\tetrad

> { *The program is invoked.* }

COPYRIGHT (C) 1987 by Causal Research, Inc.
All Rights Reserved

For help, type "help"

{ *The user plans to use the "RUN" command. The current values of
all of the output options are printed. Then the user is prompted
for a list of numbers of output options which he or she wants to
toggle. In this case the user wants to see all of the suggested
sets and the implied tetrad equations.* }

>setout

```
        Tetrad Equations                    Vanishing Partials
        -------------------                 ----------------------
1: Suggested sets     FALSE

   Statistical Info On:                     Statistical Info On:

2: All tetrad         FALSE           5: All partial        FALSE
3: Implied tetrad     FALSE           6: Implied partial    FALSE
4: Held tetrad        FALSE           7: Held partial       FALSE

                                      8: Rtpr Chart:        FALSE

Rttr Chart Info for:
9:  Measured - Measured Edges:   FALSE
10: Latent - Latent Edges:       FALSE
11: Latent - Measured Edges:     FALSE
12: Measured - Latent Edges:     FALSE

13: Correlations  FALSE               14: Standard     FALSE

Enter the numbers of options that you want to toggle: 1 2
```

{ *The output options with the new values are now automatically printed out.* }

```
        Tetrad Equations                       Vanishing Partials
        -------------------                    ----------------------
        1: Suggested sets    TRUE

        Statistical Info On:                   Statistical Info On:

        2: All tetrad        TRUE              5: All partial        FALSE
        3: Implied tetrad    FALSE             6: Implied partial    FALSE
        4: Held tetrad       FALSE             7: Held partial       FALSE

                                               8: Rtpr Chart:        FALSE

        Rttr Chart Info for:
        9:  Measured - Measured Edges:   FALSE
        10: Latent - Latent Edges:       FALSE
        11: Latent - Measured Edges:     FALSE
        12: Measured - Latent Edges:     FALSE

        13: Correlations  FALSE                14: Standard    FALSE
```

{ *No output has been created so far. The "RUN" command is now invoked to produce output about the suggested sets and the tetrad equations. Since some information needed to run the program has not been entered yet, the command prompts for the covariance file, the graph file, the significance level, and the name of the file where output is to be sent. In this case, the output is sent to a file called "firstout".* }

>**ru**

Covariance file: **d1.dat**

Graph file: **d1graph**

```
Edge:  T1->T2
Edge:  T2->T3
Edge:  T1->T3
Edge:  T1->x1
Edge:  T1->x2
Edge:  T1->x3
Edge:  T2->x4
Edge:  T2->x5
```

```
Edge: T2->x6
Edge: T3->x7
Edge: T3->x8
Edge: T3->x9
```

{ *The default value of the significance level is 0.05.* }

Output file: **firstout**

> **exit**

12.8. User Interrupts

Some of the calculations that TETRAD performs can be quite time consuming, especially if the model is a large one. For that reason, the user has been provided with a way to interrupt some calculations and return (almost) immediately to the TETRAD command prompt. The user can interrupt a calculation by *holding down* the control key and pressing the "g" key.

12.9. Errors

Two kinds of errors can be made when using TETRAD. **Syntax errors** are "grammatical" errors in the input; they include such things as improper variable names or illegal numbers.

Semantic errors in TETRAD are errors in the "meaning" of the input; they include such things as entering the wrong covariance between two variables or specifying an edge between two variables which should not be connected. Naturally, TETRAD cannot detect all semantic errors; it has no way of knowing whether the covariance between two variables should be 0.01 or 1000. However, TETRAD does detect some semantic errors.

The Form of Error Messages

An error message in TETRAD consists of either four or five parts, depending upon whether the error occurs in input that is entered from a terminal or in data read in from a file. These parts are

1. an explanation of the action TETRAD is going to take,

2. the name of the file and the line number in which the error occurred (if the error is from a file),

3. the line on which the error occurred,

4. a pointer showing the place in the line at which the error occurred, and

5. an explanation of the error.

For example, suppose a graph file contained the following line.

```
T1 x%
```

TETRAD would have the following response.

```
Warning: Input being ignored.
T1 x%
    ^Non-alphanumeric character in tail name.
```

Actions

When TETRAD discovers an error in a line of input, there are three different kinds of actions that the program may take.

1. TETRAD may simply ignore a line of input, and continue on. In this case, the line of input is simply treated as if it did not exist. Upon taking this action TETRAD writes "Warning: Input being ignored."

2. TETRAD may ignore part of a line of input. In this case, the beginning of the line is read, and the end of the line is simply treated as if it did not exist. Upon taking this action TETRAD writes "Warning: " at the beginning of the message. At the end of the

message it points to a character in the input line; all characters after that are ignored. TETRAD then writes "Rest of line ignored."

3. If the error prevents TETRAD from continuing to process its data, TETRAD will return to the command prompt without creating any output. The next time a command creating output is issued, TETRAD will prompt the user to re-enter the data. For example, if covariances between all of the observable variables are not contained in the covariance file, TETRAD will prompt the user for a new covariance file. In this case TETRAD writes "Fatal error: " at the beginning of the error message.

Agreement between Graph and Covariance Files

TETRAD receives input of two different kinds from two different sources. A covariance file specifies the correlations or covariances between various observable variables, and a graph file contains a directed graph. The covariance file should contain covariances for every pair of observable variables that appear in the graph.

It is possible that the input file might not specify covariances for every pair of observable variables in the graph. Alternatively, the covariance file might not specify covariances for every pair of observable variables occurring in the data file itself. In either case the error is fatal. TETRAD will not produce any output and will give control to the part of the program which asks the user if he or she would like to enter a new graph.

Sometimes one may wish to run TETRAD using a directed graph that contains some but not all of the measured variables in the covariance file. And sometimes one may intend to enter a directed graph that contains all of the measured variables in the covariance file, but inadvertently omit some of those variables. TETRAD cannot intuit the user's intentions, but the program does recognize the ambiguity of the situation. If the covariance file contains covariances between pairs of observable variables that do not occur in the graph, TETRAD simply issues a warning, and continues normally.

Maximum Number of Variables and Edges

TETRAD sets a limit to the maximum number of variables that can appear in an input file and graph. The exact value of this variable depends upon the kind of computer being used. Currently, for the IBM PC and compatibles, the maximum number of variables is 23 (9 for the demonstration disk accompanying this book).

If the maximum number of variables is exceeded the an error message will appear. If there are variables in your covariance file that do not appear in the graph, then removing all occurrences of these variables from the input file may reduce the total number of variables to below the maximum number allowed.

One distinctive error message that TETRAD can issue concerns the maximum number of edges that may be entered in a graph. When this total is reached, TETRAD will stop prompting for more edges and print a warning.

Memory

Memory errors occur when the computer's random access memory capacity is exceeded. Such errors may occur because

1. the model you are trying to run is too big for TETRAD,

2. the model you are trying to run is too big for your computer's memory,

3. the significance level is too large for the model you are analyzing[43], or

4. too many units of suggested sets have been requested.

Semantic Errors TETRAD Will Not Recognize

Listed below are some mistakes likely to cause TETRAD to give poor results. They are especially difficult to locate because, syntactically, there is nothing to cause an error message from TETRAD. Everything looks fine, but when TETRAD's recommendations are subjected to other methods of evaluating linear models (e.g., LISREL's chi square calculator), the results are disastrous.

1. The *data file* is *faulty*. There might be a typo in the correlations (e.g. a number was entered incorrectly), or there might be incorrect variable names bound to a correlation.

---

[43]TETRAD is forced to do more computation on the same model and data set for larger values of significance level. When significance level is increased fewer equations "hold" in the data, consequently fewer edges are prohibited from being suggested as additions. The computational demands go up when the number of admissible candidates to a suggested set of treks goes up.

2. The *graph* is *faulty*.

    a. The graph for which suggested trek additions were requested is not skeletal and has a measured variable directly connected to two or more latent variables.

    b. The wrong graph was entered.

3. The *general assumptions* were *faulty*.

    a. The initial skeleton is a poor model.

    b. The assumptions of structural equation models do not hold. (see Chapter 6, Section 2.6)

    c. The sample is inadequate or unrepresentative.

12.10. TETRAD Commands

TETRAD is not sensitive to the case of the characters that a user types in (except for variable names). Also, TETRAD recognizes any nonambiguous substring of a command. For example, if a user enters "ru," TETRAD will recognize the "RUN" command. However, if a user enters "r," then TETRAD will print an error message pointing out that "r" is ambiguous (because there is a "RUN" command and a "RTTR" command).

Types of Commands

TETRAD commands may be divided into three broad categories.

1. Output-producing commands cause information about a model to be written to a file. An example of an output command is "PARTIAL," which outputs information about which partial equations are implied by a model, and which partial equations hold in the population. (Note that the "OUTPUT" command does not itself produce output and, so, is not an output-producing command).

2. Parameter commands set various parameters (such as the significance level) which affect the output produced by the output commands. For example, the "SIGNIFICANCE" command allows the user to reset the significance level which determines whether or not a particular equation is said to hold in the data. Such a command affects the output produced by output commands such as

"PARTIAL," but does not itself produce any output. To invoke a given parameter command, simply type the name of the command; the command will them prompt for the new value of the parameter.

3. Finally, there are miscellaneous commands that are helpful in running the program but do not produce or affect the output of the program. For example, the "VIEW" command allows the user to view output files produced by TETRAD.

Switches

Each output-producing command has a (possibly empty) set of compatible switches. Adding a switch to a command limits the output of the command to some subset of the normal output. Switches must be entered on the same line as the command itself. For example, the "RTTR" command has four compatible switches, "MM", "ML", "LM", and "LL". If the user types "Rttr," then the entire Rttr chart is output. If the user types "Rttr mm," then only that part of the Rttr chart involving an edge between two measured variables is output.

It is possible to enter more than one switch on a command line. Any subset of the switches that are compatible with a given command may be entered in any combination and in any order. The effect of entering more than one switch on a command line is cumulative; that is, the output produced by a combination of switches combines all of the output that would have been produced by each switch individually.

For example, "rttr mm ml" is equivalent to "rttr ml mm." The effect of both of these command is to output that part of the Rttr chart involving an edge between two measured variables or an edge between a measured variable and a latent variable.

Prompting

Each ouput-producing command has certain required information that it needs to produce its output. For example, it is impossible to calculate which tetrad equations are implied unless a model has been specified. For that reason, if an output command is entered and some of the necessary information is missing, the command will prompt the user for the missing information. If the prompt is followed by a value between square brackets ("[", "]"), that value is the default value. Simply hitting a carriage return at that point enters the default value.

12.11. Running TETRAD in Batch Mode

Versions of MS DOS labelled 2.1 and higher are capable of redirecting input and output. To get input from a file named "A" instead of from the terminal simply type "tetrad < A." "A" should contain all of the commands to TETRAD that one would normally enter from the terminal. In Fig. 12-8 we show an example of a file which produces a TETRAD session identical to the example in Section 12.7, but in which the input is from a file instead of the terminal.

```
setout
1 2
ru
d1.dat
d1graph
firstout
exit
```

Figure 12-8: An input file for running TETRAD in batch mode.

Note that the file includes not only commands such as "SETOUTPUT" and "RUN," but also answers to prompts that TETRAD issues.

To run TETRAD in batch mode, simply create a batch file with a ."bat" extension. If input is to come from file "A," simply put in the batch file the command "tetrad < A." Then invoke the batch file by typing its name (without the ."bat" extension). For example, a file "tet.bat" could be created. The contents of tet.bat would be the line "tetrad < A." To invoke tet.bat simply write "tet."

12.12. List of Commands

This section contains a brief list of all of the TETRAD commands. In the following section each command is described in more detail. This section does *not* explain what the output means. It uses a number of concepts explained in Chapter 7 and 5.

We divide the commands into three types, *output-producing commands, parameter commands*, and *miscellaneious commands*. Output-producing commands all cause output to be sent to the current output file. Each will prompt for any parameter values that are needed but that have not been set by the user. Parameter commands change parameter values. Miscellaneous commands are self-explanatory. The parameters are not commands, but do affect the output produced by commands.

12.13. Command Summaries

In this section a description of each command is given. The commands are listed in alphabetical order. The format of each description is the same, namely:

1. The name of the command.

2. A brief description of the action taken by the command.

3. If it is an output-producing command, a description of the switches that can be used with the command. This includes
   a. The default switch (i.e. what happens if no switch is specified with the command).
   b. The name of a switch.
   c. The effect of using that switch.

4. The type (output-producing, parameter, or miscellaneous command).

5. A list of the parameters that affect the output of the command (in the case of output-producing commands) or a list of the parameters that the command affects (in the case of parameter commands). This section is left out in the miscellaneous commands.

6. If it is an output-producing command, a list of other commands that interact with the given command.

CHANGEGRAPH

Changegraph prompts for a series of edges to be added to or deleted from the current graph. First, it prints out the current graph. Then it prompts for edges to delete. If there are edges to delete, the user should enter one of these edges and press carriage return. The format of an edge is exactly the same as that used in graph files, that is, a variable name followed by at
second variable name. The command will continue to prompt for edges to delete

Output-producing commands

Correlations	Correlations of measured variables
Compare	Detailed effects of adding edge to graph
Partial	Partial equations
Rttr	Effect on tetrad equations of adding edges
Rtpr	Effect on partial equations of adding edges
Run	Various outputs depending on setoutput
Standard	Summary information
Suggested	Sets of treks that will improve graph
Tetrad	Tetrad equations

Parameter commands

Changegraph	Changes current graph
Input	Covariance and graph files
Output	Output file
Pi	Sets parameters of base model for pi
Setoutput	Menu to set parameters for a run command
Setparameters	Prompts for information about all parameters
Significance	Resets the significance level
Units	Number of significance levels for suggested sets

Miscellaneous commands

Edit	Line editor for input files
Exit	Exits program
Help	Help on each command
Print	Print a file
Status	Current value of output parameters
View	Views output files one screen at a time

List of Parameters - Affect Output

Current graph
Covariances
Number of edges in base model
Number of fixed edges in base model
Significance
TTR of base model
Units

Figure 12-9: A list of TETAD's commands.

until the user enters a carriage return at the prompt. This is taken as a signal to stop prompting for further edges to delete. Then the command prompts for edges to add in the same fashion. Finally, it prints out the graph with the changes the user has made. While it is possible to delete *edges*, it is not possible to delete *vertices*; a vertex is present even after all of the edges containing it have been deleted.

The following is an example of the use of changegraph to add the edge x1->x2 to the current graph.

>change

Edges to be deleted.

Edge: **<CR>**

Edges to be added.

Edge: **x1 x2**
Edge: x1->x2
Edge: **<CR>**

Type

Parameter

Affects parameter

Current graph

COMPARE

Compare prompts the user for an edge to add to the current graph. Compare prints out all of the equations which were implied in the original graph but are not implied by the graph with the added edge. (Note that it is not possible for an equation to be implied in the extended graph but not in the original graph). For each equation it (redundantly) prints out whether or not it is implied by the *extended graph*, whether or not it holds in the data, its residual, and its p value. At the end it specifies the Rttr, D(I-H), and D(H-I) values for that edge. Below is an example of the use of the compare command and the output it produces. (Remember, we are assuming the covariance file is d1.dat and the graph file is d1graph).

>**compare**

Edge:
>**x1 x2**

The relevant part of the output produced by this command was

Edge added: x1->x2

Tetrad Equation	Residual	Impld.	Held	P(diff.)
x1 x2, x4 x3 = x1 x4, x2 x3	0.1334			0.0000
x1 x2, x3 x4 = x1 x3, x2 x4	0.1419			0.0000
x1 x2, x5 x3 = x1 x5, x2 x3	0.0794			0.0018
x1 x2, x3 x5 = x1 x3, x2 x5	0.0821			0.0000
x1 x2, x6 x3 = x1 x6, x2 x3	0.0100		y	0.6631
x1 x2, x3 x6 = x1 x3, x2 x6	0.0083		y	0.6574
x1 x2, x7 x3 = x1 x7, x2 x3	0.0119		y	0.5992
x1 x2, x3 x7 = x1 x3, x2 x7	0.0070		y	0.7127
x1 x2, x8 x3 = x1 x8, x2 x3	0.0102		y	0.6519
x1 x2, x3 x8 = x1 x3, x2 x8	0.0029		y	0.8816
x1 x2, x9 x3 = x1 x9, x2 x3	0.0081		y	0.7237
x1 x2, x3 x9 = x1 x3, x2 x9	0.0064		y	0.7326

Rttr: 0.502   D(I-H): 4   D(H-I): 8

Each of these equations was implied by the original graph, but are not implied when the edge x1->x2 is added to the graph.

Switches

Default switch: tetrad

Common: Causes the two variables entered by the user
to be interpreted as specifying a correlated
error between those variables.

Tetrad: Print out tetrad equations defeated by addition of the edge.

Partial: Print out partial equations defeated by addition of the edge.

Type

Output producing

Parameters that affect

Covariances
Current graph
Significance

See also

Input
Changegraph
Significance

CORRELATIONS

This command prints out the correlations between each of the measured variables.

Type

Output producing

Parameters that affect

Covariances

See also

Input

EDIT

Edit is a simple line editor. It prompts for a filename to edit. If the file currently exists, its contents are read in to a buffer. Edit always has a current line, which is where commands that change the file act. Initially, the current line is set to the first line of the file. 'u' and 'd' move the current line up and down respectively. When in append mode, the user may enter a series of lines which will be entered into the file just after the current line. Append mode is ended when the user types a period (".") as the first character of a line. Insert mode is similar except that the text is entered just prior to the current line. Edit operates only on files with a maximum line length of 80 characters. It recognizes the following commands. The changes made are not permanent changes to the file until the "w" command is issued.

a	Enter append mode. (Ended by typing "." as first character of line.)
c	Prompts the user for a string. This string replaces the current line.
d	Move current line down one line. (No effect if at bottom of file.)
e	Exit editor, return to TETRAD.
i	Enter insert mode. (Ended by typing '.' as first character of line.)
l	Display the file.
r	Remove the current line.
s	Show the current line.
u	Move current line up one line. (No effect if at top of file.)
w	Prompts for a filename and writes the file.

<CR>   Move current line down one line.

The following is an example of how to use EDIT to create d1.dat.

>edit
i

{ *The user inserts the following text into the initially*
empty file. Each line is inserted into the file until
a "." is encountered as the first character in a line. }

T1 T2
T2 T3
T1 T3
T1 x1
T1 x2
T1 x3
T2 x5
T2 x6
T x7
T3 x8
T3 x9

{ *This ends insert mode. Hereafter, text entered will*
be interpreted as commands rather than as text to be
inserted into the file. }

l   { *The user lists the file.* }
T1 T2
T2 T3
T1 T3
T1 x1
T1 x2
T1 x3
T2 x5
T2 x6
T x7
T3 x8
T3 x9

*{ The user notices that there is a mistake two lines up
from the bottom of the file. Since the current position
is the bottom of the file, he or she goes up two lines
to fix it. }*

u
T3 x8
u
T x7
c   *{ The user issues a change command to fix the line. }*
T x7
Change to: **T3 x7**
w   *{ The user saves the file. }*
File name [d1.dat]: **d1.dat**
e   *{ The user exits. }*

Type

> Miscellaneous

EXIT

Closes all of the files and causes the program to exit.

Type

> Miscellaneous

HELP

Simply typing help gives a brief summary of each TETRAD command. For a given command C, typing "help C" give a more extensive description of the command. Unlike the command interpreter, "HELP" does not accept abbreviations of commands.

Help prints its information a screenful at a time, and then pauses until the user presses another key. Pressing "e" or "E" (without a carriage return) exits help and returns to the command prompt. Pressing any other key except <CR> prints the next screenful of information.

The information on each command includes what effect issuing the command has, what parameters it is affected by or affects, and how each switch modifies the action of the command.

Type

Miscellaneous

INPUT

Input first prompts the user to enter the name of a covariance file, and then prompts the user to enter the name of a graph file. If a file does not exist, the user will be reprompted for a file name until the name of a file that does exist is entered. The default value for each file is the current file.

Input doesn't check that either of the file names it prompts for exists until after both file names have been entered. For that reason, if the covariance file does not exist, the error message won't appear until after the name of the graph file has also been entered. Any error message will specify which file name is faulty.

Type

Parameter

Affects parameters

Covariances
Current Graph

OUTPUT

Output prompts for a file name, and changes the file where output is sent to the entered file name. If the file already exists, then the user will be asked if he or she wishes to append further output to the file. If the user answers no to this question, then the user will be asked if he or she wishes to overwrite this file. If the answer to this question is also no, then the user will be asked to enter another file name. If the user wishes to send output to the terminal, then he or she should enter the name "con:" in response to the prompt.

Type

Parameter

Affects parameter

Output file

PARTIAL

Partial prints out information about a set of partial equations. The membership of the set is determined by the switches. For each member of the set partial prints out whether it is implied, whether it holds at the given significance level, and the probability of obtaining the observed partial residual given that the residual in the population is 0.

Switches

Default switch: All

All: Information about every partial equations among each triple of distinct observable variables.

Held: Information about every partial equation among each triple of distinct observable variables that holds at the given significance level.

Implied: Information about every implied partial equation among triples of distinct observable variables.

Type

Output producing

Parameters that affect

Covariances
Graph file
Significance

See also

Input
Changegraph
Significance

PI

Pi is a command used to set the paramaters of the base model. In order to calculate the pi value of a model, three things must be known about the base model.

1. the number of edges,

2. the TTR, and

3. the number of fixed edges.

The value of pi depends upon the number of degrees of freedom in the base model. The number of degrees of freedom depends upon how many edges have coefficients that may vary, and how many edges have fixed coefficients. For each latent variable, TETRAD fixes the coefficient of one edge to a measured variable variable to one.

"Pi" first asks if the user wishes to use a model with one latent variable connected to every measured variable by a single edge as the base model. (Henceforth, such a model will be called a **star model**. If the user answers "y" or "Y," then TETRAD will automatically set the parameter values of the base model to equal those of the star model. The covariances among variables are those specified in the covariance file. The variables in the star model are those appearing in the covariance file. If these files have not been specified, then TETRAD will prompt for them. The advantage of using a star model as a base model is that it makes the pi value of any model nonnegative, since it implies all possible tetrad equations. If the "PI" command is never issued, the TETRAD uses the star model as a base model.

If the user answers no to the first question, then he or she is asked if the current model should be the base model. If the user answers "y" or "Y," then TETRAD will automatically set the parameter values of the base model to equal those of the current model. Once again, the current model is based upon the current graph and covariance files; if these have not been specified then TETRAD will prompt for them.

If the user answers no to the second question, then TETRAD will prompt the user to enter the number of edges, the TTR, and the number of edges with fixed coefficients in the base model.

Once a "PI" command has been issued, the base model will remain unchanged until the next "PI" command is issued. (Upon entering TETRAD, if no "PI" command is issued, the parameters of the base model are based upon the star model derived from the first covariance file entered.)

Type

Parameter

Affects parameters

Number of edges in base model
TTR of base model
Number of fixed edges in base model

PRINT

Print prompts for the name of a file, and then prints the file on a printer.

Type

Miscellaneous

RTPR

For each edge in a given set, Rtpr prints out what effect adding that edge to the current graph will have (as long as the Rtpr is greater than 0). The set of edges includes all edges that are not currently in graph, and correlated errors between each pair of variables that do not have an edge in either direction between them. The information printed includes how much the TPR of the current graph will be reduced, how much (PI-PH) will be reduced, and how much (PH-PI) will be increased. The names given to these quantities are

I(PH-PI): The increase in the number of equations that hold, but aren't implied.

D(PI-PH): The decrease in the number of equations that are implied, but don't hold.

Rtpr: The reduction in the total tetrad residual.

Switches

None

Type

Output producing

Parameters that affect

Covariances
Current graph
Significance

See also

Input
Changegraph
Significance

RTTR

For each edge in a given set, Rttr prints out what effect adding that edge to the current graph will have (as long as the Rttr of the added edge is greater than 0). The information printed includes how much the TTR of the current graph will be reduced, how much (I-H) will be reduced, how much (H-I) will be increased, and the pi value of the modified model. The names given to these quantities are

I(H-I): The increase in the number of equations that hold but aren't implied.

D(I-H): The decrease in the number of equations that are implied but don't hold.

Rttr: The reduction in the total tetrad residual.

Pi: The pi value of the model.

Switches

Default Switch: All

All: Each edge that is not already present in the graph, and each
           correlated error between pairs of observable variables
           that have no edge in either direction between them. If
           this switch is on, the other switches are ignored.

Ll: Each latent-latent edge that is not already in the
           graph, and each correlated error between pairs of latent
           variables that have no edge in either direction between them.

Lm: Each latent-measured edge that is not already in the
           graph, and each correlated error between latent and measured
           variables that have no edge in either direction between them.

Ml: Each measured-latent edge that is not already in the
           graph, and each correlated error between latent and measured
           variables that have no edge in either direction between them.

Mm: Each measure-measured edge that is not already in the
           graph, and each correlated error between pairs of measured
           variables thathave no edge in either direction between them.

Type

Output producing

Parameters that Affect

Covariances
Current graph
Significance
Number of edges in base model
TTR of base model
Number of fixed edges in base model

See also

Input
Changegraph
Significance
Pi

RUN

Run combines the output of all of the other output-producing commands in a single command. The exact output of Run depends upon the options set via the setoutput command.

Switches

None

Type

Output producing

Parameters that affect

Covariances
Current graph
Units
Signficance
Number of edges in base model
TTR of base model
Number of fixed edges in base model

See also

Input
Changegraph
Setoutput
Units
Significance
Pi

SETOUTPUT

Setoutput determines what the output of the run command will be. It prints the following menu.

Tetrad Equations   Vanishing Partials
-------------------   ----------------------
1: Suggested sets   FALSE

Statistical Info On: Statistical Info On:

2: All tetrad   FALSE   5: All partial   FALSE
3: Implied tetrad   FALSE   6: Implied partial   FALSE
4: Held tetrad   FALSE   7: Held partial   FALSE

                                                    8: Rtpr Chart: FALSE

Rttr Chart Info for:
9: Measured - Measured Edges: FALSE
10: Latent - Latent Edges: FALSE
11: Latent - Measured Edges: FALSE
12: Measured - Latent Edges: FALSE

13: Correlations FALSE   14: Standard   FALSE

The Boolean values next to each option indicate whether it is currently on or off. The default value for each option is false. In order to toggle the value of any set of options, simply type the number of each option at the prompt. After the numbers of the options have been typed in, the menu is printed again so that the user may see the effect that his input has had on the selected options.

The output produced by the run command if a given option is on is equivalent to the output of one of the other output-producing commands. These equivalences are described below.

1. Suggested sets = suggestedsets

2. All tetrad = tetrad all

3. Implied tetrad = tetrad implied

4. Held tetrad = tetrad held

5. All partial = partial all

6. Implied partial = partial implied

7. Held partial = partial held

8. Rtpr = rtpr

9. LL = rttr ll

10. LM = rttr lm

11. ML = rttr ml

12. MM = rttr mm

13. Correlations = correlations

14. Standard = standard

Setting these values has no effect on any command other than "run". However, once they have been set, they remain set until the user changes them with another "SETOUTPUT" command.

Type

Miscellaneous

See Also

> Rttr
> Rtpr
> Partial
> Tetrad
> Suggestedsets
> Correlations
> Standard

SETPARAMETERS

This command prompts the user to set all of TETRAD's parameters. These are, in order

1. Covariance file

2. Graph file

3. Output file

4. TTR of base model

5. Number of edges in base model

6. Number of fixed edges in base model

7. Units of suggested sets

8. Significance level

The following is an example of the use of the command to change the significance level, the units of suggested sets, and the output file.

> { *The items in brackets are the default values.*
> *Entering a <CR> enters the default value.* }

>setpar

Covariance file: [d1.dat] **<CR>**

Graph file: [d1graph] **<CR>**

Output file: **out2**

TTR for the base model: [6.37395] **<CR>**

How many edges in base model [11.0000]: **<CR>** ·

How many fixed edges in base model [3]: **<CR>**

Units of suggested sets [2.00000]: **3**

Significance level (between 0 and 1) [0.05000]: **.4**

Type

      Parameter

Affects parameters

      Covariances
      Current graph
      Significance
      Number of edges in base model
      Number of fixed edges in base model
      TTR of base model

SIGNIFICANCE

The significance command sets the significance level used by TETRAD to determine whether tetrad and partial equations hold in the population. If a well-formed number between 0 and 1 is not entered, then it will continue to prompt until one is entered.

Type

Parameter

Affects parameter

Significance

STANDARD

The Standard command prints out the TTR, I-H, H-I, number of tetrad equations that hold in the population, number of tetrad equations explained by the model, the pi values of the model, TPR, PI-PH, PH-PI, number of partial equations that hold in the population, and number of partial equations explained by the model.

Type

Output producing

Parameters that affect

Covariances
Current graph
Significance
TTR of base model
Number of edges in base model
Number of fixed edges in base model

See also

Input
Changegraph
Significance

Pi

STATUS

Status prints out the current value of each output parameter. The output options refer to parameters set by the "SETOUTPUT" command and used by the "RUN" command. The following is an example of the format.

Graph file: CS.DAT
Covariance file: CS.G
Output file: CSOUT

The number of edges in the base model is: 8
The TTR of the base model is: 12.09
The number of fixed edges in the base model is: 0
The significance level is: 0.05
The number of suggested sets units is: 2
The sample size is: 115

Output options (for run command only):

Suggested sets:	TRUE	Implied tetrads:	FALSE
All tetrads:	TRUE	All partials:	TRUE
Implied partials:	FALSE	Held tetrads:	FALSE
Held partials:	FALSE	Rtpr:	TRUE
LM Rttr:	TRUE	MM Rttr:	TRUE
ML Rttr:	TRUE	ML Rttr:	TRUE

Type

Miscellaneous

SUGGESTEDSETS

Suggestedsets outputs a series of significance levels. Associated with each significance level is a series of sets of treks. Each set of treks will defeat some tetrad equations that do not hold in the population at the given significance level, but will not defeat any tetrad equation that holds in the population at the given signficance level. A heuristic procedure is used to calculate the sets, so it is possible, although unlikely that there are some inaccuracies in the suggested sets output even if the current graph is skeletal. The number of different significance levels is determined by the units parameter.

The first significance level is the first level at which any suggested sets exist. Each succeeding significance level is the first level at which there are different suggested sets than at the preceding level.

Below is an example of output from the "SUGGESTEDSETS" command with covariance file d1.dat and graph file d1graph.

Sets of suggested treks at significance level = 0.0063

{ x4-x5 }

Sets of suggested treks at significance level = 0.0207

{ x3-x4 x3-x5 x4-x5 }

If units had been set at one, then only the suggested sets at significance level 0.0063 would have been suggested.

Switches

None

Parameters that affect

Covariances
Current graph
Units

See also

Input
Changegraph

TETRAD

Tetrad prints out information about a set of tetrad equations. The membership of the set is determined by the switches. For each member of the set tetrad prints out whether it is implied, whether it holds at the given signficance level, and the probability of obtaining the observed tetrad residual given that the residual in the population is 0.

Switches

Default switch: All

All: Information about every quartet of distinct observable variables.

Held: Information about every tetrad equation among four distinct observable variables that holds at the given significance level.

Implied: Information about every implied tetrad equation among four distinct observable variables.

Type

Output-producing

Parameters that affect

Covariances
Current graph
Significance

See also

Input
Changegraph
Significance

UNITS

The units command determines how many significance levels the "suggestedsets" command will print out suggested sets for. If a well-formed number is not entered, it will continue to prompt the user until one is entered. If a real number is entered instead of an integer, it will round the number to the nearest integer.

Type

Parameter

Affects parameter

Units

VIEW

View prompts for a filename. It then prints out the file a screenful at a time. It recognizes the following commands. These commands are executed immediately upon being typed in; the user does *not* enter a <CR>. It is possible to split the screen into up to eight windows. Each window may contain a separate file. It displays only the first 80 characters of a line.

b	Move up one line. (No effect if top of file on screen)
d	Print next screen. (No effect if bottom of file on screen)
e	Exit view mode, return to TETRAD.
f	Move down one line. (No effect if bottom of file on screen)
g	Get file. (Prompts for file name).
n	Move to next window.
p	Move to previous window.
r	Remove window.
s	Split window.
u	Print last screenful. (No effect if top of file on screen)

Type

Miscellaneous

Appendix:
The Grammar of the Input

The Backus-Naur notation is used to formally specify the syntax of the input to TETRAD. A complete description of this notation can be found in [110]. A short summary of the notation appears below.

form	:	a syntactical object of type form
forma formb	:	the concatenation of forma and formb
(forma formb)	:	also the concatenation of forma and formb
{form}	:	0 or 1 occurrences of form
form*	:	any number (including 0) occurrences of form
form+	:	at least one occurrence of form
'a'	:	the character a
forma | formb	:	an occurrence of either forma or formb

The correct syntax of the program's input is given below. The following conventions are used.

1. The character produced by pressing the space bar is denoted SPACE.

2. The character produced by pressing the tab key is denoted TAB.

3. The character produced by pressing the return key is denoted CR.

```
space ::=              TAB | SPACE

digit ::=              '0'  | '1'  | '2'  | '3'  | '4'
                       '5'  | '6'  | '7'  | '8'  | '9'

alphabetic :: =        'a'  | 'b'  | 'c'  | 'd'  | 'e'  | 'f'  | 'g'  | 'h'
                       'i'  | 'j'  | 'k'  | 'l'  | 'm'  | 'n'  | 'o'  | 'p'
                       'q'  | 'r'  | 's'  | 't'  | 'u'  | 'v'  | 'w'  | 'x'
                       'y'  | 'z'  | 'A'  | 'B'  | 'C'  | 'D'  | 'E'  | 'F'
                       'G'  | 'H'  | 'I'  | 'J'  | 'K'  | 'L'  | 'M'  | 'N'
                       'O'  | 'P'  | 'Q'  | 'R'  | 'S'  | 'T'  | 'U'  | 'V'
                       'W'  | 'X'  | 'Y'  | 'Z'

alphanumeric ::=       digit | alphabetic

sign ::=               '+'  | '-'

number ::=             {sign} {digit} '.' digit+

variable ::=           alphanumeric {alphanumeric}

edge ::=               variable space+ variable

number-line ::=        space* number space* CR

edge-line ::=          space* edge space* CR

input-line ::=         space* number space+ edge-line

variable-line :: =     space* variable (space+ variable)* CR

numbersgroup ::=       space* number (space+ number)

graph-file ::=         edge-line+

line-form ::=          input-line+

matrix-form ::=        variable-line numbersgroup

covariance-file ::=    number-line (line-form | matrix-form)
```

The covariance file has form covariance-file.

The graph file has form graph-file.

When TETRAD prompts the user for a number, a number line should be entered.

When TETRAD prompts the user for an edge, an edge line should be entered.

About the Authors

Clark Glymour took undergraduate degrees in chemistry and philosophy at the University of New Mexico and a doctorate in History and Philosophy of Science from Indiana University, where he also pursued minors in mathematics and chemical physics. He is the author of *Theory and Evidence* (Princeton University Press, 1980), an editor of *Foundations of Space-Time Theories* (University of Minnesota Press, 1981), and a coauthor of several historical studies on the development of modern physics. His *Freudian Connections* is forthcoming from Harvard University Press. He is presently Professor and Head of the Department of Philosophy at Carnegie Mellon University, and Adjunct Professor of History and Philosophy of Science at the University of Pittsburgh.

Richard Scheines studied the history of science at Hobart College, and is a Ph.D candidate in History and Philosophy of Science at the University of Pittsburgh. He is currently a Research Scientist for the Center for Design of Educational Computing at Carnegie Mellon University (CDEC). Besides his work in developing the TETRAD program, he is the leader of a CDEC project for developing intelligent tutors.

Peter Spirtes took degrees in physics and in philosophy at the University of Michigan, and both a doctorate in History and Philosophy of Science and a master's degree in Computer Science from the University of Pittsburgh. Formerly Research Programmer in the Laboratory for Computational Linguistics, and Research Scientist in the Department of Philosophy at Carnegie Mellon, he is now Assistant Professor of Philosophy at Carnegie Mellon.

Kevin Kelly took an undergraduate degree in philosophy at the University of Missouri-St. Louis and then received a doctorate in History and Philosophy of Science from the University of Pittsburgh. He is the author of several papers on computation theoretic aspects of computer discovery procedures. He is Assistant Professor of Philosophy at Carnegie Mellon University.

References

[1]   Aho, A., Hopcroft, J., and Ullman, J.
        The Design and Analysis of Computer Algorithms.
        Addison-Wesley, Reading, Massachusetts, 1974.

[2]   Anderson, T.
        An Introduction to Multivariate Statistical Analysis.
        Wiley, New York, 1984.

[3]   Baumrind, D.
        Specious Causal Attributions in the Social Sciences.
        Journal of Personality and Social Psychology 45:1289-1298, 1983.

[4]   Bentler, P., and Woodward, J.
        A Head Start Reevaluation: Positive Effects Are Not Yet Demonstrable.
        Evaluation Quarterly 2:493-510, 1978.

[5]   Bentler, P., and Bonett, D.
        Significance Tests and Goodness of Fit in the Analysis of Covariance
            Structures.
        Psychological Bulletin 88:588-606, 1980.

[6]   Bentler, P.
        Theory and Implementation of EQS: A Structural Equations Program.
        BMDP Statistical Software Inc., 1964 Westwood Boulevar, Suite 202, Los
            Angeles, California 90025, 1985.

[7]   Blalock, H. M.
        Causal Inferences in Nonexperimental Research.
        The Univ. of North Carolina Press, Chapel Hill, North Carolina, 1961.

[8]   Blalock, H. M.
        Theory Construction: From Verbal to Mathematical Formulations.
        Prentice-Hall, Englewood Cliffs, New Jersey, 1969.

[9]   Blalock, H. M.
        Conceptualization and Measurement in the Social Sciences.
        Sage Publications, Beverly Hills, California, 1982.

[10]   Blau, Peter, and Duncan, O. D.
        The American Occupational Structure.
        Wiley, New York, 1967.

[11] Blum, R.
Discovery, Confirmation and Incorporation of Causal Relationships from a
Large Time-oriented Clinical Data Base: The RX Project.
In W. Clancy and E. Shortliffe (editors), *Readings in Medical Artificial
Intelligence*, pages 399-425. Addison-Wesley, Reading, Massachusetts,
1984.

[12] Brophy, J., and Good, T.
Teacher-Student Relationships: Causes and Consequences.
Holt, New York, 1974.

[13] Byron, R.
Testing for Misspecification in Econometric Systems Using Full
Information.
International Economic Review 28:138-151, 1972.

[14] Campbell, D., Schwartz, R., Sechrest, L., and Webb, E.
Unobtrusive Measures: Nonreactive Research in the Social Sciences.
Rand McNally, Chicago, 1966.

[15] Cartwright, Nancy.
How the Laws of Physics Lie.
Clarendon Press, Oxford, 1983.

[16] Cicirelli, V. et al.
Report to the Office of Economic Opportunity. Volume I & II: *The Impact
of Head Start: An Evaluation of the Effects of Head Start on Children's
Cognitive and Affective Development.*
Ohio Univ. and Westinghouse Learning Corporation, Athens, Ohio, 1969.

[17] Cnudde, C., and McCrone, D.
The Linkage Between Constituency Attitudes and Congressional Voting
Behavior: A Causal Model.
American Political Science Review 60:66-72, 1966.

[18] Costner, H., Schoenberg, R.
Diagnosing Indicator Ills in Multiple Indicator Models.
In Goldberger, A., Duncan, O. (editors), *Structural Equation Models in the
Social Sciences.* Seminar Press, New York, 1973.

[19] Costner, H. and Herting, J.
Respecification in Multiple Indicator Models.
1984.
Preprint, Univ. of Washington.

[20]   Crain, W.
       Vehicle Safety Inspection Systems: How Effective?
       American Enterprise Institute for Public Policy Research, Washington,
          1979.

[21]   Cross, C.
       Studies in Modality.
       PhD thesis, Univ. of Pittsburgh, Pittsburgh, Pennsylvania, 1985.

[22]   Efron, B.
       Bootstrap Methods: Another Look at the Jacknife.
       Annals of Statistics 7:1-26, 1979.

[23]   Ehrenberg, A. S. C.
       Data Reduction.
       Wiley, New York, 1975.

[24]   Ericksen, E., and Kadane, J.
       Estimating the Population in a Census Year.
       Journal of the American Statistical Association 80:98-131, 1985.

[25]   Faust, D.
       The Limits of Scientific Reasoning.
       Univ. of Minnesota, Minneapolis, Minnesota, 1984.

[26]   Forbes, H.,and Tufte, E.
       A Note of Caution In Causal Modelling.
       American Political Science Review 62:1258-1264, 1968.

[27]   Fox, J.
       Linear Statistical Models and Related Methods.
       Wiley, New York, 1984.

[28]   Freedman, D., and Navidi, W.
       Regression Models for Adjusting the 1980 Census.
       Statistical Science 1:3-7, 1986.

[29]   Freedman, DI.
       Structural-Equation Models: A Case Study.
       Technical Report, Univ. of California, Berkeley, California, May, 1983.
       Department of Statistics.

[30]   Freund, J. E.
       Mathematical Statistics.
       Prentice-Hall, New York, 1971.

[31]   Gale, W., and Pregibon, D.
        Artificial Intelligence Research in Statistics.
        The AI Magazine :72-75, Winter, 1985.

[32]   Garnett, J. C. M.
        On Certain Independent Factors in Mental Measurements.
        Proceedings of the Royal Society 96:xx, 1919.

[33]   Giere, R.
        Bayesian Statistics and Biased Procedures.
        Synthese 20:371-387, 1969.

[34]   Glymour, C.
        The Epistemology of Geometry.
        Nous 11(3):227-251, 1977.

[35]   Glymour, C.
        Theory and Evidence.
        Princeton Univ. Press, Princeton, New Jersey, 1980.

[36]   Glymour, C.
        Social Science and Social Physics.
        Behavioral Science 28(2):126-133, 1983.

[37]   Glymour, C.
        Statistics and Metaphysics.
        Journal of the American Statistical Association 81:964-66, 1986.

[38]   Good, I. J.
        A Causal Calculus, I.
        British Journal For Philsophy of Science 11:305-318, 1961.

[39]   Gorry, G., and Barnett, G.
        Experience with a Model of Sequential Diagnosis.
        Computers and Biomedical Research 1:490-507, 1968.

[40]   Granger, C.
        Investigating Causal Relations By Econometric Models and Cross-Spectral
            Methods.
        Econometrica 37:424-438, 1969.

[41]   Guilford, J.
        Psychometric Methods.
        McGraw-Hill, New York, 1936.

[42]   Harary, F., and Palmer, E.
        Graphical Enumeration.
        Academic Press, New York, 1973.

[43]   Harre, R., and Secord, P.
        The Explanation of Social Behavior.
        Blackwell, Oxford, 1972.

[44]   Hausman, D.
        Are There Causal Relations among Dependent Variables?
        Philosophy of Science 50:58-81, 1983.

[45]   Heise, D.
        Causal Analysis.
        Wiley, New York, 1975.

[46]   Hempel, Carl G.
        Aspects of Scientific Explanation.
        The Free Press, New York, 1965.

[47]   Holland, P.
        Statistics and Causal Inference.
        Journal of the American Statistical Association 81:945-60, 1986.

[48]   Holzinger, K.
        Statistical Resume of the Spearman Two-factor Theory.
        Univ. of Chicago Press, Chicago, 1930.

[49]   Holzinger K., and Spearman, C.
        Note on the Sampling Error of Tetrad Differences.
        British Journal of Educational Psychology 20:91-97, 1926.

[50]   James, L., Mulaik, S., and Brett, J.
        Causal Analysis: Assumptions, Models and Data.
        Sage Publications, Beverley Hills, California, 1982.

[51]   Jeffreys, H.
        Scientific Inference.
        Cambridge Univ. Press, London and New York, 1957.

[52]   Joreskog, K., and Sorbom, D.
        LISREL IV User's Guide.
        International Educational Services, Chicago, 1978.

[53]   Magidson, J. (editor).
        Advances in Factor Analysis and Structural Equation Models.
        Abt Books, Cambridge, Massachusetts, 1979.

[54]   Joreskog, K., and Sorbom, D.
        LISREL VI User's Guide
        Third edition, Scientific Software, Inc., Mooresville, Indiana, 1984.

[55] Kadane, J.
Comment on Freedman and Navidi.
Statistical Science 1:12-17, 1986.

[56] Kahneman, D., Slovic, P., Tversky, A. (editors).
Judgement Under Uncertainty: Heuristics and Biases.
Cambridge Univ. Press, London and New York, 1982.

[57] Kelley, T.
Crossroads in the Mind of Man.
Stanford Uniiversity Press, Stanford, California, 1928.

[58] Kenny, D.
Correlation and Causality.
Wiley, New York, 1979.

[59] Kmenta, J., and Ramsey, J. (editors).
Large-Scale Macro-Economic Models.
North-Holland, Amsterdam, 1981.

[60] Kohn, M.
Class and Conformity.
Dorsey Press, Homewood, Illinois, 1969.

[61] Leamer, E.
Let's Take the Con Out of Econometrics.
American Economic Review 73:31-43, 1983.

[62] Lee, S.
Analysis of Covariance and Correlation Structures.
Computational Statistics and Data Analysis 2:279-295, 1985.

[63] Levi, I.
*Borzoi Books in the Philosophy of Science: Gambling With Truth; An
    Essay on Induction and the Aims of Science.*
Knopf, New York, 1967.

[64] Lewis, D.
Counterfactuals.
Harvard Univ. Press, Cambridge, Massachusetts, 1973.

[65] Lewis, D.
Causation.
Journal of Philosophy 70(17):556-572, 1973.

[66] Lieberson, S.
Making It Count.
Univ. of California Press, Berkely, California, 1986.

[67] Lindley, D., Tversky, A., and Brown, R.
On the Reconciliation of Probability Assessments.
Journal of the Royal Statistical Society 142:146-180, 1979.

[68] Lindsay, R., Buchanan, B., Feigenbaum, E., and Lederberg, J.
Applications of Artificial Intelligence For Organic Chemistry.
McGraw-Hill, New York, 1980.

[69] Ling, R.
Review of "Correlation and Causation" by David Kenny.
Journal of the American Statistical Association 77:489-491, 1983.

[70] Lorens, C.
Flowgraphs for the Modeling and Analysis of Linear Systems.
McGraw-Hill Book Co., New York, 1964.

[71] Magidson, J.
Toward a Causal Model Approach for Adjusting for Preexisting
    Differences in the Nonequivalent Control Group Situation.
Evaluation Quarterly 1:399-420, 1977.

[72] Magidson, J., and Sorbom, D.
Adjusting for Confounding Factors in Quasi-Experiments: Another
    Reanalysis of the Westinghouse Head Start Evaluation.
Educational Evaluation and Policy Analysis 4:321-329, 1982.

[73] Makridakis, S., Andersen, A., Carbone, R., Fildes, R., Hibon, M.,
Lewandowski, R., Newton, J. Parzen, E., and Winkler, R.
The Forecasting Accuracy of Major Time Series Methods.
Wiley, New York, 1984.

[74] Maruyama, G., and McGarvey, B.
Evaluating Causal Models: An Application of Maximum Likelihood
    Analysis of Structural Equations.
Psychological Bulletin 87:502-512, 1980.

[75] McCAdams, et al. (editor).
Behavioral and Social Science Research: A National Resource.
National Academy Press, Washington, D.C., 1982.

[76] McManus.
Bayesian Estimation of the Deterrent Effect of Capital Punishment.
mimeo, Univ. of California, Los Angeles, 1981.

[77]   Meehl, P.
        *Clinical versus Statistical Prediction: A Theoretical Analysis and a Review
            of the Evidence.*
        Univ. of Minnesota Press, Minneapolis, 1954.

[78]   Meehl, P.
        Theoretical Risks and Tabular Asterisks: Sir Karl, Sir Ronald, and the Slow
            Progress of Soft Psychology.
        Journal of Counseling and Clinical Psychology 46:806-834, 1978.

[79]   Miller, W., and Stokes, D.
        Constituency Influence in Congress.
        American Political Science Review 1963(1):45-56, March, 1963.

[80]   Miller, J., Slomczynski, K., and Schoenberg, R.
        Assessing Comparability of Measurement in Cross-National Research:
            Authoritarian-Conservatism in Different Sociocultural Settings.
        Social Psychology Quarterly 44:178-191, 1981.

[81]   Oakes, M.
        Statistical Inference.
        Wiley, New York, 1986.

[82]   O'Donnell, J., and Clayton, R.
        The Stepping-Stone Hypothesis--Marijuana, Heroin and Causality.
        Chemical Dependencies: Behavioral and Biomedical Issues 4:229-241,
            1982.

[83]   Osherson, D., Stob, M., and Weinstein, S.
        Systems that Learn.
        MIT Press, Cambridge, Massachusetts, 1986.

[84]   Pearson, K. and Moul, M.
        The Mathematics of Intelligence, I. The Sampling Errors in the Theory of a
            Generalized Factor.
        Biometrika 19:246-291, 1927.

[85]   Rosenthal, R.
        Experimental Effects in Behavioral Research.
        Appleton-Century Crofts, New York, 1966.

[86]   Rossi, P., Berk, R., and Lenihan, K.
        Money, Work and Crime.
        Academic Press, New York, 1980.

[87] Salmon, W. C.
Probabilistic Causality.
Pacific Philosophical Quarterly 61:50-74, 1980.

[88] Savage, L.
The Foundations of Statistics.
Wiley, New York, 1954.

[89] Scheffe, H.
The Analysis of Variance.
Wiley, New York, 1959.

[90] Schoenberg, R., and Richtand, C.
Application of the EM Method.
Sociological Methods and Research 13:127-150, 1984.

[91] Schultz, T.
Monographs of the Society for Research in Child Development. Volume
47: *Rules of Causal Attribution.*
x, x, 1982.

[92] Searle, S.
Linear Models.
Wiley, New York, 1971.

[93] Simon, H.
Causal Ordering and Identifiability.
In *Models of Discovery*, pages 53-80. D. Reidel, Derdrecht, Holland, 1953.

[94] Simon, H.
Spurious Correlation: A Causal Interpretation.
In *Models of Discovery*, pages 93-106. D. Reidel, Dordrecht, Holland,
1954.

[95] Simon, H.
Models of Discovery.
D. Reidel, Dordrecht, Holland, 1977.

[96] Langley, P., Simon, H., Bradshaw, G., and Zytkow, J.
Scientific Discovery: An Account of the Creative Process.
MIT Press, Boston, 1986.

[97] Sims, C.
Money, Income, and Causality.
American Economic Review 62:540-552, 1972.

[98] Skinner, B. F.
About Behaviorism.
Vintage Books, New York, 1976.

[99] Skyrms, B.
Causal Necessity.
Yale Univ. Press, New Haven, Connecticut, 1980.

[100] Sorbom, D.
Structural Equation Models with Structured Means.
In Joreskog, K. and Wold, H. (editors), *Systems Under Indirect Observation: Causality, Structure, and Prediction.* North-Holland, Amstemdam, 1981.

[101] Sorbom, D.
Detection of Correlated Errors in Longitudinal Data.
British Journal of Mathematical and Statistical Psychology 28:138-151, 1975.

[102] Spearman, C.
General Intelligence Objectively Determined and Measured.
American Journal of Psychology 15:201-293, 1904.

[103] Spearman, C.
The Abilities of Man.
Macmillan, New York, 1927.

[104] Spearman, C.
Pearson's Contribution to the Theory of Two Factors.
British Journal of Psychology 19:95-101, 1928.

[105] Spirtes, P., and Glymour, C.
Space-time and Synonymy.
Philosophy of Science 39:xx, 1983.

[106] Suppes, P.
A Probabalistic Theory of Causality.
North-Holland, Amsterdam, 1970.

[107] Thurstone, L.
The Vectors of Mind.
Univ. of Chicago Press, Chicago, 1935.

[108] Timberlake, M., and Williams, K. R.
Dependence, Political Exclusion, and Government Repression: Some Cross-National Evidence.
American Sociological Review 49:141-146, 1984.

[109]   Van Fraassen, B. C.
        The Scientific Image.
        Oxford Univ. Press (Clarendon), London and New York, 1980.

[110]   Welsh, J. and Elder J.
        Introduction to Pascal.
        Prentice/Hall International, Englewood Cliffs, New Jersey, 1982.

[111]   Wheaton, B., Muthen, B., Alwin, D., and Summers, G.
        Assessing Reliability and Stability in Panel Models.
        In D. Heise (editor), *Sociological Methodology 1977*, pages 84-136. Jossey-
            Bass, San Francisco, 1977.

[112]   Wishart, J.
        Sampling Errors in the Theory of Two Factors.
        British Journal of Psychology 19:180-187, 1928-29.

[113]   Zeisel, H.
        Disagreement Over the Evaluation of a Controlled Experiment.
        American Journal of Sociology 88:378-389, 1982.

[114]   Zellner, A.
        Philosophy and Objectives of Econometrics.
        In Currie, D., Nobay, R., and Peel, D. (editors), *Macroeconomic Analysis:
            Essays in Macroeconomics and Econometrics.* Croom Helm Publishing
            Co., London, 1981.

Index